Living with
the Mind of Christ

Living with
the Mind of Christ

Mindfulness in Christian Spirituality

Stefan Gillow Reynolds

DARTON·LONGMAN+TODD

First published in Great Britain in 2016 by
Darton, Longman and Todd Ltd
1 Spencer Court
140 – 142 Wandsworth High Street
London SW18 4JJ

ISBN 978-0-232-53250-0

A catalogue record for this book is available from the British Library

Phototypeset by Kerrypress Ltd, St Albans
Printed and bound by ScandBook AB

For Alex Duncan (1970–1989) who reminded me,
and to the Sacred Heart of Jesus who makes all things possible.

Many thanks also to Demetri Grey, Dr Margaret Lane, Laurence
Freeman OSB, Dr May Ngo and the Cistercians of St Mary's Abbey,
Glencairn for their help and advice.

In an attempt to use a more inclusive style of language, some quotations have been slightly altered, usually changing a gender-exclusive pronoun to a more inclusive one. Where such changes seemed to infringe on the integrity of the text, the original language is left intact.

CONTENTS

Contents

Foreword by
Laurence Freeman OSB

We cannot escape from the metaphor of life as a journey. And yet the journey is into an experience of the unity and simultaneity of things. Abstract as this might sound it is in fact a very ordinary experience of the transformation of perception and behavioural response that takes place in those who sustain a contemplative practice in daily life. Gradually, although nothing at times seems to happen during the meditation periods, a new creation begins to take shape embracing and blessing us as the world bursts alive with fresh colours and vivacity.

Our urbanised, digitalised, ever-accelerating and increasingly virtual world is pining body and soul for this deeper and more human experience of reality known directly rather than on a screen. As we see the worsening symptoms of our contemplative deficiency, a new way of living and perceiving, nourished by the very spiritual traditions that failed us for so long, is waiting to be born.

Stefan Reynolds is a voice from one of these traditions, the Christian mystical transmission. He is also in touch with the painful problems and urgent needs of our time. By engaging with the phenomenon of 'mindfulness' that has become a potent spiritual fashion largely because it presents itself as wholly secular, he does a number of valuable things that the reader - and contemporary seekers generally - will benefit from. First, he sees why there is this irrepressible aspiration in our crisis-ridden culture for peace, contemplative wisdom and for recovering a way of living in the present. Then, he also sees how the 'mindfulness' movement has put a foot in the door of the over-secularised mind, allowing a wisdom stream of great hope and depth to seep into the institutions and mindsets, which have rejected them for so long.

The wise scribe brings out of his treasures things both new and old (Matthew 13:52). *Living with the Mind of Christ* is a work of scholarship and wisdom that makes contemplation contemporary. Stefan Reynolds has a strong theological and historical connection with the Christian contemplative tradition. This enables him to recognise what might seem 'new' hopes and remedies as being also manifestations of a perennial and universal wisdom. This is a necessary awakening for the modern mind. It is a delightful surprise to see that we inextricably belong to a tradition of wisdom even when we think we are inventing things for the first time. For the Christian, this book will lead to a deeper understanding of the 'mind of Christ' – a source of fresh and conscious living that lifts us up and beyond dour familiar woes.

The Second Vatican Council speaks of 'scrutinising the signs of the times and interpreting them in the light of the Gospel' (Gaudium et Spes, 4). *Living with the Mind of Christ* does exactly that - expressing the Christian contemplative tradition in a language intelligible to this generation. Today's desire for inner peace, and freedom from anxiety, finds an echo in the hearts of Christians. *Living with the Mind of Christ* bridges the gap between today's interest in Mindfulness and Christian contemplation as practiced through the ages. It also shows it is possible for Christians to find connections with non-religious forms of therapeutic mindfulness. For those seekers who journey without a name or habitation yet are willing to learn from their encounter with fellow pilgrims Stefan Reynolds will be a welcoming and illuminating companion.

Laurence Freeman OSB

Second Foreword by Professor Anne Buttimer

'There is a centre in us all', Robert Browning once wrote, 'where truth abides in fullness'. 'And to know', he continues, 'rather consists in opening out a way where this emprisoned splendour may escape than in effecting entrance for a light supposed to be without.' Mindfulness in this book could be regarded as a fresh invitation for centring. It not only re-affirms the reciprocity of analytical and reflective modes of thought in the acquisition of knowledge and understanding, but also the importance of meditation in the rediscovery of wholeness in life experience, in being and becoming. Evoking an awareness of the here-and-now enables one to feel 'at home' with oneself and one's world - surely an exciting prospect for individuals and communities. But mindfulness here has a broader global appeal: in most world religions and cultural traditions, this same appeal could be found beyond the apparent differences in belief systems, on the one hand, and specialists in secular therapeutic practices on the other hand.

Living with the Mind of Christ: Mindfulness in Christian Spirituality is a really evocative and challenging read with an appeal that stretches from personal to global levels, deriving insights from both spirituality and science, views on the sacred and the secular, theoretical and applied knowledge. Its great promise is to enable us to transcend the current waves of fundamentalism in 'religious' identities, tunnel-vision scientific specialisation, with hopes for 'centring' individual and group identities in ways beyond drug addiction and divisive rhetorics. Christians might find in many other cultural worlds the whisper: 'Be still and know that I am God'.

Professor Anne Buttimer
Vice-President of Academia Europaea,
Former President of the International Geographical Union

Introduction: Minding the Gaps

In the London Underground when the train doors open there is a rather solemn, slightly shrill but emphatically slow voice that announces, 'Mind the gap.' Everyone gingerly steps over the gap between the train and the platform (a gap which varies depending on which station you are at). This book will mind the gaps between mindfulness practice as taught today and Christian mysticism. At times it seems there are rather large gaps: belief in God being one of the wider ones. However, in the London Underground the gap doesn't mean you cannot pass from the platform to the train or vice-versa. This book will encourage a little more ease of passage. Mindfulness and Christian mysticism are not the same. The analogy of train and platform becomes contentious, however, if one implies that one moves and the other doesn't! Still Christian mysticism – like a train – takes you to somewhere where you are not: whereas Mindfulness – like a platform – encourages the experience of being where you are. The experience from the perspective of the traveller may, however, be more similar than external observation allows: people on the platform wait for the train to come, people in the train wait for the platform to arrive. Journey and arrival tend to interact in anticipation and in memory.

In the present moment we are always and only where we are. The Christian mystics can remind those practising mindfulness that the present moment may be part of a long journey, which goes way beyond what we imagine or expect. Mindfulness teachings can remind Christian mystics that no journey can be made unless one places one foot carefully ahead of another.

Many years ago I was living in France working with L'Arche, a community of assistants and people with learning difficulties living together. I was inspired by the ideals of its founder, Jean Vanier. The experience of living with people who approached life directly and not through books and historical, political and theological opinions brought me down to earth. It was the sort of bump that Jean Vanier calls 'learning the language of the heart.' I became (and still am) only semi-fluent in that language. It did point me towards the Christian mystics though, and a way of prayer that was more about being and body language than thinking. I learnt how to stop prioritising my thoughts and to recognise that I was body and that like every-body I was leaning out to be loved. I also stayed at Plum Village, a monastery/lay community set up by the Vietnamese Buddhist monk Thich Nhat Hanh in the south of France. It was my introduction to mindfulness, and from the one who is now considered the 'God-father of mindfulness'. As at L'Arche, I had to learn to let go and be in the present moment, doing the tasks I was allotted with as much attention as I could and being with the other people on retreat without talking to them (it was a silent retreat). I learnt that one communicates through awareness.

I practised mindfulness as a Christian. That experience, more than twenty years ago now, is maybe the beginning of this book. Over the years, and returning to work in universities and retreat work, I have studied and taught Christian mysticism. Even before my year in France I had discovered meditation. I went to a Benedictine boarding school in England to which I will always be grateful for introducing me to an open-minded and prayer-based faith. On leaving school I took a year out living and working in India. It was there that I learnt meditation from two Christian mystics

I was privileged to spend time with: Mother Teresa of Calcutta and the Benedictine monk Bede Griffiths. I was introduced to the teaching of another Benedictine monk John Main whose advice on meditation practice I have continued with for the last 25 years. These teachers led me to make a distinction between mindfulness and meditation. The former keeps the attention on oneself and the other takes the attention off oneself. Meditation leads to mindfulness, self-awareness in daily life. Mindfulness practices can prepare the way and support a daily practice of meditation.

Shaun Lambert's *A Book of Sparks: A Study of Christian Mind*Full*ness* introduced me to the idea of creating 'a Christian scaffolding, drawing on Biblical and historical roots, for the development of mindfulness within the Christian tradition.'[1] Though Lambert dips into the Christian mystical tradition he limits his reflections mainly to the Gospel of Mark. *A Book of Sparks* prompted me to fill in the gaps: mindfulness was not just a practice of Jesus recovered today but has been a practice of the Church through the centuries, though often neglected and repressed. The figure of Jesus is, of course, key. The Christian mystics express partially that 'fullness from which we have all received' (Jn 1:16); each mystic, in their own way, showing something of the Way.

Meditation and mindfulness practice within Christianity is not well known. To pass the buck as an authority in this field is part of the tradition itself. Jesus passed the buck to his Father in heaven who he seems to have seen as the source for all his words and actions. Christians taking up Jesus' warning not to call themselves teachers or instructors pass the buck to the 'one teacher, the Messiah' (Mt 23:10). When asked for a word of wisdom the Desert Fathers and Mothers passed the buck to what they had heard from their elders or others in the desert, 'I heard Abba Moses said...' It seems to have been quite a game not to take credit for any saying. Such anonymity and deference to wise authorities seems to be at the heart of the monastic tradition from which much of the meditation and mindfulness teachings I will look at are drawn. It is not the style of all the Christian mystics though; Augustine of Hippo thinks things out for himself so thoroughly that most people (including me) find the heights or depths of his speculation a little hard to follow. Meister Eckhart was famous, or infamous, for saying, 'You have heard that so-and-so Church Father has said this, but I say to you…' and goes on to say something that seems never to have been said before. Julian of Norwich felt she had authority to teach from the revelation that was given to her, but that didn't make her shy of giving her own interpretation of it.

Many - maybe all - of the mystics, were thinking outside the box of what had been handed on to them. Or at least unpacking the box so as to make it a little wider and more spacious. And what they say is true. We are probably all more mindful and more mystics than we give ourselves credit for (those who think that they are mindful and are mystics we may well be advised to be wary of). Mysticism in Christianity of course is not just meditation; mysticism or as I define it 'the direct experience of God' is found in our work – especially if that involves areas of justice and peace and care of the environment. It is involved in our relationships: fairness in business, truth in politics, kindness in families, generosity and warm heartedness in service to others. Mysticism is also expressed in our thinking – there is nothing necessarily anti-intellectual in mysticism. Some of the mystics I look at certainly saw a danger in thinking too much (the Desert Fathers, the *Cloud of Unknowing*, Teresa of Avila, Brother Lawrence, Simone Weil), but then others were the great thinkers and intellects of their time (St Augustine, Meister Eckhart, Julian of Norwich, Søren Kierkegaard, Simone Weil). Paradoxical as the mystics are they often fit both camps. But it certainly is possible to think mystically. Lastly, or maybe primarily, mysticism for Christians is expressed in liturgy. Gesture and word, silence, song and symbol all speak of God's presence. More than that, they enact God's presence. Just before the most sacred part of the Orthodox liturgy begins the Deacon says to the Priest, 'It is time for the Lord to act.'

The mystics I will be looking at are all from the Christian tradition. This book presumes an openness of mind from mindfulness practitioners to Christianity and from Christians to mindfulness practice. As Thich Nhat Hanh writes in his book *Living Buddha, Living Christ*:

> In true dialogue, both sides are willing to change. We have to appreciate that truth can be received from outside of – not only within – our own group [...] We have to allow what is good, beautiful, and meaningful in the other's tradition to transform us.[2]

For those who are not comfortable with mindfulness as it is presented either in its Buddhist or in its non-religious form then this book will give them access to equivalent though also distinctively different practices from within the Christian tradition.

One last piece of advice, to return to the beginning, 'Mind the Gaps.' There is a way of reading mindfully that in the Christian monastic tradition is called *Lectio Divina*. This involves reading something not just to get information but also to ponder on it, taking time, allowing yourself to enter into the ideas, feelings, images, and intentions in and behind the quotations. Some mystics have called this being aware of the gaps between the words, the space around them. There is an old Jewish saying that only half of the meaning of the Torah is in the words; the other half is in what isn't written. One can of course only read because there are gaps between lines and words, delete all gaps and the words become meaningless. What do the gaps provide? They provide room for you yourself as the reader. Mindful reading is to be aware of what is going on within you as you read. Watch what comes up. Give yourself time to ponder. At times you will learn much more from closing the book and sitting still than from reading on. In the end we only really learn what is valuable when it comes from our own experience.

The main part of this book offers something of a resource book for those who want to find a Christian framework for mindfulness and meditation practice. *Lectio Divina* is a way to Christian mindfulness because it involves the combined practice of attention and awareness, savouring a text and the feelings, thoughts and responses that arise in us as we read it. To enable this direct encounter with the mystics I allow them to speak in their own words. Relating these sources to a contemporary or at least Buddhist practice, which was not the concern of the authors, necessitates the commentary. Christian mysticism needs to be brought into relation to our experience today so as to be accessible. I believe the contemporary interest in mindfulness provides a remarkable and opportune moment for this. We live in a crazy world; all the voices for sanity, truth, goodness and love need to work together.

Chapter 1

Jesus, Teacher of Mindfulness

You know me and you know where I come from: and yet I have not come from myself. (Jn 7:28)

Putting on The Mind of Christ

Mindfulness in the Christian vision is to 'let that same mind be in [us] that was in Christ Jesus' (Phil 2:5). The mystics are those who 'have the mind of Christ' (1 Cor. 2:16). Why begin with Jesus? Jesus didn't begin with himself but imitated the Father. 'Very truly, I tell you, the Son can do nothing on his own, but only what he sees the Father doing' (Jn 5:19). The Apostle Philip implored as we might, 'Lord, show us the Father, and we will be satisfied' (14:8). Jesus replies by pointing back to his non-duality with the Father, 'Whoever has seen me has seen the Father' (14:9). That doesn't necessarily help, we cannot see Jesus in his bodily form, he now dwells 'in an unapproachable light, whom no one has ever seen or can see' (1Tim 6:16). If the dwelling is unapproachable how much more so the one who dwells in it. So we have to begin where we can, in what the Gospels say about Jesus' life and teaching. Jesus is the completely other-centred person, centred on the Father. His whole being is a response to another. It is this openness that makes him much more than a historical figure, more than a mystic. Christians believe his relationship to God was so unique that he fully expressed God; he was 'the Word of God'. His other-centeredness means he is not just a model to emulate, but also a teacher who dwells within. He is the ground of our being, 'all things were made through him' (Jn 1:3). He is 'the true light that enlightens everyone' (1:9). Enlightenment in the Christian vision is knowledge of Jesus.

Pontius Pilate asked Jesus sardonically 'What is truth?' (18:38). The modern mind tends to be sceptical if not downright cynical about anything that presents itself as the truth, or as truthful. Are the Gospels 'mere myth', fabrications of Jesus' followers? There are inconsistencies between the accounts of Jesus' life. Still, considering the Gospels derived from different communities of early Christians and different geographical contexts, the consistency is remarkable. The search for the historical Jesus is only possible through the memory of the Gospels. They do not claim scientific, or even journalistic, standards of accuracy. They tell a story. A story, which until it was written down had been an oral memory of those who knew Jesus, passed down within communities.

Four gospels became the official canon of the New Testament in the fifth century. Other written narratives about Jesus survive. Before looking at them a brief introduction to the official four: Three, known as The Synoptic Gospels, were composed between AD 70–90 (or CE). Mark was probably the first composed, Matthew uses a lot of Mark and more, and Luke draws from some still unidentified common source of all three. All are written in Greek. Matthew seems to have written for Jewish Christians and there is some polemic in his Gospel against Gentile Christians who didn't follow the Jewish law. Mark probably wrote for Roman Christians, Luke for Christians in Greece and Syria. Speaking to different communities they show different perspectives. Their diversity rests on a remarkable unity of vision though, which has prompted scholars to search for a common source document 'Q', which has never appeared. None of the Gospels are a direct first-hand record of any eyewitness to Jesus; they witness to an oral tradition.

The Gospel according to John is more of a theological commentary on memories about Jesus' life. It has been called the 'mystical Gospel', but this does not mean the facts are mythical. Theology is added to real reminiscences to bring out new and deeper meanings. It was probably written between AD 80–100 in Ephesus or Syria in a Hellenistic Jewish mentality. The style is more poetic, the tone of Jesus' teaching voice more solemn than in the synoptics. The contradictions with the earlier Gospels in the chronology of Jesus' ministry does not change the nature of the faith professed. This is also the case with some other accounts like the Gospel of Thomas, rediscovered in 1945 in an earthenware jar in Nag Hammadi in Upper Egypt. Fifty per cent of the sayings of Thomas are found in the Synoptic Gospels. Elaine Pagels believes they were recorded at much the same time as John's Gospel and in a similar geographic area – around Syria. Conflict between the two visions of Christian mysticism, and the eventual triumph of the Johannine account of Jesus, may explain why the sayings recorded in Thomas were edged out of the canon.

A refrain in all Gospel accounts is, 'Be on your guard, stay awake, because you never know when the time will come' (Mk 13:33, Lk 21:36). In Matthew Jesus says it could be any day, any hour (24:42 & 25:13). When Jesus is betrayed and arrested in the garden of Gethsemane he says 'the hour is at hand', his disciples 'could not stay awake with [him] one hour' (26:40 & 45). Wakefulness must be a daily programme, an hourly effort. It comes to a crux in times of calamity. Simone Weil (1909–1943) says that at the time of testing compassion becomes the driving force of attentiveness. The present moment occasions the place where we arrive at openness to God and neighbour, but Weil believed it was only in a state of affliction, in extreme suffering, that we are stripped of past and future. Our minds range backwards and forwards because of the difficulty they have in being with what is 'at hand'. Wakefulness starts with acceptance of the present moment; its fruit is right action motivated by compassion. Mindful living involves linking what we are doing with being in the moment, knowing, as Jesus said, 'for this purpose I came to this hour' (Jn 12:27). Mindfulness is about not postponing the decisive moment when we respond to the need of another. To be mindful, therefore, we have to be open to the experience of others, especially their troubles. 'Today it is not really enough to be a saint,' Weil writes, 'we must have the saintliness demanded by the present moment, a new saintliness, itself without precedent.'[1] Its newness is its emphasis on embodiment as the way to discover the difference between responding and reacting. Reacting comes from our pre-set aversion or attraction to what life presents. Responding involves living with compassion. To really be with someone means being physically present. Jean Vanier asks:

> How can we bring news that is truly good to the poor and the dispossessed? It is not by telling each person: 'God loves you'. It is by saying 'I love you in the way Jesus does'. That is what it means to be present to them in the flesh, because it was in the flesh that Jesus was present to the poor and told them 'I love you in the way God does'.[2]

Coming back to our Senses

In the face of our own suffering and that of others it is hard not to want to distract ourselves. Jesus tells the story of the prodigal son who, realising he had squandered his life 'came to himself' or 'came to his senses' (Lk 15:17). This is mindfulness. However, for the prodigal son, the next step is to turn back to his father, 'I shall go back to my father.' This is Christian prayer. These two stages are expressed in the *Gospel of Truth* – a second-century text found at Nag Hammadi: 'The man who repents is like one who awakens from drunkenness, returning to himself [...] He now knows where he has come from and where he is going.'[3] The Greek word used for 'repentance' here (and in all the Gospels) is *metanoia*, 'change of mind'. Kallistos Ware, renowned scholar of Greek spirituality, calls *metanoia* 'mental watchfulness with alertness to the present moment.'[4]

One of Jesus' favourite sayings, it seems, was 'If anyone has ears let him hear!' It occurs eight times in the Gospels (many more than 'Repent and believe the Good News').[5] In the Gospel of Mark, Jesus expands hearing to include sight: 'They may indeed look, but not perceive, and may indeed listen, but not understand' (4:12). 'Do you have eyes and fail to see? Do you have ears and fail to hear? And do you not remember?' (8:18). Jesus may be speaking metaphorically here, asking us to look beyond physical appearances by connecting what we perceive with what we understand and remember. The verb 'to see' has both perceptual and cognitive meanings. However, for one who opened the eyes of the blind and made the deaf hear it could well have a literal meaning. Our senses are blocked. As William Blake said, 'Man has closed himself up, till he sees all things through narrow chinks.'[6]

> They brought to [Jesus] a man who was deaf [...] [Jesus]
> put his fingers into his ears [...] And looking up to
> heaven, he sighed and said to him, 'Ephphatha,' that is, 'Be
> opened.' And his ears were opened. (Mk 7:32–35)

It could be that what the bodily senses are actually doing – seeing, hearing, feeling, etc. – is what Jesus asks us to be attentive to.

In mindfulness a key practice is the body scan, being aware of what the senses are telling us. Why is it only when we come back to the body that we can come to insight into what is happening? Because the body is in the present moment. Jesus tells us that the time is fulfilled; the kingdom of heaven is 'at hand' (Mt 3:2; 4:17; 10:7, Mk 1:15). The kingdom is not something we have to wait for; it is something we can touch here and now. This is why it is Good News. As the proverb says, 'Hope deferred makes the heart sick, but a desire fulfilled is a tree of life' (Proverbs 13:12). To realise the kingdom here and now our senses have to be involved. The declaration of the early Christians was 'what we have heard, what we have seen with our eyes, what we have looked at and touched with our hands' (1Jn 1:1). St Paul puts it even more succinctly: 'In [God] we live and move and have our being' (Acts 17:28).[7]

The body is in the here and now. The mind lives in the future. We do things now for the sake of some future circumstance but Jesus says, 'Don't worry about tomorrow' (Mt 6:34). Be mindful of today, 'each day has enough trouble of its own.' He doesn't say don't plan for the future but, as Hanh says, 'The best way to take care of the future is to take care of the present moment.'[8] Ware's advice is to 'think about the future only as far as it depends upon the present moment.'[9] The first letter of St Peter links these two aspects of present moment awareness – acceptance and wakefulness: 'Cast all our anxiety on God, because he cares for you. Discipline yourselves; keep alert' (1Pet 5:7–8). Mindfulness is to let go of anxiety about what will be and give our attention to what is at hand, accepting what has been given, doing what needs doing. Jesus told his disciples after the Resurrection not to be afraid, he commissioned them to go out and preach the Good News.

Christian practice encourages us to discover embodiment as our way to God, as the sacred language of our faith. 'Present their bodies as a living sacrifice,' writes St Paul, 'holy and acceptable to God, which *is* your spiritual worship' (Rom 12:1). Spiritual is physical. Our bodies are temples of the Holy Spirit.[10] As Blake said, 'If the doors of perception were cleansed we would see everything as it is – infinite.'[11] In self-awareness we discover our own value but we also see our blind spots. We must take 'the log out of [our] own eye' (Mt 7:5). The antidote to judging others is to see ourselves. Mindfulness similarly encourages the non-judgmental mind. 'To work for peace you must have a peaceful heart,' writes Hanh, 'With mindfulness – the practice of peace – we can begin by working to transform the wars in ourselves.'[12] St James says that the origin of fighting is the cravings that are at war within us. All of us have these conflicting desires, all of us create war; 'So who then are you to judge your neighbour?' (4:12). 'Looking deeply' leads to understanding, forgiveness, and compassionate action.

The more you see the more you Love

Christian practice, like Buddhist meditation, is about not blocking awareness through premature conclusions or making judgments from the appearance of things. We have to present to the moment to be able to respond accordingly – 'Do not pronounce judgment before the time,' St Paul writes (1Cor 4:5) 'Do not judge by appearances,' Jesus says, 'but judge by right judgment' (Jn 7:24). Not all judgments are wrong, but they must be impartial, free from personal animosity. 'Hate the sin, but love the sinner,' an old but valid guide. Loving those who hurt us means not reacting from our wounds. If we have a clear discrimination of right and wrong we can stand up against what they do without hating them. In the early Christian community wrongdoing was not ignored but carefully pointed out. If one is not listened to (and to ensure the critique is not motivated by personal animosity) impartial witnesses are brought along. Matthew 18:15–18 is an Ecclesial prefiguration of the Jury system. In the end the buck stops with the *sensus fidelium* – the collective discernment of the faithful. The challenge is to be impartially merciful and kind as our heavenly Father making 'the sun rise on the evil and the good alike' and yet at the same time to 'judge for ourselves what is right' (Mt 5:45, Lk 12:57).

Mindfulness practice, looking beyond the surface of our reactive thoughts and emotions, should help to show the difference between discernment and criticism and improve our ability to tell right from wrong. Attentiveness must bear fruit in compassion and working for what is right. 'Looking deeply', the Buddhist scholar Alan Wallace says, should not make us blind to moral categories, what is helpful and what is downright harmful. One of Wallace's critiques of reductionist approaches to Buddhist meditation is that they encourage the dropping of discriminatory consciousness. There is a danger in distilling attentiveness practices from other complementary Buddhist practices.[13] Mindfulness in the Christian vision is linked not only to ethical values but to social justice. We cannot mindfully walk by in contemplative pose while ignoring those in distress who have fallen by the roadside. Busyness makes us choose not to see, it makes us blind to what is inconvenient, disruptive and incompatible with our plans and timetables. But piety can have the same effect if we rate our religious affiliation and purity codes above others' needs as the Priest and Levite did in Jesus' story of the man robbed, stripped and beaten on the road to Jericho. 'Who is my neighbour?' It is the one God places with us in the present moment, the ones we meet on the way, not necessarily those we plan to see.

Wake up and see what is in front of you! There is enough in this world to move us to continuous compassion if we but saw it. Mindfulness is at its hardest when what is in front of us is very painful: Jesus' disciples deserted him when he was arrested and were not present at the foot of the cross. If we did see properly we might be moved with compassion and realise that there is something much more important being demanded from us in the moment. The mystic Edith Stein (1891–1942) said, 'As for what concerns our relations with our fellow men, the anguish in our neighbour's soul must break all precept. All that we do is a means, but love is an end in itself.' Mindfulness involves seeing what is there, not what we want to see. Often it involves paying attention to the inconvenient other who, like Lazarus in Jesus' story, may be lying at our gate. 'Even the dogs would come and lick his sores', Jesus recounts of the compassion of animals, but the rich man ignores the one outside his self-protecting gate (Lk 16:19–21).

A great medieval mystic St Catherine of Siena said, 'The more you can see the more you can love.'[14] She did not mean being a busy tourist cramming in all the sights; she meant seeing deeply into what is going on in this moment. Mindfulness is not just about peace but can be about allowing ourselves to be troubled. It is those we find it hardest to notice with whom Jesus is most identified – 'I was a stranger and you welcomed me in […] I was locked away and you visited me' (Mt 25:35–36). He was very unimpressed with those who called him Lord yet were unmindful of the needs of others. There is no excuse if we say, 'Lord, when was it that we saw you […] and did not take care of you?' for he comes to us in disguise and it is our duty to recognise him (Mt 25:44–45). There is no better disguise for a Lord than to come as one who is poor.

Mindfulness is about seeing that all people are worthy of our compassion. In the moment we are not called to judge who is deserving of our love. We are free to respond. 'So speak and so act as those who are to be judged by the law of liberty,' St James writes (2:12). In fact it is we are judged ('without mercy') for not responding, not opening our hearts, for not being merciful in the moment. If a boat is sinking, instead of tearing off planks of wood to make a raft for ourselves – and thereby adding to the impossibility of the situation – we can stay with the plight of others. From the perspective of compassion we might see where the hole in the boat is, and actually be of some help. Christians believe that there is a helper, an advocate, a consoler for all of us in our weakness: the Holy Spirit. This advocate turns around all our preconceived ideas about sin, and righteousness and judgment (Jn 16:8). She helps us to 'throw down' our self-accusation and the guilt we may have internalised from others (Rev 12:10). She takes our part (Rom 8:26). She 'reminds us' (Jn 14:26). 'Re-mind' is Kabat-Zinn's favoured description for growing in awareness.[15] The Spirit brings us back to mindfulness, reconnecting us with our teacher and guide every moment, breathing into us a sense of our and other people's worth. Hanh says, 'When you practise mindfulness you touch the Holy Spirit.'[16]

Mindfulness as taught in therapy today does not see itself as a 'spiritual' practice. It confines itself to bringing us back to our senses. However, to promote mindfulness over mindlessness and altruism over selfishness implies a set of values, meaning and purpose in life. In the past Christian apologetics were critical of any search for value, meaning and purpose in life that did not profess Christ. However, the experience of inter-religious dialogue and non-religious humanitarianism has led to a re-evaluation of any claim for monopoly of the Holy Spirit within the Church. 'The Spirit blows where it will' (Jn 3:8). During the Second Vatican Council the Roman Catholic Church affirmed its regard and reverence for 'those ways of conduct and of life, those precepts and teachings which, though differing in many aspects from the ones she holds and sets forth, nonetheless often reflect a ray of that Truth which enlightens all people.'[17]

A Christian approach to mindfulness would do well to follow this lead. Instead of dismissing meditative practices that are not explicitly Christian, it could take the stance of 'dialogue and collaboration' urged by the Council: 'Carried out with prudence and love and in witness to the Christian faith and life, we are called to recognise, preserve and promote the good things, spiritual and moral, as well as the socio-cultural values found among different practices.'[18] Christians can not only practice mindfulness but, insofar as it is helpful to others, promote it! 'Insofar' is important though. St Paul urges his readers to openness but with discernment: 'Do not quench the Spirit [which may be blowing where we don't expect it] but test everything; hold fast to what is good; abstain from every form of evil' (1 Thess 5:19–22). The classic criterion of Christian discernment is to look at the fruits. Is mindfulness practice leading to an increase of love, joy, peace, forbearance, kindness, goodness, faithfulness, gentleness and self-control? Then the Holy Spirit is at work in it (Gal 5: 22–23). But these virtues are not passive or self-orientated; they are responses to life. Mindfulness as self-therapy should lead to compassion in action. To be aware of where injustice is perpetrated and stand up to it, of how we can bring peace into a troubled world.

Religion is not about becoming more efficient cogs in a system. It involves seeing and challenging where the system is wrong and striving and suffering for what is right. The happiness and wellbeing which therapeutic mindfulness serves finds its deeper basis in the eight beatitudes, which undermine any idea of happiness as self-serving. The Beatitudes have parallels with the Buddhist teaching on right effort and right letting go.[19] Buddhism deepens mindfulness in its teaching on altruism and compassion. 'Deep is calling on deep,' as the Psalmist says (Ps 42:7), and Christianity and Buddhism may have much to learn from each other. Buddhist mindfulness is focused on being aware of thoughts and feelings so as to let go of them – not get involved with them. Buddhists seek to calm the mind by not getting attached to any emotional state. They would not see mindfulness as prioritising awareness of suffering, let alone seeking it out, it is concerned only with not reacting with aversion to suffering. Right effort is focused on not getting sucked into human dramas, right letting go means not avoiding suffering if it is present. Christian mindfulness would put more emphasis on responding to any situation of human need. The emphasis in Christianity is on taking responsibility for our thoughts and feelings because they affect others. For Christians the gift of mindfulness would be through seeing clearly enough, and peacefully enough, that we may be able to help.

Prayer as Awareness

There is a close overlap between the body and the unconscious. The autonomic nervous system works independently of our control. We are rarely aware of our heartbeat or breathing. Body language and symptoms speak of unexpressed feelings and unknown traumas. That is why a key practice in mindfulness is to give attention to something that we are normally unaware of – breathing, for example. We think we can tell our story: we are this because of that, right back to our childhood. However, in mindfulness practice we move from narrative thinking to an experiential sense of our self, gained through our senses. The first step is to come back to a 'felt sense of self', being aware of what we see, what we can hear, the taste of something, the texture of something we touch, the smell of a flower or freshly baked bread or coffee brewing. Coming back to the senses we come out of the narratives of our mind and the domination of our emotions. We let go of fixed ideas about ourselves, habitual emotional responses, and come into the present moment by being aware of sensations.

The leitmotiv of 'trans-personal psychology' is 'transcend and include.'[20] This school of psychology like the religious wisdom it draws from points out that letting go of thought and emotion is important because it leads to discernment, to insight. We let go of our attachment to thoughts: 'Do not believe every spirit,' St John tells us (1Jn 4:1). 'But,' he goes on, 'test them to see whether they are from God.' Detachment should give birth to discernment. In mindfulness practice we learn to observe thoughts and emotions from a place of acceptance and freedom. But not all thoughts and emotions are helpful and we have to separate the wheat from the chaff. Mindful breathing calms our emotions but also gives insight into the root of them. By giving our attention to sense perception we can also learn about what lies hidden in the unconscious. Thomas Keating speaks of centring prayer as 'a divine psychotherapy' in which the unconscious is purified by being raised into awareness. Facing the dark side of our personality, accepting ourselves as we are, allowing childhood trauma to be released are as much the work of contemplation as of analysis. They happen as the mind lets go of its control. Keating says that by cultivating 'a neutral attitude towards the psychological content of your prayer' we develop 'the capacity to accept what comes down the stream of consciousness as an essential part of the discipline.' But 'the purpose of centring prayer is not to experience peace [...] but the permanent and abiding awareness of God that comes through the mysterious restructuring of consciousness.'[21]

The inter-relation of inner and outer awareness is a key message of Jesus. 'Recognise what is before your eyes and the mysteries will be revealed to you,' he says in the Gospel of Thomas, 'for there is nothing hidden that will not be revealed' (5). In Luke's account of the two disciples on the road to Emmaus he says that, after walking with Jesus all day, at the breaking of the bread 'their eyes were opened and they recognised him' (24:30–31). Mindfulness is about recognising what has been with us all the day, 'Keep your eyes open,' Jesus says (Mt 25:13). 'Look at what is before your eyes,' St Paul echoes (2Cor 10:7). The tendency of the mind is to add a narrative to what we see, reading things in terms of past experience or of what we think will happen. The disciples on the road to Emmaus had their own gloomy narrative of what had happened. It was this that kept them from seeing what was right before their eyes. To recognise Jesus involves a complete rethinking of the past and the future in terms of the present. This 'restructuring' was working as Jesus spoke to them along the road, opening their hearts. But it often needs something physical – like the breaking of bread – for us to open our eyes.

If we interpret things in terms of cause and effect, of past experience shaping our anticipation of the future, we miss what is happening *now*. Jesus said to the crowd:

> When you see a cloud rising in the west, you immediately
> say, 'It is going to rain'; and so it happens. And when
> you see the south wind blowing, you say, 'There will be a
> scorching heat'; and it happens. You know how to interpret
> the appearance of earth and sky, why do you not know how
> to interpret the present time? (Lk 12:54–56)

There is a difference between the mind when it works with cause and effect, and the mind when it dwells in 'the present time'. In the former our thoughts create our reality. If we are negative about things, things will be experienced as negative. Thinking affirmative thoughts creates a positive reality.[22] Mindfulness is, however, not just positive thinking. We don't try to shape the present moment. Things are experienced in their pristine freshness without thought coming in to explain or predict. One of the mystics we will look at, Jean Pierre de Caussade (1675–1751) shows Jesus as acting spontaneously, unconditioned by the past:

> Jesus Christ did not limit his own action to what he had previously said; he did not even obey literally his own maxims. One moment he says, 'I will not go up to the festival', next moment he does go. The Divine Spirit perpetually inspired his holy soul; having always been abandoned to that divine Breath there was no need to consult the preceding moment in order to determine the following one. The breath of grace formed all his moments.[23]

The Kingdom of Heaven is 'at Hand'

Gospel of Thomas points to Christ's presence 'at hand' in the moment: 'They said to Jesus, "Tell us who you are that we may believe in you." He said to them, "You search the face of heaven and earth, but you have not come to know the one who stands before you, and you do not know how to understand the present moment" ' (91). We have to look deeply. In the Biblical vision all things point to a source beyond them, life manifests God's Word. 'The heavens proclaim the glory of God and the firmament shows forth the work of his hands' (Ps 18:2). 'God's eternal power and divine nature, invisible though they are, have been understood and seen through the things he has made' (Rom 1:20). Or, as the Wisdom of Solomon puts it, 'From the greatness and beauty of created things comes a corresponding perception of their Creator' (13:5). In the New Testament creation's source became visible, took human form and was born in human likeness. In Thomas's Gospel Jesus points to the incarnation as the source of Christian enlightenment: 'If they say to you, 'Where have you come from?'

say to them, 'We have come from the light, from the place where the light came into being by itself, established itself, and appeared in their image' (50).

In receiving the light we in turn shine, like a mirror reflecting God's glory. The light of awareness is not just an inner, spiritual light placed 'under the bushel basket or under the bed' or 'in a cellar' it is placed on a lamp stand 'so that all may see' (Mt 5:15, Mk 4:21, Lk 11:33). What is unconscious is uncovered; 'For there is nothing hidden, except to be disclosed; nor is anything secret, except to come to light' (Mk 4:22). In Matthew and Luke's Gospels enlightenment specifically relates to the body, the eye symbolising awareness: 'The eye is the lamp of the body. So if your eye is healthy, your whole body will be full of light' (Mt 6:22). 'If then your whole body is full of light, with no part of it in darkness, it will be as full of light as when a lamp gives you light with its rays' (Lk 11:36).

Mindfulness can come through attentiveness to anything. Christ is present in the universal and the particular, macrocosm and microcosm. In Thomas's Gospel Jesus says, 'I am the light that is over all things. I am all. From me all came forth, and to me all extends. Split a piece of wood, and I am there. Lift up a stone, and you will find me there' (77). Because the presence of God is ubiquitous it cannot be limited to any particular thing (that would be idolatry). Awareness of God's Kingdom is, therefore, more about receiving than seeking. The fish has no need to seek the water it lives in. Jesus manifested God's Kingdom but also said, 'The Kingdom does not admit of observation, you cannot say look here it is or there it is, for in fact, it is within you and among you' (Lk 17:20).[24]

Mindfulness, Jon Kabat-Zinn says, is a 'non-doing' – not indolence or passivity but an 'effortless activity': 'There is no exertion of the will, no small-minded "I", "me", or "mine" to lay claim to a result, yet nothing is left undone.'[25] The Christian equivalent of 'effortless activity' is the contemplative action that comes from faith. The message of the early Church is that righteousness is not something achieved; it is received by faith. St

Paul states it thus: 'I live no longer, but Christ lives in me, and the life which I now live in the flesh I live by faith in the Son of God' (Gal 2:20–21). In St John's Gospel people ask Jesus 'What must we do to perform the works of God?' Jesus replies: 'Believe in him whom God has sent' (6:29). As with works, so with love; what is important is 'not that we loved God but that he loved us' (1Jn 4:10). Even self-knowledge in Thomas's Gospel is the premise to being known by God and discovering who we are in relation to him: 'When you know yourselves, then you will be known, and you will understand that you are children of the living Father' (3). Likewise contemplation is not about success, goals and expectations. With St Paul we must be content with whatever comes, accepting having little, accepting plenty. The art is one of patience, waiting on God as a farmer for his crops to grow, without doing anything.

One of the key practices of mindfulness, to stop, sit and be aware of our breathing needs patience. Likewise, if we use a prayer-word we must, as John Main says, 'be content to say your mantra.' But the practice of patience overflows in other times of our lives as well. We learn to let go and let things unfold according to their own nature. In moments of wisdom we let our lives unfold in the same way. As Kabat-Zinn puts it:

> We don't have to let our anxieties, and our desire for certain
> results, dominate the quality of the moment, even when
> things are painful. When we have to push, we push. When
> we have to pull, we pull. But we know when not to push
> too, and when not to pull. Through it all, we attempt to
> bring balance to the present moment, understanding that
> in patience lies wisdom, knowing that what will come next
> will be determined in large measure by how we are now.
> This is helpful to keep in mind when we get impatient
> in our meditation practice, or when we get frustrated,
> impatient, and angry in our lives.[26]

The value of 'not-doing' is illustrated in the story of Mary and Martha in Luke's Gospel (10:38–42). Martha 'welcomed [Jesus] into her home' – in Jewish families of the time this was the role of the oldest female member of the household. Mary, Martha's sister, 'sat at the Lord's feet and listened to what he was saying.' As a younger sister her role would have been to help. Jesus was on his way up from Galilee to Jerusalem, travelling with his twelve male disciples and the women disciples. From Galilee to Bethany – one can assume the guests arrived hungry. Martha sets about preparing a meal, it seems she was happy enough to leave Mary sitting. 'But,' the Gospel says, 'Martha was distracted by her many tasks; so she came to [Jesus] and asked, "Lord, do you not care that my sister has left me to do all the work by myself? Tell her then to help me." ' Martha is the only person in any of the Gospel accounts who tells Jesus what to do!

Martha is distracted by busyness. Modern research has shown the value of multi-tasking as something of a myth. Doing many things at once means nothing is done properly. It is also proven to lead to stress.[27] Martha is stressed, has lost her cool and feels unloved ('do you not care?'). She is annoyed with her sister but doesn't approach her directly, but via Jesus. She has a strong sense of what *should* be done – Mary should do this, Jesus should do this. Mary has broken all cultural norms for women and taken the place of a disciple learning from her Rabbi (in the same way as St Paul 'sat at the feet' of Gamaliel).[28] She has broken the cultural norm of a younger sister who should be at the disposition of her elder in housework. Maybe Mary had heard Jesus' teaching that 'The Son of Man did not come to be served but to serve' (Mk 10:45, Mt 20:28).[29] Faith is more about receiving than doing. Indeed, 'the Lord answered her, 'Martha, Martha, you are worried and distracted by many things; there is need of only one thing.' What is the one thing? That 'man shall not live by bread alone, but by every word from the mouth of God' (Lk 4:4). What Jesus is saying is more important than what they are going to eat. They could keep the catering simple.

When we have visitors 'the one thing necessary' is to enjoy and benefit from the visit. How many times are we so stressed by catering for guests that we are unable to relax and really enjoy their company? The important thing is not what we do but the quality of our presence. A cheese on toast with love is better than a family fight over a roast. The problem was not Martha's business but her distractedness. Mindful washing-up is one of Hanh's favourite practices. Amid the tasks of life we need only be awake, aware, and alert. 'Seek first the Kingdom of God and everything else will be given to you as well' (Mt 6:33). If Martha had sat down as well maybe the male disciples, or Jesus himself, would have put his teaching into practice and juggled the pots in the kitchen.

Jesus ends by saying, 'Mary has chosen the better part, which will not be taken away from her.' Freedom to choose is not to be taken away because of social and gender expectations. In Mary's case her right to learn as a disciple, and become maybe a teacher herself, is not to be taken away. A traditional interpretation is that Mary is illustrative of the contemplative life, and Martha of the active. In heaven, contemplation 'will not to be taken away' though we will no longer need to work. Being still in body is a necessary antidote to busyness. It also unhooks us from clinging to an identity among things that are impermanent. 'Everything is changing,' the Buddha said, 'It arises and passes away. The one who realises this is freed from sorrow.'[30] St Paul advises 'those who have to deal with the world not to become engrossed in it, I say this because the world as we know it is passing away' (1Cor 7:31).

The Intimacy of the Name

The early Christian message was that the promises God made to the prophets had been fulfilled in Jesus (Acts 3:18). While the Jewish people were in exile in Babylon six centuries before Christ, the Prophet Isaiah (49:8) consoled the exiles with God's message, 'At an acceptable time I hear you, in the day of salvation I help you.'

The tenses of the Ancient Hebrew verbs don't relate to time but to action. The verbs 'hear' and 'help' can be read either as perfect tense – action completed, or imperfect – action still being done.[31] St Paul writing in Greek which has past, future and present tenses, emphatically directs the early Christian community to the present: '*Now* is the acceptable time, *Now* is the day of salvation' (2Cor 6:2). The 'I Am' sayings for Jesus reveal him to be the embodiment of the present moment in time. In the book of Exodus (3:14) God revealed himself to Moses as 'I AM.' He also revealed himself as 'the God of Abraham, of Isaac and of Jacob' but, as Jesus points out, this does not mean he is a God of the past: from the perspective of God all are alive (Lk 30:28). To the scandal of many of his hearers Jesus aligns himself with the eternal Now, prior to God's revelation in history: 'Before Abraham was born, I am' (Jn 8:58).

Mindfulness is the art of being open to what life presents, moment by moment in its newness. Letting go of what has been is particularly hard when we have experienced a joy. When someone we love dies we are sorrowful because of the joy we had from their company. Sorrow is joy that has passed. If we want to have a continuation of the past we will be disappointed. Blake says in his poem 'Eternity':

> He who binds to himself a joy
> Doth the winged life destroy;
> But he who kisses the Joy as it flies
> Lives in eternity's sunrise.[32]

Though Jesus knew where he came from and where he was going 'he did not cling' to that identity (Phil 2:6). We, who have very limited awareness of ourselves, should all the more let go of identities that derive from the past or future. Where I was born, where I went to school, my job, my plans, my foreboding: are they really me? If our identity does not come from 'the world' where does it come from? St Paul gives three stages to self-knowledge:

letting go, allowing our minds to be remade, and becoming a new creation – a child of God. 'Adapt yourselves no longer to the pattern of this present world, but let your minds be remade and your whole nature thus transformed' (Phil 2:5–6). Mindfulness covers the first two stages; grace alone can achieve the last.

To live in eternity's sunrise is not something to be achieved. It is already there. The servant sees things the same way as his master. At a deeper level the servant lives no longer but Christ lives in him, teaching from within. Jesus' parting gift to his disciples was his own peace, not what comes from security and worldly comforts. In meditation we access peace in the difficult situations of life. After his Resurrection – and all he and his disciples had been through – Jesus reiterates, 'Peace be with you' (Lk 24:36, Jn 20:19). The peace we practice in mindfulness enables us to receive the Holy Spirit. Jesus is our teacher of prayer because, through the Spirit he has given, he prays in us, with us and for us. 'In sighs too deep for words' God breathes in our heart, opening it to the flow of God's love. (Rom 5:5, 8:26). The Benedictine monk John Main (1926–1982) sees the fruit of meditation not only as mental wakefulness, but predominantly in an open heart:

> In meditation we seek to disassemble the barriers we
> have set up around ourselves, cutting us off from our
> consciousness of the presence of Jesus within our hearts [...]
> Once we enter into the human consciousness of Jesus, we
> begin to see as he sees, to love as he loves, to understand as
> he understands, and to forgive as he forgives.[33]

John Main revived a way of Christian prayer with a prayer word or *mantra,* which has its roots in the Gospel. Being attentive to the sound of the word focuses our hearts on Christ. This is the Christian equivalent to the attentiveness to the breathing taught in mindfulness practice. Either word or breath becomes a way of unhooking from our thoughts, letting distractions pass, bringing healing and peace into our bodies and emotions. The prayer word or *mantra* is not something we think about or analyse; the sound draws our attention.[34] Main recommends the word *Maranatha* ('Come Lord' in Aramaic) as a perfect Christian prayer of calling and receiving. The fact *maranatha* is not in our language helps, as it is the resonance of the word, not reflection on its meaning, which leads us beyond thoughts into the experience of Christ's presence.

People often ask why the teaching of meditation is not in the Bible, why it is so unfamiliar for Christians? But we need only look more carefully at Scripture and at the practice of the Christian mystics. The Psalms urge us to 'calm and quiet our soul', to 'Be still and know that I am God' (Ps 131 & 46). The practice of using a sacred word has roots in an ancient Jewish practice: Already in the third biblical generation 'people began to call upon the name of the Lord' (Gen 4:26). God encouraged the prophet Jeremiah (29:12), 'Call upon Me.' 'Everyone who calls on the name of the Lord will be saved,' said the Prophet Joel three hundred years later and three hundred years after Joel Paul charges his disciple Timothy to pursue spiritual things 'with those who call on the Lord out of a pure heart.'[35]

What was this 'name'? The most important and most often written name of God in Judaism is הוהי (YHWH). This *Tetragrammaton* appears 6,828 times in the *Biblia Hebraica Stuttgartensia*, a very early edition of the Hebrew Masoretic text. Because Judaism forbids pronouncing the name outside the Temple in Jerusalem (which was destroyed in the first century) the saying of the 'name' has since then been a silent practice. *Yahweh* cannot be said out loud in synagogue liturgy, hence when reading the text of the Torah, it is substituted by *Adonai* ('my Lord'), and is thus translated in Christian Bibles. 'Lord' is a title, however, not a name. Calling on the name was an intimate practice, 'Call upon *Yahweh* while He is near,' Isaiah says (55:1,6). As Richard Rohr observes,

> The Jewish name for God – Yahweh – was not spoken, but
> breathed. Its correct pronunciation is an attempt to imitate
> the sound of inhalation and exhalation [...] The one thing
> we do every moment of our lives is therefore to speak the
> name of God. This makes it our first and our last word as
> we enter and leave the world.[36]

Like breathing we must 'pray unceasingly' (1Thess 5:17). Prayer
is spiritual breathing.

The fact that repeating of the name was a common in Jesus'
time is witnessed by his saying; 'Not everyone who says to me
'Lord, Lord (*Yahweh, Yahweh*) shall enter the kingdom of heaven,
but only those who do the will of my father in heaven' (Mt 7:21).
As with his other teachings on prayer Jesus doesn't reject Jewish
practice but wants sincerity. Sincere prayer doesn't seek approval
of others: 'Go into your private room and pray' (6:6). Of course
most Jewish people didn't have private rooms, the private room
is the heart. Sincerity involves silence: 'Do not heap up empty
phrases as the Gentiles do; for they think they will be heard for
their many words. God knows what you need before you ask'
(6:7-8). One word expressing the intention of the heart is enough.
The 'Our Father' in Aramaic is a succession of rhythmic phrases
directing attention to God and expressing our needs. When we
want to learn something by heart we repeat it. Saying a word or
phrase with increasing attention and interiority is key to 'prayer of
the heart'. When Jesus prayed on the Mount of Olives the disciples
heard him 'saying the same words over again' (Mt 26:44, Mk
14:39). Mark preserves the Aramaic word '*Abba*' as the heart of
Jesus' prayer at this crucial moment.[37] This word, which can be
translated as 'daddy', expresses the affectionate intimacy of a child.
St Paul sees the Spirit praying this word within us (Rom 8:15, Gal
4:6).

Names in the biblical tradition are not just labels; they carry the
meaning, presence and power of that which they signify. Hence

the question that the Priests asked St Peter after the healing of a lame man: 'By what power or by what name have you done this?' (Acts 4:7). The wearing of the name YHWH by the High Priest and its invocation three times under the breath in the Holy of Holies on the Jewish feast of *Yom Kippur* started the process of atonement and the restoration of creation.[38] In the 'Our Father' hallowing the name comes before praying that the 'Kingdom come'. The 'Name' invokes the 'Kingdom'. In the Jewish understanding a 'name' carried with it the qualities of a person. Abram became Abraham (meaning 'father of a multitude') when he responded to God's call. Simon became Peter, *Petros* in Greek (a play on the word *petra* meaning 'rock') when he made his profession of faith. The name Jesus in Aramaic is *Jeshua* meaning '*Yahweh* saves' (Hebrew *Yah'shua*).[39] In John's Gospel Jesus says he has revealed the name of his Father to his disciples. He then says, 'This is the name you [Father] gave me' (17:11). Clearly this is *Yahweh, Yah'shua, Jeshua*. St Paul says God 'has given [Jesus] the name which is above every name' (Phil 2:9). So when St Peter says, 'there is no other name under heaven given among men by which we must be saved' (Acts 4:12), he is speaking of the name of God. Jesus' name contains within it the power and presence of God. The 'Jesus prayer' in the Orthodox tradition understands this.

Yahweh or Jesus has never been considered the only term of evocation in the Jewish and Christian traditions. The same meaning, presence, power can be expressed in various ways and under other forms, and maybe most especially under the form of silence. Karl Rahner sees 'anonymous Christians' as those who seek truth without naming it explicitly as Christ. Mindfulness practice could be included in this category. For them, as Meister Eckhart says, 'God is a word, a word unspoken.'[40] Jesus can be present in the wisdom of all religions. He is definitely present in our neighbour in their need, but also, as Simone Weil says, in friendship and in the beauty of the world.[41] Mindfulness should, however, be open to the mind of Christ for to name the mystery is to go deeper into it. Christ's is no narrow mind; there is room in his awareness for everything for 'without him not one thing came into being' (Jn 1:3). It is shame that any who practise mindfulness would not be open to him. For his name enables us to discover our true identity beyond what we can think or imagine: 'He came to what was his own, and his own did not accept him. But to all who received him, who believed in his name, he gave power to become children of God' (1:11).

The wise man Simeon, encountering the child Jesus in the temple, prophesied he would be 'a sign that is opposed' (Lk 2:34). 'The stone rejected by the builders has become the cornerstone,' was a prophecy of Psalm 118. The religious legalism of Jesus' time, and of any time, tries to come to God by keeping rules. Jesus showed rather that vulnerability is the place we encounter God's grace. Simeon concludes his prophecy by saying that through Jesus 'the secret thoughts of many hearts will be laid bare.' Revealing the unconscious motivations of our thoughts is the work of prayer as much as psychoanalysis. Stubborn opinions, grudges and conditioned thinking can be a major block and obstacle to the fullness of life. Prayer, the Desert Fathers said, is the active work of laying aside our thoughts.[42] The later monastic tradition clearly emphasised that this was done in relation to Christ. To live in God's presence, St Benedict says, we must 'lay hold of [our] thoughts while they were still young and dash them against the rock, which is Christ.'[43] Jesus 'the Divine therapist' breaks open our fixed thinking and opens our mind and heart to God's love.[44]

Jesus undoes those blocks by presenting us with the greatest block of all. Letting go of thoughts and action is the renunciation of power and control expressed in Christ's Passion. Christ crucified is, therefore, 'a stumbling block', as St Paul says, for those who would control life through right action or intelligence (1 Cor 1:23). Like with Jesus, so with us, God only needs our humanity, not our spirituality. God tells St Paul, 'My grace is sufficient for you, for my power is made perfect in weakness' (2 Cor 12:9). St Paul modelled this in his own life:

When I came to you, brethren, I did not come with superiority of speech or of wisdom, proclaiming to you the testimony of God. For I determined to know nothing among you, except Jesus Christ, and Him crucified. I was with you in weakness and in fear and in much trembling. (1 Cor 2:1–3)

The link between vulnerability and openness: an open non-judgmental mind, a forgiving heart, alertness to whatever the moment presents, shows these are not states to achieve. We have only to remove the blocks, let go of what constricts our awareness. The work of letting go, of acceptance, is the work of contemplative prayer. 'The mind of Christ' that rises as we let limited consciousness fall, is true mindfulness.

Chapter 2

What is Mindfulness?

*'There is no form of happiness to be compared with
inner silence.'[1]*

Separating Meditation from Faith

The secularisation of meditation has opened the door for
mindfulness and meditation to reach a far wider audience than
is afforded through exclusive religious domains. By taking
meditation and mindfulness out of its exclusive religious domain
and perceived origins the benefits of these practices have become
available for the secular community. Mindfulness as a form of
'secular contemplation' has been able to penetrate areas like
businesses, hospitals and state schools where religion has usually
been barred. In that sense it has become more 'incarnate' than
religion, which tends to be encountered only in the 'sacred' aspects
of life – Sundays, births, deaths, marriages. Surely the message of
the incarnation is that the humdrum *vie quotidienne* is the place
where we encounter God (especially work and family duties where
we learn what it is to serve others). Christ did not cling to the
sacred dimension of life but emptied himself (Phil 2:6).

However, the average mindfulness group has its own rituals,
emphasis on communal practice and doctrine or ethic of non-
judgmentalism. This has prompted some to see it as a semi-
religious cult 'tailor-made for the secular West.'[2] Any tree must
be judged by its fruits though: Mindfulness does seem to help
many with mental health, grounding people in a stronger sense

of reality and detaching them from unhelpful ways of thinking. No doubt if the contemplative practices of the traditional religions were accessed the same effect would be achieved. Studies for many years have shown that religious people are happier and prayer and faith-based meditation have beneficial effects on the brain.[3] Mindfulness, one might say, should humbly join the queue. However, in terms of the modern world it has an advantage: it manages to get under the radar of 'religious proselytising'.

If contemplative practice becomes ever increasingly absorbed into mainstream culture the foundations might be laid for an openness to the deeper aspects of the 'whole package' of contemplative wisdom which includes ethics and trans-personal meaning. It may be possible for secular institutes to bring in these values without necessarily associating them with religion. This has been proposed by the Dalai Lama and by Christian theologians like Hans Kung. Compassion, truthfulness, fairness are human values irrespective of religion. But how do mindfulness and faith-based meditation practices relate? Would 'living in the present moment' be in any way different, deepened or distracted by belief in an ultimate reality present yet also always beyond the horizon of any momentary experience?

The adoption of mindfulness as a therapeutic technique has happened quite independently of any movement to integrate spirituality into psychological treatment. Therapeutic mindfulness' dissociation from religion or spirituality may be a denial that for many people faith may be a strong motivation for mindfulness practice. Religion can provide a strong motivation for mindfulness practice: to dis-identify with mental activity not just for the sake of personal mental health but also for union with God. The mystics of the world religions witness that peace and transcendence go together. Mindfulness by packaging itself as secular may be neglecting a potential resource for human flourishing. In most parts of the world religion and spirituality are not peripheral to self-identity. A distinction can be made between 'religion' and 'spirituality' yet they can and often do work together. While religion plays a social and motivational role, spirituality contributes to personal acceptance and empowerment. As meditation and mindfulness is practised as much, and maybe more, in groups as in individual practice, so the resources of faith communities and traditions of wisdom and even of religion may be the natural context for the deepening of spirituality into service of others.[4]

In the meditative practices of the world religions there is also practical guidance: if mindfulness is being present in the moment then meditation is training the mind to do that. In mindfulness practice the aim is to unhook us from fixed thought patterns, the aim is not necessarily self-transcendence. Meditation in the contemplative traditions of the world may take us that one step further, to take the attention off ourselves completely. Mindfulness, as it is taught today in secular institutions, keeps itself absolutely separate from religion and even spiritual concerns. Could today's interest in mindfulness open the doors, and finally the minds, of secular institutions to a more profound contemplative consciousness? In the end a technique which is practised for personal and corporate benefits, may become a journey into the reality of self-giving love.

Feelings and ideas about ourselves are, for better or for worse, shaped by verbal culture, which includes religion. Mindfulness practices can help de-emphasise verbal control – the internalisation of imposed cultural values – by cultivating the space to be who we are. But as part of this 'acceptance' it remains important for the therapist to understand and appreciate the client's religious perspective *if* that perspective is a source of motivation not repression. If it is a detrimental influence too, that should not be ignored but brought to the light of a healthier faith perspective. Religion and spirituality if accessed appropriately could be an asset for therapist and client. To access meditation through the client's own religious or spiritual outlook would activate previously dormant resources for therapy, turning a client's spirituality into a relevant personal strength. In religious cultures or with clients who profess religious faith, the presentation of faith-based meditation would enhance the credibility of mindfulness. More importantly it would make the practices relevant to the client's spiritual concerns.

This is not to say that, in terms of stress and mental health, those who profess religion are any different to those who don't. It can be appropriate for doctors and therapists to point those in need to secular clinical mindfulness to help with specific vulnerabilities. Once the practices are engaged with and some of the benefits achieved, however, there should be an opportunity to point out equivalent (or ways of doing the same) practices within the contemplative traditions of the world religions. For example, as it is possible that someone doing mindfulness practices for personal health and wellbeing may be led to the deeper teachings of Buddhist meditation and motivated to realise the truths expressed in that tradition, so it is natural for those drawn to Christian faith to link what they learn in mindfulness with their experience of prayer. By putting mindfulness within a faith or wisdom perspective in whatever religion there is an opportunity to connect mindfulness with a broader spectrum of life skills nurtured in religious commitment: ethics, discrimination of truth, community, commitment, meaning.

The challenge of mindfulness practice to the more 'belief' orientated aspect of religion is the use of the body and physical processes like breathing and sense experience as the object of focus. This is also its claim to universal applicability as no particular religion owns the breath. Everyone alive is able to notice what they hear, see, taste and touch so the body-scan encouraged in mindfulness can hardly be called a Buddhist preserve. Watching the in-breath or out-breath at the nostrils or the rise and fall of the abdomen can hardly be considered Buddhist proselytising (as some Christian critics of mindfulness have seen it). Such techniques don't involve emptying the mind, or evoking unknown spiritual forces, they simply involve giving the mind a physical focus thus helping to bring mind and body together. And in this context, it is perhaps understandable that non-Buddhist teachers don't feel any need to call mindfulness 'spiritual'.

However, the bridge between the body and the spirit is something the world religions need not feel uncomfortable with. Much religion helps explain it: for Christians God expresses himself not in a book, in rules or beliefs but in flesh. Christianity is a theology of the body. Buddhist mindfulness uses bodily awareness as a tool but not as an end. Though normally non-theistic, most Buddhists would identify their lifestyle as 'spiritual practice'. To see Buddhism as *a*theistic or even 'without beliefs' is challenged by Buddhist scholars like Alan Wallace and the Dalai Lama. The silence of the Buddha on metaphysical questions was not a denial that there is a realm beyond our physical senses but more a conviction that this is encountered more through mindful practices than through speculation. Body awareness is for the Buddhist a key to enlightenment because it brings us into the here and now.

The breath is also central to the Christian story. From Genesis 2:7 God formed man from the dust of the ground and breathed into his nostrils the breath of life. Our breath comes from God, and enlivens the body. The Psalmist sings, 'You withdraw their breath [creatures] return to dust, You send forth your Spirit they are created' (Ps 104: 29–30). The Hebrew word for spirit and breath *ruah* is the same (as in many ancient languages: Sanskrit *atman*, Greek *pneuma*, Latin *spiritus*). In the Acts of the Apostles we read, 'Jesus breathed on [his disciples] and said "Receive the Holy Spirit" ' (Jn 20:22). Where St John says, 'God is Spirit', the monk and theologian Maximus the Confessor (580–662) changes one letter in the Greek, saying 'God is breath.'[5] 'Do you not know,' St Paul tells the Christians in Corinth, 'that your body is a temple of the Holy Spirit?' (1 Cor 6:19–20). Another aspect of the body emphasised in Christian prayer is the heart. 'The love of God has flooded our inmost heart,' writes St Paul (Rom 5:5). 'Lead the mind into the heart,' say the teachers of the Jesus prayer. One of the early bishops of the Church, Diadochos of Photiki (fifth century), speaks of 'an unceasing mindfulness of God' which comes from 'keeping our eyes always fixed on the depths of our heart.'[6]

Alan Wallace, for one, sees a deep parallel between Christian teaching on watchfulness and discernment and the Buddhist understanding of mindfulness and introspection. In both cases the two go together. Mindfulness, Wallace says, 'holds the attention' on an object while introspection examines 'the state of one's body and mind' in relation to this object.[7] Meditation, in this sense is inherently relational (even if that which we are getting to know is ourselves). But the object of contemplation can also be God. The Christian mystical tradition keeps in mind that we cannot *see* God. Without this proviso Wallace is wary of 'mythical' religious language distinguishing as he does 'the empiricism of experience' from 'faith based religion'.[8] However, for the Christian it is faith, which relates us to what cannot be seen. Wallace wishes to include spiritual experience within the realm of the empirical – he is concerned with what meditation and spiritual practice can reveal about consciousness and the universe in scientifically verifiable data. But could this also not be the idolatry of trying to *see* God?

The great scholar of Christian mysticism, Bernard McGinn, sees faith as the conceptual and motivational basis for Christian prayer even when ideas and desires are left behind.[9] If relation with God, or Jesus as the human face of God, shapes the 'prayer of quiet' or 'union' how much more, he says, in the preparatory stages of mindful self-recollection. The Christian mystics have always seen self-knowledge, the facing up to our thoughts and inclinations, and letting go of what is not helpful, as something instilled into us through faith, hope and finally love. Having a faith perspective on life may not necessarily make one more mindful but it does instil a sense that 'there is more to life than meets the eye'. What is scientifically verifiable in spiritual experience is not really what is most important. For, St Paul says, 'in hope we were saved. Now hope that is seen is not hope. For who hopes for what is seen?' (Rom 8:24). The patience instilled in Christian mindfulness comes from being open to and waiting for what faith gives us the assurance of, 'the evidence of things *not* seen' (Hebrews 11:1). It is good to look at the view but also to be aware of the horizon. In a sense not-seeing is the key to believing.

It has been said faith is universal: non-religious people put their faith in scientific understandings or humanistic and environmental values. But religious faith has the particular characteristic of looking beyond this world. This shouldn't lead to a neglect of things in this world but it does involve recognising that 'what is seen was made from things that are not visible' (Hebrews 11:3). In the case of Christian faith, therefore, one should say it is not strictly empirical nor is it 'mythical'. The language of religious belief points beyond empirical verifiability to the transcendent. Myths are shaped in the imagination but mindfulness or meditation practised in faith would help us not only to be present to the here and now through our senses but would attest to 'what no eye has seen, nor ear heard, and no mind has imagined' (1 Cor 2:9).

Seeing Beyond the Horizon

Religious people can see mindfulness as 'self bound'. Sitting concentrating on our breathing may be a remedy for stress but does it help us take the attention off ourselves and be aware of others who are in need? Loving-kindness meditation may well be good but does it translate into action? Do we feed the hungry, visit the prisoner, etc.? A dichotomy between self-awareness and self-transcendence doesn't really fit with the wisdom of the world religions, which have always seen a link between active and contemplative life. Mindfulness of self and others should go together. However, the default tendency to relate all experience to ourselves may not be challenged by mindfulness. Faith in something beyond our ego would help with letting go of obsessive thoughts, which revolve around the thought 'me!' Relating what happens to ourselves – what we do or don't like – may be cured better in caring for another than through cultivating a peaceful ego. This is the problem of distilling one bit of Buddhism and teaching it without reference to the other aspects of Buddhist faith and practice. Religions develop slowly, incrementally. What can seem to modern secular viewers as eccentric or boring bits play an important role.

To take an analogy from the sphere of medicine: No one doubts the benefits of conventional medicine in treating symptoms of illness – we take an aspirin when we have a headache – but the cause of the symptom is often not addressed. Moreover, pharmaceutical medicine can have negative and uncomfortable side effects. Holistic medicine, in contrast, takes the body as a whole, encouraging all systems to work together harmoniously. Holistic medicine focuses on prevention – identifying at-risk areas of health before they become a problem. Conventional medicine has become little more than disease management. Most conventional drugs used today originated from the natural healing properties found in herbs. Aspirin was originally derived from willow bark for its salicylic content. However, scientists found ways to isolate beneficial compounds found in medicinal plants and create them synthetically in a lab. Conventional medicine may be beneficial for acute injuries, such as a car accident, broken bones, heat stroke, frostbite, and the like; however chronic conditions such as the flu, diabetes, heart disease, and cancer can all benefit from a more holistic approach that incorporates herbal remedies into a regimen of care. Mindfulness Based Stress Reduction (MBSR) isolates a particular practice of Buddhism in the same way that conventional medicine takes an 'active ingredient' from herbs. It is still herbal medicine but is now packaged to treat a particular symptom – stress. The other 'bits' of traditional religion are left behind as modern medicine discards the rest of the herb.

These other bits play an important role, however, in limiting a side effect of modern mindfulness practice – the fact that it could leave us as selfish as ever. Moreover, the question whether mindfulness really treats the cause of mental health issues or whether it helps to create an acceptably functional level of peacefulness depends on one's philosophy of life. Thomas

Merton notes how, examined at his trial by psychologists, Adolf Eichmann, superintendent at Auschwitz, was found to have no symptoms of insanity: 'He was calm in his mind, had no sense of guilt, never lost his ability to sleep or his appetite, but merely felt he was doing his job.'[10] This could be a description of business-based-mindfulness. Merton concludes that to be well-adapted and peaceably functional without questioning what on earth we are doing is the most dangerous form of madness.

Viktor Frankl's classic and experiential analysis of how people survived concentration camp concludes that what kept people going was not physical or mental strength, nor acceptance of the way things were, but the ability to make meaning out of the difficulties of life. Frankl noted that real meaning came neither from beliefs or a sense of wellbeing – both of which were undermined by life – but from a sense of calling, as a summons. Meaning is made as a response to something outside of ourselves:

> Ultimately, we should not ask what the meaning of his life is, but rather must recognise that it is we who are asked. Each of us is questioned by life; we can only answer to life by answering for our own life; we can only respond by being responsible [...] By declaring that man is responsible and must actualise the potential meaning of his life, I wish to stress that the true meaning of life is to be discovered in the world rather than within man or his own psyche, as though it were a closed system. I have termed this constitutive characteristic 'the self-transcendence of human existence'. It denotes the fact that being human always points, and is directed, to something or someone, other than oneself – be it a meaning to fulfil or another human being to encounter. The more we forget ourselves – by giving ourselves to a cause to serve or another person to love – the more human we are and the more we actualise ourselves. What is called self-actualisation is not an attainable aim at all, for the

simple reason that the more one would strive for it, the more he would miss it. In other words, self-actualisation is possible only as a side-effect of self-transcendence.[11]

This sense of 'otherness' I believe is the gift of Christianity to mindfulness: Who we are in relation to others and the great other who is God.

In God whose glory 'was in the beginning, is now and ever shall be' past and future need not be rejected in favour of the present moment. All things are present to Him. Even for us mortals, as Frankl's 'Logotherapy' points out, the meaning of our lives lies as much in our potentialities 'to be fulfilled in the future' and 'actualised, saved and delivered into the past, wherein they are rescued and preserved from transitoriness.'[12] Anticipation and memory are part of meaning. This is why Frankl says choice is so important in giving an indelible meaning in our lives, 'a footprint in the sands of time'. Such choice, however, demands responsibility not just for ourselves but for others, and ultimately, for Christians, to the other that is God. As Frankl always proposed, if there is a Statue of Liberty off the East Coast of America there should be a Statue of Responsibility off the West Coast. Freedom from past and future is not a panacea for human problems for, like God in whose image we are made, we find our meaning in what is, was, and will be. To live 'faithfully' is to live in this continuity between what we received in the past, live in the present and hope for in the future. It is to live mindful that we are part of a story much bigger than ourselves and the meaning of our own life comes as a response to others and to the 'other' who calls us.

Exclusive and Inclusive Christianity

What are the theological hurdles that Christians face in allowing Mindfulness to be accepted within their ranks? According to the Gospels Jesus claimed universal relevance – 'I am the Way, the

Truth and the Life,' he said, 'No one comes to the Father except through me' (Jn 14:6). However, in this saying he was speaking as the Word of God incarnate not from the ego. The ego is shaped by ideas about ourselves that we received as children and, later in life, from the projections and expectations of others. When René Descartes (1596–1650) said 'I think therefore I am', he was describing the ego. The true self has no self-image, but has its identity from being itself. A misreading of the high Christological statements of Jesus can lead to a rather egoic picture of Jesus. When Jesus says, 'I am the Way, the Truth and the Life' he speaks as the true self, the selfless self. Jesus points away from himself to the source: 'Anyone who believes in me believes not in me, but in the Father who sent me' (Jn 12:44). The Gospels show in deed and word Jesus never acted from himself but in obedience to his Father. So no one comes to the Father unless they leave their limited sense of self behind. The true self, drawing from the source of life, is not separate from anything that lives. Living from the truth, it is united to all that is true. If mindfulness helps to let go of the ego then it shares in Christ, it is part of the way, the truth and the life and it can lead to the Father.

Seeing and doing things in just one way, having fixed conclusions, and not wanting to learn, is what the mindful-theorist Ellen Langer calls 'mindlessness.' It could also be called fundamentalism. An 'exclusive' claim on truth is dangerous when narrow-mindedness seems to be prescribed by God. Christians can have a narrow view of what it means to say 'Jesus is Lord.'

Imagine saying something and it immediately comes to be. 'God said "Let there be light!" and there was light' (Genesis 1:3, etc.). 'God has spoken only one Word, but in that Word there is everything,' says St John of the Cross.[13] Jesus is the speech of God. Not only through him all things were made but he became something 'made' in the womb of Mary. The Christological debates of the fifth century concluded that all the sayings of Jesus in the Gospels could be attributed to both his Divine and his human nature because both inhered in the person of Jesus. The only 'I' that can say, 'I am all' is God.[14] This 'I' entered historical contingency, was limited in time, space, gender, became man, but never ceased to be 'the true light, which enlightens everyone' (Jn 1:19). This Divine predicate makes universal mediation possible.

The fifth-century Fathers believed that by a translation of terms what was said of one nature in the person of Christ could be said of the other. So, for example, when Jesus says 'I thirst' this expresses his human bodily thirst and also divine longing to bring all things to completion. Its literal meaning refers to his incarnate nature (only bodies thirst!) but symbolically it can be read to His divinity. The saying 'I am the Way, the Truth and the Life, no one comes to the Father except through me' on the other hand starts the other way: literally it applies to Christ's Divine nature; then, by analogy, to his human nature as *Logos ensarkos,* the enfleshed Word. The problem with Christian fundamentalism is that the nuance of different levels of interpretation is missed. All readings of Scripture are flattened to the literal sense. In this particular case the analogical reading is taken as the literal and one is left only with a human being who claims to be God and denies that identity to anything else. The early Church Fathers, however, saw the Divine nature predicated in the 'I' and 'me' of Jesus' claim. Through the incarnation the universal 'Way, Truth and Life' was manifested in human form.

All people are in relation to Christ from the fact that they exist, 'not one thing came into being except through Him' (Jn 1:9). One can only make universal and exclusive claims about a single limited human life when that life points beyond itself to something much bigger. Consider C.S. Lewis's comment:

> A man who was merely a man and said the sort of things
> Jesus said would not be a great moral teacher. He would
> either be a lunatic – on the level with the man who says he
> is a poached egg – or else he would be the Devil of Hell. You

must make your choice. Either this man was, and is, the Son of God, or else a madman or something worse.[15]

This human being was God's self-expression. When we speak our breath carries our words so the Father expresses his Word through the Spirit. The Holy Spirit is what enables people to enter into a conscious, mindful, relationship with the source of their being. We realise that more than being created by God we are children of God. We enter into the same relationship with God as Jesus' had. This is the invitation of Christian mysticism: 'God became human so that human beings might become Divine.'[16]

If spirit and body are so closely related in Christianity that a 'translation of terms' from one to the other is possible then the universal human embodied capacity to be mindful could be a way of relating to Christ. However non-religious the language of therapeutic or educational mindfulness, as an embodied response to life it always remains potentially a spiritual act. We come to God by being fully human. It is possible to arrive at a mindful state (as Langer says) without meditation. It is likewise possible through the wise practices of Buddhism, Christianity and contemplative traditions throughout the world. Mindful awareness practices are therapeutically important because they can lead to fuller, happier, and more humane living. This is what makes such practices spiritually significant also, for, as Thomas Aquinas said, 'Grace builds on and perfects nature.'[17]

It is true, however, that medieval Christian theologians spoke of *cognita Dei experimentalis,* the experimental knowledge of God. Spiritual empiricism is no preserve of the East. A distinction can be made between faith, which is at roots an experience, and belief, which is the conceptual framework in which that experience is understood. If belief is the map then faith is the journey. We have to walk the walk. Faith that 'merely believes what it ought to believe,' St Anselm describes as 'dead.'[18] The experimental within Christianity is set within the context of transcendence. In

Christian theology belief is the premise of gnosis: 'I believe so that I may understand,' said St Anselm.[19] But if understanding is really led by faith it has to pass through unknowing: 'If I understand it,' St Augustine said, 'it's not God.'[20] Unknowing involves letting go of the idea and launching into the reality. This journey is a way of love, reaching out to the one who summons us into being, inviting us to be more than we can imagine. In this sense belief always remains the horizon of Christian faith. *Cognita* and *experientia* are a response to the transcendent as it has revealed itself in time.

Can the Real Mindfulness Please Stand Up!

There exist variously nuanced 'educational' and 'meditative' approaches to mindfulness. Recently, and with a big impact, a new angle has come into being – 'therapeutic' mindfulness. Unlike some pedagogic models this uses meditational practices but within a strictly secular paradigm. With these different versions is it possible to say what mindfulness is?

The word can be traced back to the Old English word *gemyndful* meant 'of good memory'. Old English also had an adjectival form *myndig* meaning 'recollecting' or 'thoughtful'. It passes into Middle English as '*myndful*'. As such it appears in the King James Bible where mindfulness is a quality shown pre-eminently by God: 'What is man, that Thou art mindful of him?' (Ps 8:4). As an English word it derives from the Latin *memor* (memory). It is worth noting though, as the sentiments of the Psalms demonstrate, that the Hebrew meaning is not just to remember, but also to show concern, to act with loving care. It further implies putting things into practice. The second letter of St Peter in the King James Version encourages us to 'be mindful of the words spoken before by the holy prophets.'

Recently the word 'mindfulness' has been loosely employed to translate certain Buddhist technical terms, such as the Sanskrit *smrti* or equivalent Pali term *sati*.[21] In the early Buddhist text *Dīgha*

Nikâya the Buddha defines *sati* as the ability to remember, to keep in memory what was said and done long ago. This can seem rather different to the 'living in the present moment' emphasis of recent mindfulness teaching. However, according to Wallace, in early Buddhist practice it came to imply not just 'calling to mind' but also 'taking hold' of whatever presents itself in awareness through an act of attention. It also implied a certain 'guarding of the mind' to discern what in the field of awareness was wholesome and what was unwholesome. In this sense, in early Buddhist understandings of mindfulness, awareness is not just a passive acceptance of what is, but active vigilance against what is unhelpful and cultivation of positive states of mind.[22]

The word itself obviously does not, *per se*, imply a Buddhist meaning and has been used in educational studies without any reference to meditative practices. Harvard psychologist Ellen Langer has been called 'the mother of mindfulness' through her research. For Langer mindfulness describes the simple human capacity to notice things. When thought is caught in preconceived ideas then the human person loses their openness to what is new and different to our expectations. By way of antonym, the prevention of 'mindlessness' is to see things in terms of their possibilities, what they 'could be'. It involves drawing novel distinctions between things, responding creatively to what each moment presents, looking to our own experience and to the multiple perspectives of others rather than to fixed conclusions.[23] Mindfulness, Langer says, is the basis of any true learning.[24] But for her it doesn't imply meditational practices. Mindfulness doesn't involve trying to stop thinking but stopping to think:

> We need to stop and actually *think* about what we're doing, how we're reacting, and perhaps even reflect on why we're reacting in the way we are in the moment. We make so many choices in our lives on 'autopilot', we don't always

spend the time actually *thinking* about what choices we are making.[25]

Langer sees learning as furthered more by focusing on varying stimulus than through single-pointed attention. Mental flexibility stops us falling into mindless responses conditioned by the past. Mindful health is about 'freeing ourselves from constricting mindsets.'[26] It involves 'the simple act of actively noticing things.'[27]

> I don't see mindfulness as simply being optimistic or 'thinking will make it so'. Instead, it's trying to put your thoughts into some sort of context – in the moment you're doing something – to become more connected not only with yourself, but with those and the world around you.[28]

Mindfulness should not, she says, be an effort: when we notice change, newness, then things become naturally interesting. In classrooms creative distraction would be more pedagogic than telling students to 'sit still', 'pay attention', 'focus', 'concentrate'. Educators, she believes, should make students aware of the multiple perspectives on any subject, and encourage them that changing their mind is part of being open and inquisitive.

Langer sees the need for certainty as at the root of 'mindless' behaviour. Her studies have avoided the field of religious belief but religious views, tending to be absolute, could play into the one perspective mentality. Fundamentalism is a prime example of a mind that has closed down in its certainties. Langer does, however, give two antidotes to mono-track thinking that need not necessarily relativise religious beliefs. She advocates: 1) Understanding there are various perspectives on any object and, to bear in mind that although we may not take on every perspective, we have the ability to recognise other points of view could be held with integrity by others; 2) Realising, even when we have our point of view, that we are always changing, as we change and adapt to new circumstances our beliefs are related to in new ways. Certainly Langer's studies challenge any group that see themselves as 'knowers' rather than learners. For believers in God this should be self-evident: God is infinite, we only ever have partial knowledge when it comes to knowing him. Moreover, knowledge of God comes through God's self-revelation; it is never through our own understanding. Still, religion always carries the danger of operating in rigid categories without being able to create new ones. As Shaun Lambert puts it:

> 'If God loves me then he shouldn't let me suffer at all,' is a very limiting and untrue category. 'If it's from another religion it must be bad,' is a limiting and wrong category of thinking – as well as an automatic one. When it comes to God and life, we need an openness to new categories and new perspectives, which requires an orientation in the present moment. As Christians we are people of faith, but sometimes faith is taught as absolute certainty. We don't have an absolute certainty. Faith tells us that we have conditional certainty, otherwise it wouldn't be faith.[29]

However, alongside humanist perspectives, such as Langer's, there exists the long tradition of Buddhist 'mindfulness' – the foundation stone of the meditative practices of that religion. Buddhist practices cultivate the focusing of the mind onto single-mindedness, thereby calming it (*samatha*) and giving it the energy to look deeply at 'what is' (*vipassana*). In his book *The Miracle of Mindfulness* Hanh gives practical meditation practices like doing tasks with full attention – 'when washing the dishes wash the dishes' – walking mindfully, awareness of breathing, tasting, touching, hearing and seeing with as full presence as possible.[30] The inspiration for these applied meditation practices are ancient Buddhist texts that Hanh has made accessible: *Satipatthana Sutta* (Four Establishments of Mindfulness), *Anapanasati Sutta*

(Full Awareness of Breathing) and *Bhadekaratta Sutta* (Sutra on Knowing the Better Way to live Alone).

The *Satipatthana Sutta* teaches that all feelings, whether of compassion or irritation, should be welcomed, recognised, and treated on an absolutely equal basis as part of who we are. To think in terms of either pessimism or optimism oversimplifies the truth, we have to see reality as it is. In mindfulness one not only cultivates rest and happiness but alert wakefulness. Meditation is no evasion; it is a serene encounter with reality. The *Anapanasati Sutta* teaches that the breath is the bridge, which connects life to consciousness, uniting our body to our thoughts. Whenever the mind becomes scattered it advises using the breath as the means to take hold of the mind again. The *Bhadekaratta Sutta* extends this focus of awareness to all we encounter and do during the day. Being present is the way to be in the present moment.

Hanh sees such practices as valuable for all people whether Buddhist or not. Practitioners from the West especially are urged to build bridges with their Christian heritage. 'Mindfulness is very much like the Holy Spirit,' Hanh believes, 'Both are agents of healing.'[31] Jesus' baptism in the Jordan is equated with the Buddha's enlightenment under the Bodhi tree. According to the Gospels the heavens opened above Jesus and the Holy Spirit descended in the form of a dove, God speaks of him as his beloved child. For Hanh this is symbolic of the open, transparent, peaceful, pure consciousness whereby we know ourselves as infinitely valuable. Jesus went on from this experience to spend forty days in the Desert – this, Hanh says, was to consolidate his practice of mindfulness. Christian saints echo this experience. Hanh loves the story of St Francis looking deeply at the almond tree in winter and asking it to speak to him about God, and the tree was instantly covered with blossoms.[32]

As a Buddhist teacher Hanh leans towards a Universalist understanding of the value of meditation. Another Buddhist teacher who does this is Alan Wallace. For Wallace mindfulness refers to a spiritual experience that is in no way the privilege of Buddhism.

Forms of single pointed attention (*samatha*) are found to varying extents in all the world's great contemplative traditions. Buddhism gives it a particular texture both in terms of motivation and in how contemplative experience is interpreted. Christianity offers another texture. For traditional Buddhism, however, mindfulness is preparatory for investigating reality, for insight and wisdom, the practice of *vipassana*. 'Mindfulness includes not only present-centred mindfulness,' Wallace believes, 'but also retrospective memory of your experiences.'[33] It is the cumulative, depository quality of insight that builds religious traditions. Tradition means 'handing on'. For Wallace mindfulness is truncated if seen only in personal terms and practised for personal benefits, its true value is transpersonal and altruistic – for the sake of others.

Therapeutic Mindfulness

Therapeutic mindfulness developed out of Cognitive Behaviour Therapy (CBT) as a way of dealing with stress, depression, compulsive disorders and other mental health issues. In contrast with earlier CBT techniques, Mindfulness Based Cognitive Therapy (MBCT) looks at whether trying to control our thoughts or emotions is helpful, or part of the problem. Negative feelings are not to be avoided or manipulated away by 'positive thinking'. Avoidance of negative feelings limits full experience and leads to pathology. What about accepting thoughts and emotions as they are? The therapy client or patient is encouraged to embrace whatever is present in the moment. The client is not prompted to change what they think, but rather to look with a new detachment at whatever passes through their mind or emotions. This 'spaciousness' allows the client to refrain from immediate identification with thoughts and feelings and open up new ways of reacting to what is going on in and around them.

Behaviour therapists try to use strictly secular language in Mindfulness theories. Stripping mindfulness from any religious connotations makes it available to non-Buddhists. Mindfulness is used strictly as a therapeutic tool, instrumental to mental health, stability and cognitive clarity. 'Mindfulness-Based Stress Reduction' (MBSR) maintains something of the Buddhist emphasis on the realisational potential of mindfulness: mindfulness is not so goal orientated – for the achievement of better mental health – but is a 'way', a way of understanding 'what is', a path of insight and life-wisdom. It is not just a way of doing therapy. It is meditation.

MBSR was developed by Kabat-Zinn and colleagues at the University of Massachusetts Medical School. MBSR is transparent about its origins in Buddhist meditation practices. However, as Kabat-Zinn says, to call mindfulness Buddhist is like saying that gravity is British because Isaac Newton discovered it! MBSR prefers to see mindfulness as a universal human capacity for awareness and attention irrespective of religious belief. MBSR sees meditational practices as useful in secular therapeutic contexts. The client is encouraged to distinguish between first and second-degree suffering. Life will always be to some degree unsatisfactory (the Buddhist concept of *Dukha*), but we add to this when we say, 'this should not be.' Unhappiness arises from the craving of what isn't and rejection of what is. Kabat-Zinn advises, 'When you look at thoughts as just thoughts, purposefully not reacting to their content and to their emotional charge, you become at least a little freer from their attraction or repulsion.'[34]

MBSR facilitators prefer not to call such practices 'spiritual' but rather ways of learning to 'be' through letting go of self-analysis. MBSR, like Hanh, encourages fixing the attention on one thing (usually the breath or bodily sensations) and then developing awareness of the quality of attention itself. Paying attention in the present moment leads to what Kabat-Zinn calls 'heartfulness'. The other pillars of mindfulness are non-judging, patience, a beginner's mind, trust, non-striving, acceptance and letting go. MBSR tries to cultivate an open, curious mind that notices things and isn't caught in its own moods or opinions. In addition to Buddhism MBSR elicits mentors from American literature and

Native American wisdom. The witness of contemplative prayer in Christianity is rarely, if ever, referred to.

While CBT tries to unblock debilitating judgments and assumptions by changing behavioural attitudes, MBSR proposes a simple acceptance of things as they are. Because of a suspicion of analysis, *why things are the way they are* is addressed less in MBSR. Respect for their world-view, experience and ethical values are part of client autonomy, but in MBSR any trans-personal or metaphysical approach to meaning is considered beyond the preserve of this particular therapy. But meaning is part of healing. It cannot be imposed, but to assume that only a purely secular mindfulness is appropriate presumes a default atheist outlook, which is not the case for many clients. It may be that when faced with multiple religious perspectives secular mindfulness is a common denominator, which can be applied across the board. The danger, however, is that in terms of 'meaning' it becomes a lowest common denominator and doesn't go deep enough. The question arises within therapeutic mindfulness – 'And what next? Is this really only about me getting well?'

For the Buddhist, calming of the mind goes hand in hand with insight into reality, an insight expressed objectively in the *Dharma*. For Christians being still is so we know God (Ps 46:10). Wallace, for one, believes that accounts of mindfulness adopted by psychologists run the risk of departing from traditional Buddhist teachings on meditation. 'Simple attention', 'capacity to notice things' – seen by pedagogic, therapeutic and many recent Buddhist *vipassana* teachers as the heart of mindfulness – does not, in Wallace's view, correspond to Buddhist accounts of *sati* (Sanskrit – *smrti*) which includes *retrospective* memory of things in the past and *prospective* remembering to do something in the future as well as attention to a present reality. Likewise, when mindfulness is equated simply with attention it leaves out the ethical-discriminatory aspect of Buddhist practice. This is also essential in cultivating wholesome states of mind and stopping unwholesome states. Wallace writes:

Buddhist meditation can quickly devolve into a vague kind of 'be here now' mentality, in which the extraordinary depth and richness of Buddhist meditative traditions are lost [...] A sniper hiding in the grass, waiting to shoot his enemy, may be quietly aware of whatever arises with each passing moment. But because he is intent on killing, he is practicing wrong mindfulness. In fact, what he's practicing is bare attention without an ethical component [...] Right mindfulness has to occur in the context of the full Noble Eightfold Path: For example, it must be guided by right view, motivated by right intention, grounded in ethics, and be cultivated in conjunction with right effort.[35]

To take one type of Buddhist meditation out of its context distorts it. Mindfulness may not be a distillation of Buddhism but an aspect of it, which only works when related with others. Practised within a materialistic world-view mindfulness may relieve stress but could be a short-change form of Buddhism. This shouldn't mean that one has to take on the whole of Buddhism in order to practise mindfulness. But it does mean a broader *context* for mindfulness should be encouraged that includes social, ethical, and philosophical values. Mindfulness needs to be an integral practice. The question is whether, alongside Buddhism and secular humanism Christianity can also serve as a broadening and deepening *context* for mindfulness? I propose the Christian mystics can provide this.

Who were the Christian Mystics?

Did not the mystics find God within them, in their own psyche? The Christian mystical tradition is that part of Christianity which speaks of personal experience of God normally in the context of silence and stillness. In most forms it involves a practice of interiority or withdrawal of the senses from multiplicity towards what Aquinas called 'the simple enjoyment of the truth'.[36] The step of self-awareness ('that we are') is normally seen as a stepping-stone to self-transcendence ('that God is'). Most Christian mystics speak of finding and losing themselves in God. The Divine in this tradition is both 'the other' to whom the self relates and the 'ground of being' in which all people live. McGinn sees the umbrella characteristic of the great variety of Christian mysticism as 'awareness of the presence of God'.[37] If this is different from 'ordinary' Christian ways of experiencing God it is because of its 'unmediated quality': It is not necessarily through Scripture, Sacrament, human fellowship or even practices of prayer and reflection that God is encountered. For the mystic God is encountered directly in their own soul. Though McGinn goes on to explain, somewhat circuitously, that unmediated contact with God is often experienced through means.

John Main clarifies this by making a distinction between 'experiences in prayer' – which have to be let go of and ignored – and 'experience of prayer' which leads to an unselfconscious state. 'To have the eye of our heart opened is to lose the very sense of the 'I' that sees,' John Main says.[38] Christian mysticism cannot be expressed through any idea: 'The reality Jesus has uncovered for us,' Main says, 'is the new age of presence.'

> Our elaborate theories and systems simply crumble before the power of the actual experience, one that is so evident, so simple it defies adequate verbal expression. It can indeed only be communicated by sharing the experience-in-itself. Any description of it alienates it from the authenticity of the present when we try to treat it as observable.

However, Main also says that meditation is a practical discipline through which we verify the truths of faith 'in your own experience'. Unmediated experience makes mediated experience more real. This is very similar to what John Henry Newman said about the need to move from 'notional ascent' to 'real ascent'. The idea of union with God stands in relation to the actual state as 1) intention does to realisation, 2) stimulation does to practical action, and 3) as abstract truth in relation to personal apprehension of it.[39] We can notionally assent to a proposition such as 'London is a beautiful city' without ever having been to London since we have in our minds the concept of 'beauty' and of 'city', but *real* ascent would require us to have been to London and to recollect our mental image of London as beautiful. In this way 'real experience' can verify what we 'believe'. It can also make us review our beliefs – if our experience of London was bad. The correlation of notional and real ascent develops over time and with regular revisitings. So it is with God. Meditation and mindfulness as a daily practice show us both the unreality of our ideas and also make possible their *real*isation.

A great scholar of mysticism, Evelyn Underhill, believed mysticism involved 'putting to sleep of that "Normal Self" which usually wakes, and the awakening of that "Transcendent Self" which usually sleeps'.[40] If this is interpreted as an altered state of consciousness then mysticism could be understood in rather individualist and esoteric ways rather than being seen as a natural state of other-centredness, a state of self-forgetting love. Newman quipped (rather tongue in cheek as he himself was a mystic) that mysticism 'begins in mist and ends in schism'. He left out the 'i' in the middle. Some have added to the defamation by saying mysticism always centres on 'I'! Mysticism has always had a mixed reception in Christianity. Underhill believed it was 'One of the most abused words in the English language [...] it is much to be hoped that it may be restored sooner or later to its old meaning, as the science or art of the spiritual life'.[41] Maybe the time has come for its rehabilitation. The great Jesuit theologian Karl Rahner said, 'The Christian of the future will be a mystic or he will not exist at all.'[42]

For our purposes a definition of mysticism – more difficult than a definition of mindfulness – is not necessary. Rather I propose to look at particular texts and people who through the spectrum of Christian history have written of the practice of the presence of God through silence, stillness and simple awareness. In this I have not chosen to look at 'visionary mysticism', nor at the type of mysticism – dominant in the early Church – concerned with Scriptural interpretation. These are valid approaches – and include within their respective camps great mystics like Hildegard of Bingen and Origen – but their parallels with contemporary views of mindfulness are minimal. Neither will I look at the great tradition of poetic mysticism represented by say Hadewijch of Brabant, Richard Rolle, Thomas Traherne and William Blake. My focus will be on practices of meditation and mindfulness and not on the language of mysticism or its expression in theology or religious life. Many of the great theologians, legislators and reformers of the Church could be seen as mystics but I will only touch briefly on Benedict of Norcia, Francis and Clare of Assisi and Thomas Aquinas or Martin Luther.

Christian mysticism might ask for something of Ellen Langer's multi-perspectival awareness. Any single viewpoint as to 'what is mysticism' leads to a simplification. Many social and political activists were mystics – Trevor Huddleston, Dorothy Day, Martin Luther King or Mother Teresa. Many had powerful experiences of love and forgiveness – like Nelson Mandela in prison – without necessarily seeing them in terms of Christianity. One could say that there are as many 'mysticisms' as there are mystics. There are, however, 'schools', 'traditions' and 'lineages' within Christian mysticism which link individual experiences. This book looks at those who use meditation as a way of awareness. I touch on the tradition of *nipsis* or 'wakefulness' among the ascetics of the Christian East but focus mainly on 'Western' Christianity. The mystical tradition within Christianity can help discipleship and prayer to be more embodied, less cerebral. Faith is something lived with our whole being. Mysticism is not, therefore, about otherworldliness but about the fullness of life here and now. The variety among the mystics highlights that it is a fully human, fully personal response to God. Like Langer's heuristic approach to learning each gives workable models to emulate and inspire without saying 'this is the only way.' The mystics show that the life of Christ expresses itself in myriad ways.

Ways of Learning

'No servant is greater than his master, but a fully trained servant is like his master' (Mt 10:24). The Christian mystics look for that likeness. The root of Jesus' mysticism was his sense of oneness with God ('I and the Father are One') and his responsiveness as 'Son' to the Divine source of his being. Those who followed his 'Way' drew from Jesus' teaching and from the gift of the Spirit leading them into the same experience of non-duality with God. During certain historical periods the *zeitgeist* and personalities of the leading mystics highlight particular aspects of being a child of God. As the Spirit leads into 'all truth', the body of Jesus continues mystically in the community of his followers and in the sacraments, which expand Christ's ministry beyond the time and place of his human life. The Christian mystics were, therefore, nourished by 1) the teaching of Jesus; 2) his experience made accessible through the Spirit; 3) the living out of Christian life in a community of faith (faith being as much about response as about belief); and 4) the augmentation and substantiation of that faith in lived experience through the Sacraments.

When Christianity was accepted by the Roman Empire there was a danger that 'Christianity' would become a convention, even something imposed on people, rather than a community of followers of the 'Way'. Those who went to the desert in the fourth and fifth centuries wanted to make a real and personal response to Jesus. Religious practice was not for them about external observances – doing things right – but inner watchfulness and a self-knowledge. Though living in the same era St Augustine – philosopher, Bishop, apologist for Christian faith even in its institutional form – did not take the path of the desert. However, he did share a concern for self-knowledge as the way to real and personal faith. He emphasised grace more, the Desert Fathers and Mothers emphasised practice. Both, however, drew from Christ's teaching on using mindfully the 'talents' given to us.

The medieval mystics reflect on the value of the present moment as the point of access to the Divine perspective. To see things as God sees them frees us from the past and enables us to act spontaneously. C.S. Lewis in *The Screwtape Letters* remarks that God wants us to attend chiefly to two things, 'to eternity itself, and to that point of time which [we] call the Present.'

> For the Present is the point at which time touches eternity. Of the present moment, and of it only, humans have an experience which [God] has of reality as a whole; in it alone freedom and actuality are offered them.[43]

The eternal moment is the source of compassion and loving-kindness: to see ourselves as God sees us is to know we are loved, to look at the world as God does is to look with pity not with blame. The medieval mystics also looked at how awareness of the body can be a distraction but also a way to an immediate sense of God's presence. Awareness of the body doesn't mean being self-conscious about our appearance, anxious about our health, centred on our comforts or discomforts; rather it is a way of enjoying the simple experiences of life. It offers a way of being mindfully in the world without being 'worldly'.

The sense of God's presence in all things is expressed in *Canticle of Creatures* of St Francis of Assisi (1181–1226). All created things are brothers and sisters to Francis. To be aware of them is to be mindful of God. Brother Sun, the source of all light, is a symbol of God; Sister Moon 'bright and precious and fair'; Sister Water 'humble useful and chaste'; Brother Fire, lights up the night and is 'handsome, jocund, robust and strong.' If we are mindful of 'Our Sister Mother Earth' then we will flourish for 'she teaches us and feeds us with fruits and coloured flowers and herbs.' Francis rejects nothing as of little value: the birds, the blades of grass, even bodily death, are companions on the way, brothers and sisters. His first biographer, Thomas of Celano wrote:

> St Francis praised the Artist in every one of his works; whatever he found in things made he referred to their Maker [...] In beautiful things he came to know beauty itself. To him all things were good. They cried out to him, 'He who made us is infinitely good.' By tracing his footprints in things, Francis followed the beloved wherever he led. He made, from created things, a ladder to his throne.[44]

Seeing all things as sacraments of God's presence and appreciating the small things of life is a special characteristic of French spirituality in the early modern period. St Francis's mother was French – that is where he got his name from, *Francesco*. But Francis is a universal model of what Christian mindfulness is like. Even Søren Kierkegaard from a quite different tradition than the French mystics (though the same era) recognised St Francis as having lived out the Gospel injunction to 'consider the lilies' and to 'look at the birds of the air.'

Mindfulness of nature and of God's presence in things is balanced by some recent mystics who evoke the *via negativa* which has been used by Christian mystics over the centuries to remind us that God is 'no thing'. Though creation can represent God – make God present again – God's nature is beyond space and time. So, as Simone Weil puts it, 'God is only present in this world under the form of absence.'[45] To take the representations as God would be idolatry. John Main, the last mystic I look at, bridges the gap encouraging a sense of God's presence in our lives through removing our thoughts and images about God. We have to learn to be with God not through any particular form but as the root and ground of all existence. The value of poverty (which St Francis lived outwardly in having no possessions so as to be open to all) is read by Main inwardly (as the Desert Fathers read it) – leaving behind the riches of thought and imagination during the time of prayer, limiting ourselves to one pointed attention. Or, as Kierkegaard put it slightly differently, 'Purity of heart is to will only one thing.'

The Christian mystics revisit each other; they make new emphases, 'bringing forth out of [their] treasure things new and old' (Mt 13:52). It is a like a symphony where the notes in an earlier movement reappear later in combination with new score. It is not so much one mystic imitating another – though there are lineages as with any tradition (from the Latin *trans dare*, 'handing on'). Rather they are coming from a common source. We have to be mindful of our own way, not imitate the way of another (even that of Christ as an exterior model). When St Francis was lying on his death bed he said to his Franciscan brothers, 'I have done what was mine to do; may Christ teach you what is yours to do.'[46] The harmony and diversity of the Christian mystics – separated as they are by many centuries – prompts one to think that however distinctive the musicians may be, the symphony has but one composer.

In the Middle Ages Mary Magdalene was considered the archetypal contemplative 'for she loved much' (Lk 7:47). At the end of St John's Gospel, at 'the tomb where they laid him', she is distracted with grief. Jesus is alive and speaking to her but she does not recognise him. She is caught up with the past. She remembers him as he was, not as he is. Mindfulness has to be in the now. Jesus calls her by her name, 'Mary'. She turns to him, turns to the one who is present to her, who knows her, and she says '*Rabbuni*, which means teacher' (Jn 20:11–16). For the Christian mystics meditation on the historical life of Christ prepares us for the encounter with the living Christ, the discovery that it is not us who try to hold him in mind but he who has always been mindful of us. It is the experience of being known and loved by another. In that love we discover who we are.

Chapter 3

Cognitive Therapy of the Desert

O that today you would listen to God's voice! Harden
not your hearts. (Ps 94)

There is a voice, which cries to us until our last breath,
and it says: Now is the time.[1]

Getting Real with Prayer

It could be said there was an anti-mystical strand among the
Desert Fathers and Mothers of the fourth and fifth centuries.
They were not interested in visions, in extraordinary phenomena,
miracles or esoteric teaching on prayer, but this, as we have seen,
is not really the essence of mysticism. There are two collections of
'sayings' from the Desert Fathers and Mothers: The *Anonymous
Sayings* collated in the fifth century and the longer *Alphabetical
Sayings* collated in the sixth. Alongside the *Sayings* we have the
more systematic (and earliest written) presentation of the desert
teaching in the writings of Evagrius of Pontus (345–399) and
his disciple John Cassian (360–435). All sources show the desert
teachers were eminently practical. Their concern was everyday life,
living the ordinary with extraordinary love. They were concerned
with the difficulties everyone faces when they come up against the

distractions and restlessness of their own minds. These things that blocked them in contemplation of God and love of neighbour they called demons, objective forces ranged against them.

Even the battles with demons they portray as a grimly realistic affair – the passions being the battlefield. In no way are they interested in mysticism or spirituality unless it had a concrete effect on healing the human soul. Anthony the Great (251–356), known as the founding *Abba* in Egypt, could foresee the future but refused to talk about it. Knowing the future wouldn't help people in what really concerned them – the present moment and its troubles. The Desert Mother Amma Syncletica said, 'It is dangerous for anyone to teach [prayer] who has not been first trained in the 'practical' life.'[2] By this she meant dealing with the unintegrated passions of the soul. Abba Agathon warns not to be impressed by anyone who raises the dead, but is unable to control their own temper.

In this the Desert Fathers and Mothers have common ground with therapeutic mindfulness, which prefers to read practice as cognitive therapy rather than spirituality. Jon Kabat-Zinn for example avoids 'the inaccurate, incomplete, and frequently misguided connotations of that word [spirituality].' He sees mindfulness as a 'consciousness discipline' but this shouldn't necessitate belief systems or notions that we have to get anywhere other than where we are. In Kabat-Zinn's opinion 'ideas of spirituality frequently ring with a slightly holier-than-thou resonance [...] the idea of transcendence can be a great escape, a high-octane fuel for delusion.'[3] If we get into spiritual ideas and ideals, we often avoid dealing with the real issues of our life. The Desert Fathers and Mothers would concur with this. For them the place of practice was everyday life. There was no special realm or activity that was 'spiritual'. All things could be sources of inspiration.

St Benedict – a slightly later Desert Father – says, 'Do not aspire to be called holy before you really are, but first be holy that you may more truly be called so' (The Rule of Benedict (RB) 4:62). We need to breathe in before we can breathe out. So it is in the spiritual life. The word 'spirit' comes from the Latin *spirare* meaning 'to breathe'. Spirituality should be an in-spiration not an as-piration. We shouldn't be trying to be holy but should let God be God in us. Then we can breathe freely, both in and out. Our inner and outer lives will connect. If spirituality is an inspiration then it is not an end in itself. The end, as St Benedict says, is the 'good life', life in all its fullness. We shouldn't aspire to a spiritual life, we should aspire to life, learn to appreciate life as it is.

Belief in God and a sense of Divine presence inspires us to do the humble practice of being present to what is. Spirituality does not mean trying to impress ourselves, or others. It means getting real. The aspiration of Christians is to be like Christ. But to do that we have to be inspired – given the Spirit – we have to breathe in Christ who breathed out his Spirit to the Father: '"Father into thy hands I commend my Spirit"; and having said this he breathed his last' (Lk 23:46). After his Resurrection Jesus breathed again, this time over the apostles: 'He breathed on them and said receive the Holy Spirit' (Jn 20:22). In the beginning God spoke creation into being and the breath that carried that word was the Spirit. In breathing in Jesus by being present to the whole of creation – life in all its fullness – we receive the Spirit that makes us holy, the Holy Spirit. 'Breathe only Christ', St Anthony of the Desert said.[4] Then all life's happenings become a source of in-spiration.

The Desert Fathers and Mothers read spiritual practice broadly as ways of being aware of all that goes on, in and around us. Making sure we 'inspire' before we 'aspire' means continually checking what inhibits our breathing – the various passions which keep us short of breath. Spirituality for them was not about supernatural experiences or esoteric theories but about how to deal with the blocks that keep us from fullness of life. There is a cautionary tale in the sayings of Abba Poemen: A very distinguished foreigner once visited him, he had come specially to see him, he was ushered into Poemen's presence and started talking. But Poemen averted his gaze and refused to speak to him. In dismay, the visitor went out and asked Poemen's disciple what was going on. The embarrassed disciple went inside to plead that his master would say something to the visitor who had travelled so far. But Poemen explained to his disciple, 'Our visitor is from above and speaks of heavenly things, but I am of the earth and speak about earthly things. If he had spoken to me about the passions of the soul, then I should have answered him. But if he speaks of spiritual things I know nothing of them.' The visitor tried again by saying, 'What shall I do, Abba, I am dominated by the passions of my soul?' Abba Poemen said, 'Now you are speaking rightly.'[5]

Taking Good Care

Mindfulness is motivated by a sense of value and interest in what presents itself to consciousness however mundane or even awkward. It is not really our opinions, views and philosophies which are interesting but what goes on underneath. That is why the Desert Fathers and Mothers have been called the first psychotherapists. Spiritual life, for them, was dealing with the hidden unconscious motivations that rule our life – the passions. Mindlessness, on the other hand, is unwillingness to pay attention to what is happening in and around us. We prefer fantasyland. The opposite of being mindful is being forgetful. The Desert Fathers and Mothers said that three things go before all sin: forgetfulness, negligence and desire: 'For truly every time forgetfulness comes, it engenders negligence; and from negligence desire proceeds; and desire causes a man to fall.'[6] The Desert Fathers and Mothers are not very interested in morality. Measuring behaviour as good or bad was really not their business. But they were worried about carelessness, of not facing up to what one was doing. This made one a liability to oneself and to others. 'Unawareness is the root of all evil,' one monk said.[7] For the Desert Fathers and Mothers this laxity came from a state of mind they called *acedia*, which can be translated as listlessness, despondency or boredom. *Acedia* makes us want to distract ourselves. It keeps us from being simply present to what is unfolding here and now.

However, *acedia* is not exactly the same as sloth or laziness. The person suffering from *acedia* can be very busy, but doing the wrong thing. Evagrius in his book *Practikos* (The Practical Way) says that diligence starts with the mind, not with trying to amend our behaviour exteriorly: 'The mind is easily moved indeed, and hard to control,' he writes, 'the war fought on the field of thought [is] more severe than that which is conducted in the area of things and events.'[8] Cassian tells the story of a monk whose fixation on a task distracted him from any time for rest that he desperately needed to recover.[9] Workaholics try to give meaning to their life through what they do, rather than discovering that life has meaning in itself. The witness of the early monastics is that a sense of value and interest in life is augmented and encouraged by a belief that 'the divine presence is everywhere' (RB 19:1). Spirituality inspires but should we aspire to be spiritual?

St Benedict was deeply influenced by the desert tradition, particularly as handed down through Cassian. But he lowers the level of aspiration from the 'pure spirituality' that was something of a tendency in the Desert. Instead of saying that we should get rid of our thoughts he advises people to seek God 'as ever present *within* our thoughts' (RB 7:14). Benedict's *Rule* shows how God indwells all life experience; our thought, the people we meet and live with, the activities of our day. There is no split between the religious and the secular. 'All guests who present themselves [from the outside world] are to be welcomed as Christ' (53:1). One doesn't need to be spiritual to carry the presence of Christ, all people do by the fact of their existence for 'not one thing was made except through Him.' The utensils and tools of the monastery kitchens and workshops 'are to be regarded as sacred vessels of the altar' (31:10). 'All our actions, everywhere, in the workshops, in the fields, on a journey, not just in the Oratory, are in God's sight' (7:13).

Living in God's sight means learning to live with ourselves, facing up to who we are. Gregory the Great (540–604) in his *Life of*

St Benedict says that in his cave 'Benedict lived alone with himself but under the gaze of God.' Gregory goes on analyse what it means to 'live with oneself':

> Every time we are drawn outside of ourselves by too much mental agitation, we are not 'with ourselves', even though we think we are. Because we wander here and there in our minds we do not see ourselves [...] I would say that this venerable man 'lived with himself' because he was always on guard and watchful. He was always aware of being before the eyes of the creator. He was constantly examining himself and he did not let the eye of his mind wander about.[10]

For the Desert Fathers and Mothers it is not what we do that is important; what matters is that there should be a real human being there to do it. 'If you have a heart you can be saved,' Abba Pambo said.[11] Mindfulness involves accepting our situation as imperfect human beings who are loved by God and capable of loving others through all mishaps and mistakes. Mindfulness is not about perfectionism. It is a way of being real, humble, down to earth. Humility offers a way of facing our negative tendencies, without collapsing into guilt and low self-esteem. St Benedict believed the more humble we are, the more rooted in the rich soil of self-awareness, the more we are able to bear fruit in good works. 'No lotus without the mud,' as Thich Nhat Hanh says. At the end of Benedict's list of good works he reminds the monk that even if he fails to keep any of them he should 'never despair of God's mercy' (RB 4:72).

Humility should be balanced by vigilance though. Benedict's predecessor and mentor in the East, Basil the Great (330–379) already believed 'the mind is idle and careless for a lack of belief in the presence of God.'[12] If we were to meet the Queen or the Pope our eyes would remain intent – we would not look here and there; so with a sense of God's presence the mind becomes intent and focussed. The Desert Fathers emphasised the preciousness of time: 'An old man said, "He who loses gold or silver can find more to replace it, but he who loses time cannot find more." '[13] When the monks prayed, 'Give us today our daily bread' it was not so much for physical food – for that they had to work – but for attentiveness to receive the unique gift of each day: 'An old man said, "Having arisen in the early hours, say to yourself, 'Body, you must work to feed yourself; soul, be vigilant in order to receive the inheritance'".'[14] For St Basil the sense of Divine presence is the first step in prayer, the second step is to let go of the day's impressions, of worries and fears that smother the soul. To 'care' doesn't mean being anxious and careworn. We must learn to care in a carefree way. But to take good care we must learn to be still.[15]

The Laying aside of Thoughts

The Greek word for the withdrawal of thoughts from past and future and coming back to the present moment is *anachoresis*, literally ἀνά – back, and χώρησις – to the original. *Anachoresis*, St Basil says, enables us 'to carry about with us, in all that we do, the holy thought of God stamped upon our souls.'[16] Basil does not propose adding a thought of God from outside, so to speak, to every task and activity. This would mean doing one thing and thinking about something else. Such mental duplication would be distracting and impossible to maintain. Rather, for Basil, the awareness of God is stamped within us as we go about our daily tasks. In his Episcopal homilies Basil extends *anachoresis* beyond monastic practice to the simple pleasures of life. When eating a raisin be aware, be grateful.

> When you sit down to dinner with your families, pray!
> When you take bread, thank the giver! When you
> strengthen your weak body with wine, think of him who

is giving you this gift for the delight of your heart and the elimination of your weakness! When you put on a garment, give thanks to him who gave it to you. When you slip on your overcoat, grow in your love for God who has provided us with suitable clothes for summer and winter [...] When you look up to the sky, contemplating the beauty of the stars at night, pray to the lord of the Universe who, in his wisdom, has created everything [...] By keeping all things in mind in gratitude you will in this way pray without ceasing, not limiting your prayer to words, but uniting yourself in your whole life, inner and outer, with God, so that your life is a continuous appreciation of God's presence in all things and so you will come to uninterrupted prayer.[17]

We tend to say someone is holy when they go to Church a lot, or when they say a lot of prayers, or talk about 'spirituality' but all this is 'outer'. Inner holiness, Benedict says, comes from not trying to be holy but from being holy in ourselves. We only become holy when we open our hearts to God's Spirit, God's inspiration. We do this in meditation. In saying the mantra or being mindful of the breath we are not aspiring to be spiritual in our eyes, in the eyes of others or in God's eyes, we are being open and attentive to God's Spirit always with us. Humility is not about aspiring to be spiritual but, as St Benedict says (repeating to God the verse of the Psalm) it is about recognising 'I am of no account and lack understanding, no better than a beast in your sight, yet I am always in your presence' (RB 7:13). Like St Basil, Benedict reminds us that God is present in everything we do; eating, drinking wine (not to excess), getting dressed, looking at nature. Being holy is letting God be God in us.

Benedict in his *Rule* says we should 'seek after peace and pursue it.' Peace comes from living each day as 'God's today.' This is the wisdom of both Western and Eastern monasticism. A young

monk once asked a Russian Elder: 'Father Tichon, how can we
attain to peace of heart?' The answer was:

> Live in the present. We ought not to live either in the past
> or the future. We ought to live in the present, for the present
> day, and we are to thank God for everything.[18]

In Mindfulness meditation it is attention to the breath that
keeps us in the present moment. For those who practise Christian
meditation taught by John Main attention to the mantra plays a
similar role. Different disciplines suit different people. The Desert
tradition puts more of an emphasis on the 'word' but still links this
with the breath. 'One should remember God more often than one
breathes,' Evagrius writes, 'Join to every breath a sober invocation
of the name of Jesus.'[19] The tradition of breath awareness was
maintained in the *hesychast* tradition of the Orthodox Church.
Some generations after Evagrius, Hesychius of Jerusalem promised,
'If you wish to live in peace and ease and keep your heart watchful
without difficulty, let the prayer of Jesus cleave to your breath and
you shall succeed before long.'[20] Nearly a thousand years after
Evagrius, St Gregory Palamas (1296–1357) wrote 'In Defence of
Those who Devoutly Practise a Life of Stillness':

> Since the mind of those recently started on the spiritual
> path continually darts away again as soon as it has been
> concentrated, they must continually bring it back once
> more; for in their experience they are unaware that the
> mind itself, of all things, is the most difficult to observe and
> the most mobile. That is why some teachers recommend
> them to pay attention to the exhalation and inhalation of
> their breath, and to restrain it a little, so that while they are
> watching the breath, the mind, too, may be held in check.[21]

Whether the focus is the repetition of the name, or awareness of breath, the aim is to let go of everything else. We let go of the past – our memories are not necessarily images of what really happened but only our perception of things, what we thought happened. We let go of the future – our hopes and fears too have no basis in reality; expectations will always be more or less inaccurate. One of the great contemporary attractions of mindfulness is that it gives actual practices for coming into the *Now* which can be followed. John Cassian while he was discussing prayer with Abba Isaac (Conf 10:8–11) recognised the need for an actual method. Inspiring talks do not necessarily steady the mind. Cassian describes the busy mind: 'Thoughts wander from spiritual contemplation and run hither and thither [...] One thought succeeds another, without stopping, in a perpetual flux in which the mind neither perceives the origin of its thoughts nor is aware of their flight and disappearance.' What was needed in his opinion was something 'precise, as a formula for instance would be, to which we can recall our wandering mind.' The mature question is not 'what' but 'how.' Abba Isaac explains the use of a set phrase in prayer. The Hebrew tradition of 'calling on the name' finds a new expression in the formula 'Oh God come to my aid', repeated continuously.

The advice Cassian was given by Abba Isaac is similar to the one pointed attention cultivated in mindfulness of the breath. The teaching of the Egyptian desert fathers puts more emphasis on the use of a phrase in conjunction with the breathing. The phrase recommended by Isaac sums up the Lord's Prayer – putting attention on God, recognising our need. Cassian also links the simplicity of this practice to the first Gospel beatitudes: 'Blessed are the poor in spirit': 'The mind should unceasingly cling to this formula until, strengthened by constant use and by continual meditation it casts off and rejects the rich and full material of all manner of thoughts. It restricts itself to the poverty of this one verse.' A Syrian contemporary of Cassian, Macarius in his *Spiritual Homilies*, emphasises a different practice, which parallels the Buddhist practice of the body-scan taken over into therapeutic

Mindfulness whereby we bring thought back to the sensations of the body. Macarius says our thoughts are like straying children; we need to gather them together and 'lead them into the home of [our] body', focusing our attention within ourselves so that the thoughts do not escape and wander about.[22]

The use of a fixed prayer phrase, continuously repeated during the time of prayer, is the basis of the Jesus Prayer; silent repetition of the name of Jesus linked with a call for help: 'Lord Jesus Christ, have mercy on me'. 'Confine your minds within the words of the prayer', advises St John Climacus, the seventh-century monk of Mount Sinai in Egypt.[23] St Francis of Assisi in the thirteenth century used the phrase 'My God and My All'. He was heard to repeat it – and nothing else – all night long.[24] The fourteenth-century treatise *The Cloud of Unknowing* (Ch.7) recommends the use of a shorter word 'of one syllable' like 'Love' or 'God' as an 'arrow prayer' fixed continually to the heart. The contemplative traditions of other world religions have parallel practices. 'God has revealed himself in many and varied ways', as the Letter to the Hebrews says (1:1). When looking at other people's practices the way forward is not to judge but to discern.

Not Judging but Discerning

Contemporary mindfulness practice encourages us to be 'non-judgmental': not to be attached to our opinions about ourselves, others, and the world around us. Being trapped in a chain of thought is to have our mind in chains. We are bound by our fixed opinions. Letting go of ideas about who we are – conditioned as they are by notions of what we should be – means we become adaptable. St Paul in his earlier life felt he should keep the Jewish law fastidiously, this in turn made him intolerant to those he felt did not keep it. He persecuted the followers of Christ as lawbreakers. After his conversion he let go of holding both himself and others up against an external standard of behaviour: 'To the weak I became weak, that I might win the weak. I have become all things to all people' (1 Cor 9:22). This openness to others St Paul describes as 'being poured out as a drink offering' (Phil 2:17, 2 Tim 4:6). It was more than evangelical availability – buying drinks for everyone – for a drink offering in the Temple was offered on top of the main sacrifice. St Paul describes his self-gift as a response to one 'who loved me and gave himself for me' (Gal 2:20). Acceptance of others and ourselves comes from the experience of being loved and forgiven, despite our mindlessness. Jesus prayed on the cross, 'Father, forgive them for they know not what they do' (Lk 23:34). It was this experience that helped St Paul to realise that 'Love keeps no store of wrongs' (1 Cor 13:5).

The knowledge of being called prompted Paul to spend time in the desert of Arabia (Gal 1:17). He became a prototype for the Desert Fathers and Mothers three centuries later in their cultivation of receptivity and acceptance. His words echo in many of their sayings:

> The old men used to say that we should each of us look upon our neighbour's experiences as if they were our own. We should suffer with our neighbour and weep with him, and should behave as if we were inside his body; and if any trouble befalls him, we should feel as much distress as we would for ourselves.[25]

St Paul's letters were also key to the early monastic ideal of prayer. His injunction to 'pray without ceasing' was not taken as saying lots of prayers but carrying the spirit of prayer in the heart.[26] In the nineteenth-century Russian classic *The Way of a Pilgrim* it was this ideal that motivates the author's search for 'a way of keeping the mind centred in God's peace.'[27] Three other sayings were key to early monasticism: 'To be spiritually minded is life and peace' (Rom 8:6). Living peaceably as the aim of all practice. 'Do not be conformed to the world but be transformed by the renewing of your minds' (12:2). The mind unconditioned by the world is the beginner's mind, the simplicity and directness of a child. The beginner's mind transforms our values from those of success and achievement to that of life and peace. Lastly, 'Take captive every thought to make it obedient to Christ' (2 Cor 10:5). Work is needed to be free from conditioned patterns of thinking. *Anachoresis* involves bringing the mind back to its original, the mind of Christ, taking control of every thought so they serve Christ.

Living these exhortations came to a head in the practice among the Desert Fathers and Mothers of not judging. There are innumerable stories of the elders refusing to pass judgment on any who were seen to fall short:

> Whenever [Abba Agathon's] thoughts urged him to pass judgment on something which he saw, he would say to himself, 'Agathon, it is not your business to do that.' Thus his mind was always recollected. [...] Abba Poemen said, 'If you want to find rest here below, and hereafter, in all circumstances say, Who am I? and do not judge anyone.' [...] A brother at Scetis committed a fault. A council was called to which Abba Moses was invited, but he refused to go to it. Then the priest sent someone to say to him, 'Come, for everyone is waiting for you.' So he got up and went. He took a leaking jug, filled it with water and carried it with him. The others came out to meet him and said to him, 'What is this, Father?' The old man said to them, 'My sins run out behind me, and I do not see them, and today I am coming to judge the errors of another.' When they heard that they said no more to the brother but forgave him. [...] Abba Xanthias said, 'A dog is better than I am, for he has love and he does not judge.'[28]

This includes not judging ourselves, for how can we learn to love our neighbour unless we love ourselves?

> Abba Poemen said that his friend Abba Paphnutius used to say, 'During the whole lifetime of the old men, I used to go to see them twice a month, although it was a distance of twelve miles. I told them each of my thoughts and they never answered me anything but this, "Wherever you go, do not judge yourself and you will be at peace".'[29]

We are not our thoughts; our minds are bigger containers than our thoughts. Other people are bigger than our thoughts as well. Not being judgmental means recognising we can never really say what another person is like. We can dislike someone's behaviour – and often rightly – but we can't say they are 'like that.' In the Biblical vision of Genesis 1:26 the only image and likeness we have is that of God. Life is more than our ideas about it. Science provides us with hypotheses about how things work but they are regularly re-evaluated and replaced, they remain approximations. The solid divisible matter of Newtonian physics dissolves into waves and anti-matter. We can never understand an infinite universe, how much more God? Religions provide symbols of reality – the Greek word for symbol is *dogma*. The Creed and doctrines of the Church evoke in image and idea the reality they represent. They express intuitions arising from the *sensus fidelium*, confirmed in the light of theological discernment over centuries. Used properly they are windows onto heaven and earth. Misused, however, religions close the shutters so we see only the window. We become fixated with signposts and do not walk the journey.

Hamlet said to one of his narrow minded friends, 'there are more things in heaven and earth, Horatio, than are dreamed of in your philosophy.'[30] Doctrine, if it is alive, is never fixed. At times it can morph into unexpected meanings, while always remaining the same deposit of truth handed down in the Church.[31] Letting go of our thoughts involves realising we cannot take in the whole picture. It is part of the humility which realises we only ever see partially. 'I have not gone after things too great,' the Psalmist sings, 'nor marvels beyond me, but truly I have set my soul in silence and peace' (Ps 131:3–6). So how do we make domineering and belligerent thoughts captive so as to allow our minds to be remade so as to live peaceably and pray unceasingly? The Desert Fathers and Mothers gave basically three answers to this: 1) By not being captive to fixed ideas, don't let thoughts and moods have authority over us. 2) Let them go as clouds passing through the sky, identifying rather with the spaciousness around them. 3) Create an observing distance from our thoughts by characterising afflictive thoughts as demons, they are not us, we are afflicted by them. These three approaches are summed up in a saying of the fathers:

> They said that seven monks lived on St Anthony's mountain. At the time of the palm harvest, one of them had to keep guard to drive away the birds. Now there was an old man there, and when it was his day to watch he began to cry out, 'Go away you bad thoughts inside and you birds outside.'[32]

A final approach emphasises not so much rejecting thoughts as discerning between them. So, 4) Instead of trying to push away what is unpleasant, observe what is of value and what isn't: 'An old man said, "What condemns us is not that thoughts enter into us but that we use them badly; indeed, through our thoughts we can be shipwrecked, and through our thoughts we can be crowned."'[33] Receptivity and acceptance is the key to not spending our energy evaluating all our experience in terms of what we think is good or bad (usually for us!). This is difficult when we have to live with things that we feel aversion to. When faced by restlessness, physical pain, agitation or emotional worries Thomas Keating advises that we allow pain itself to become our object of focus.

> One of the best ways of letting go of an emotion is to feel it. Painful emotions, even some physical pains, tend to disintegrate when fully accepted [...] By allowing our attention to move gently toward the emotion and by sinking into it, as though you were getting into a nice Jacuzzi, you are embracing God in the feeling [...] Emotional swings are gradually dissolved by the complete acceptance of them: 'Yes, I am angry, I am panicky, terrified, restless.' Every feeling has some good. Since God is the ground of everything, we know that even the feeling of guilt, in a certain sense, is God [...] 'Letting go' is not a simple term; it is quite subtle and has important nuances – depending on what you are intending to let go of. When a thought is not disturbing, letting go means paying no attention to it. When a thought is disturbing, it won't go away so easily, so you have to let it go in some other way. One way you can let it go is to sink into it and identify with it, out of love for God.[34]

Acceptance, therefore, goes hand in hand with self-knowledge: not avoiding but knowing what is going on inside us. One of the main practices shown by the Desert Fathers and Mothers is 'paying attention to oneself'. 'If you wish to know God? Learn first to know yourself,' said Evagrius, 'the pious are not at variance with themselves!'[35] The virtue of spiritual discernment could only come from self-knowledge. Discernment meant being able to diagnose exactly what is going on at any given moment. This seems to have been a particular gift of the Desert Mothers. The *ammas* are underrepresented among the *Alphabetical Sayings* though many of the *Anonymous Sayings* may have originated with them. Some characters stand out though. Whereas many of the Father's sayings emphasise ascetical feats, the *ammas* emphasise responding to what life presents. Amma Theodora, the wife of a Roman tribune who retired to the desert, summed up the art of monastic life as 'knowing how to profit from circumstances.'[36] The purpose of asceticism was not to reject physicality but to accept that 'the body is for Him who made it.' In Amma Theodora's battle with demons she realised what many fierce ascetics forgot:

> 'What makes you demons go away? Is it fasting?' They
> replied, 'We do not eat or drink.' 'Is it vigils?' They replied,
> 'We do not sleep.' 'Is it separation from the world?' 'We live
> in the deserts.' 'What power sends you away then?' They
> said, 'Nothing can overcome us, but only humility.'

Amma Syncletica, one of the great teachers of the desert, says, 'We must direct our souls with discernment.' The troubles of life, she says, come both from outside and from within: 'The soul is like a ship when great waves break upon it, and at the same time it sinks because the hold is too full.' What keeps us from peace is at least halved when we let go of 'the interior onslaughts of our thoughts.' Discernment, she says, involves the Gospel advice to 'be wise as serpents' (Mt 10:16). 'Being like serpents means not ignoring attacks and wiles of the devil,' she says, for 'like is quickly known to like.' This remarkable psychotherapy rests on the insight that we shouldn't ignore that we have a shadow side; it is best to fight the enemy on his own ground. Getting to know ourselves is key. For Syncletica this doesn't necessarily involve renouncing anything exteriorly. The real place of practice is not the desert but our own mind.

> Amma Syncletica said, 'There are many who live in the
> desert and behave as if they were in the town, and they are
> wasting their time. It is possible to be a solitary in one's

mind while living in a crowd, and it is possible for one who is solitary to live in the crowd of his own thoughts.'

Solitude in the end is being oneself, for there is only one of us in the world. To be ourselves we have to accept ourselves as we are. To be in the crowd is to compare ourselves with others, measuring our so-called achievements and failures with them. This seems to have been a besetting problem in the desert where worldly success was replaced by ascetical prowess. The monks tended to compete with each other, to outdo each other in their practices. The Desert Mothers seem to be a wise voice against this crowd mentality. Discernment involved humble and realistic self-knowledge. The monastic cell was the place where one practised mindfulness. 'Go, sit in your cell,' many of the Fathers said, 'your cell will teach you everything.' Non-judgment meant not comparing ourselves to others. Amma Sarra said, 'I shall not ask that all men should approve of my conduct, I shall pray instead that my heart might be pure towards all.'[37]

Mindfulness as Health of the Soul

The most systematic treatment of the inner life among the Desert Fathers is in the writing of Evagrius of Pontus. He was the first to analyse the eight passionate thoughts and how they interact.[38] Like Theodora and Syncletica he believed that discernment came with keeping centred. Trying to gain the applause of others only makes us live in a world of shadows. 'If your spirit still looks around at the time of prayer, then,' Evagrius says wryly, 'you are no better than a man of affairs engaged in a kind of landscape gardening' (*Chapters on Prayer* 43/61–62). Resisting judgment based on comparison and coming to insight in self-knowing, in Evagrius' view, was the sign of a healthy soul. In *Practikos* he gives the desert practice of inner mindfulness. Like Amma Theodora he believed it was counter-productive to fight the passions. Purity of heart helps us see the roots of unmindful behaviour. External self-discipline only deals with the symptoms. It is 'like a man fighting in the darkness of night' (83/37).

For Evagrius there are two moderators for balancing external behaviour: prudence and temperance. Prudence enables the right use of things, so as to 'arrange affairs according to the requirements of the times' (88/38). 'Prudence gives birth to mindfulness.'[39] Temperance helps us deal with those things that would make us lose our centre. It 'enables us to look upon those affairs which cause irrational phantasms, remaining the while free of passion.' Prudence and temperance lead to health of soul, which also frees us from any oppressiveness in religion. Those who are healthy 'no longer remember the law or commandments or punishment,' Evagrius says, 'Rather they say and do what excellent habit suggests.' It is one of the insights of therapeutic mindfulness that a calm mind leads to appropriate behaviour while 'untoward emotions' or 'disturbing impulses' are at the root of behavioural dysfunction. 'Excellent habit' is our capacity to imitate God in his goodness. 'Nothing makes someone resemble God as doing good to others,' Evagrius says, 'But in doing good to them, one should take great care not to transform these good deeds into a thought.'[40] If we try to cultivate specific virtues we end up being tempted by their opposites. If we focus on our sins we ignore our essential goodness. 'Both the virtues and the vices only make the mind blind.' We cannot become mindful merely from action that proceeds from the exterior to the interior. 'The effects of keeping the commandments do not suffice to heal the powers of the soul completely,' Evagrius, says, 'They must be complemented by a contemplative activity.'

If this is true of outward behaviour so it is true of thoughts. Even pure thoughts are a distraction to mindfulness: 'One who has become free of disturbing passion does not necessarily pray truly,' Evagrius warns, 'It is quite possible for a man to have none but the purest thoughts and yet to be so distracted mulling over them.' Kabat-Zinn says that mindfulness is not 'replacing one thought with another one that we think may be more pure. Rather, it is to understand the nature of our thoughts as thoughts and our relationship to them, so that they can be more at our service rather than the other way round.' Mindfulness is not to be confused with positive thinking: 'If we decide to think positively, that may be useful, but it is not meditation. It is just more thinking. We can as easily become a prisoner of so-called positive thinking as of negative thinking.'[41] Mindfulness doesn't involve changing our thinking by more thinking. The practice is to watch our thoughts without being drawn into them. We become less identified with habitual thought patterns. Evagrius proposes such impartial observation, a near scientific objectivity:

> Let the monk keep careful watch over his thoughts. Let him observe their intensity, their periods of decline and follow them as the rise and fall. Let them note well the complexity of their thoughts, their periodicity, the demons which can cause them, with the order of their succession and the nature of their associations. Then let him ask from Christ the nature of these data he has observed. (*Practikos* 50/29–30)

The last line shows that for Evagrius observation is always tied to insight, *samatha* to *vipassana*. A slight danger of contemporary mindfulness teaching lies in the assumption that thought patterns change simply by observing them. Alan Wallace argues they don't.[42] The witness of Buddhist and Christian contemplation is that insight is needed to propel us from self-awareness to self-knowledge. For Evagrius insight was the fruit of faith. Faith for him is not just a set of beliefs but is 'an interior good, one which is found even in those who do not yet believe in God' (81/36). Faith is a psychic dynamism, the power of attention whereby we see through our thoughts into reality. Christians see that reality as God, but anyone who cultivates attentive mindfulness has the psychic dynamism, the inner resources, which put them into contact with God. 'When attention seeks prayer it finds it,' Evagrius says, 'For if there is anything that marches in the train of attention it is prayer; and so it must be cultivated' (*Chapters on Prayer* 149/79). The opposite of faith is not unbelief it is agitated thinking:

> A man in chains cannot run. Nor can the mind that is enslaved to passion see the place of spiritual prayer. It is dragged along and tossed by those passion-filled thoughts and cannot stand firm and tranquil. (71/67)

The psychic dynamism of faith, for Evagrius, therefore, rests on passionlessness. According to John Eudes Bamberger *apatheia* is the 'keystone of Evagrius' whole structure of ascetic practice.'[43] 'Passionlessness' may not be the best translation, however, as the idea is not stoic (though the term is taken from stoic sources). *Apatheia* was used two hundred years earlier in Christian thought by Clement of Alexandria. For both Clement and Evagrius it means not a rejection of desirousness *per se*, but the resolving of disordered passions into abiding calm. At various points in his work Evagrius calls *apatheia*; 'Kingdom of heaven,' 'true knowledge of existing things,' 'health of the soul,' 'a habitual state of imperturbable calm,' and 'faith'.[44] It is closely involved with purity of heart, tranquillity and stability. A good translation would be mindfulness.

For Evagrius *apatheia* it is conceived by obedience, preserved by fear of the Lord, and gives birth to love. *Apatheia* never fully stabilises but must be guarded and protected. With vigilance it can become a more or less permanent state, not temporary. Evagrius charts its degrees and growth and limits: he does not expect even monks to literally love all equally. Natural attraction and compatibilities mean we are more close to some than to others. Moreover, for the achievement of *apatheia* grace is needed. Evagrius' stress on *apatheia* as the sole goal of life has led some recent commentators to feel that the sixth-century Ecumenical Councils may not have been wrong in their judgment that his thought should not be seen as representative of Christianity. Hans Urs von Balthasar, a great scholar of Evagrius, concludes 'the mysticism of Evagrius was closer to that of Buddhism than that of Christianity.'[45] However, with the new interest in mindfulness as a universal practice it may be time to revisit his controversial life and thought.

Evagrius of Pontus

What we know about Evagrius comes from the *Lausiac History* written by his disciple Palladius (363–431) and the anonymous *Historia Monachorum* written before 400 AD. Evagrius was born in 345 in Ibora in present day Turkey or Iberia in Georgia.[46] As a young man he went to the area of Pontus on the south-eastern part of the Black Sea. There he lived and studied with the Cappadocian Fathers and was ordained deacon by St Gregory Nazianzus after the death of St Basil in 379. As a theologian he was active at the Second Ecumenical Council in Constantinople in 381 and continued to teach and serve as a Deacon at the Imperial court in Constantinople. It was there, the *Lausiac History* recounts, that he fell in love with the wife of a prominent member of high society. He felt deeply threatened by the whole situation and was in near despair one day over the struggle to control his passions. That night he dreamed that he was being accused in a court of a vague crime that he had perpetrated, though he was aware of being innocent. In order to escape punishment he swore an oath on the spot that he would leave Constantinople and 'watch after his soul'. When he woke in the morning he gave a good deal of thought to his dream and decided that 'though I was asleep, yet I took the oath'. The next day found him aboard ship, sailing for the Holy Land.

In the Holy Land Evagrius met one of the Desert Mothers, St Melania the Elder, widow of a Roman patrician who had become a disciple of Macarius the Great at Scetis in Egypt. Melania felt called to combine contemplation with charitable work, leaving Egypt she ran a monastery and a hospice for pilgrims on the Mount of Olives. Here Evagrius settled, living a semi-monastic life while also enjoying something of the high society in Jerusalem. He fell gravely ill however, and when Melania found out that he hadn't kept a promise he had made to 'watch after his soul' she persuaded him to follow a much stricter monastic calling advising him to go to Nitria and Scetis in Egypt where she had taken her training in desert spirituality. He took to the life there with complete dedication. He soon became spokesman for the Greek-speaking monks in northern Egypt. Most Egyptian monks of that time were illiterate. Evagrius, a highly educated classical scholar, is believed to be one of the first people to begin recording and systematising the erstwhile oral teachings of the monastic authorities. Eventually, he also became regarded as a Desert Father, and several of his sayings appear in the *Vitae Patrum* written after his death. He himself wrote both pastoral and dogmatic treatises based on the teachings of the elders of the desert.[47] His use of Greek philosophical terms alienated him from many of the more simple Coptic monks though they never doubted his holiness.

Evagrius's reputation suffered posthumously, however, in the mid-sixth century. Like the other Cappadocian fathers Gregory of Nazianzus and Basil of Caesarea, Evagrius was an avid student of Origen of Alexandria (c. 185–250 AD), and he further developed certain esoteric speculations regarding the pre-existence of human souls and the natures of God and Christ. Origen's thought was declared heretical at the Fifth Ecumenical Council in 553 (under Justinian). Although Evagrius is not mentioned by name in the Council's 15 anathematisms, in the eyes of most contemporaries, the 553 Council did indeed condemn Evagrius, together with Origen. These anathemas were repeated in subsequent ecumenical councils with clearer implication of Evagrius. The accusations of heresy meant that many of his more speculative writings were lost in the original Greek. Since, however, by the sixth century, many of his writings had been translated into Syriac and Armenian (traditions unaffected by the decisions of the 553 Council) these works survived in these translations (and some of these sixth-century Syriac manuscripts survive today). Many of Evagrius's more ascetic works survive in Greek, often in manuscripts of the tenth century and attributed to other more 'orthodox' writers.

If we translate *apatheia* as 'mindful attention' and follow Evagrius' adage that prayer follows close in its train then *Practikos* and *Chapters on Prayer* show the deep end of mindfulness practice. 'The proof of mindfulness (*apatheia*),' he says, 'is had when the spirit begins to see its own light, when it remains in a state of tranquillity [...] it maintains its calm as it beholds the affairs of life' (*Practikos* 64/33–34). 'The soul which has mindfulness (*apatheia*) is not simply the one which is not disturbed by changing events but the one which remains unmoved at the memory of them as well' (67/34). The first step remains the same though; letting go of busyness in action, conceptualisation and memory: 'You will not be able to arrive at mindfulness (*apatheia*) if you are completely caught up with material affairs and agitated with unremitting concerns, for prayer is the rejection of concepts' (70/34). Also, 'when you pray keep your memory of past events under close custody.'[48] 'Strive to render your mind deaf and dumb at the time of prayer.' Do not try to control the outcome of your practice or cultivate an image of God internally or externally. Just persevere. 'Pay no heed to the concerns and thoughts that might arise the while.' 'If certain matters are suggested to your mind, giving you the impression that they are pressing concerns demanding attention then do not stir up the memory of these matters or move your mind to search into them.' 'Stand guard over your spirit, keeping it free of concepts at the time of prayer so that it may remain in its own deep calm.'

Apatheia/mindfulness establishes health in the parts of the soul that deal with anger and desire:

When you find yourself tempted or contradicted, or
when you get irritated or when you grow angry through
encountering some opposition or feel the urge to utter some
kind of invective – then is the time to put yourself in the
mind of prayer. You will find that the disordered movement
will immediately be stilled.

Evagrius knows that these parts of the soul are connected
strongly to the body. That is why mindfulness heals the body.
However, Evagrius would not say that one could create mindfulness
through body awareness. For Evagrius the mind is immaterial,
'the immaterial icon of the immaterial God.'[49] At times he seems
to say that it is only this immaterial icon (which he calls *nous*)
and not the body or soul which is the place of contact with God.
'Whereas others derive their reasonings and ideas and principles
from the changing states of the body, yet God does the contrary',
he says, 'God descends upon the mind (*nous*) itself and infuses
his knowledge into it as he pleases' (*Chapters on Prayer* 63/65).
Yet Evagrius still concludes, 'God brings calm peace to the body's
disturbed state through the mind.'

In his *Letter to Melania*, the Desert Mother who guided him, he
speaks of the work of prayer as integration of the whole person:

> Mind will stand again in its first creation [when] body, soul
> and mind, through the renewal of their wills, will become
> one entity [...] There will be a time when the human body,
> soul, and mind cease to be separate, with their own names
> and their plurality, because the body and the soul will be
> raised to the rank of the mind.[50]

When we are mindful (in *apatheia*), the parts of the soul dealing
with anger and desire work together to maintain the soul in the
state of quietude. Through them the body is re-linked to mind so
that the whole person becomes mind-full. Desire reaches out for

virtue and knowledge. Anger chases away harmful or unnecessary thoughts. Both desire and anger, therefore, play their part in a healthy soul, stopping habitual thinking from becoming ingrained. The stuck mind is to be feared more than anything. 'Self-opinion,' Evagrius says, 'prevents self-knowledge.'[51] When our thoughts, opinions, judgments become immovable they unleash disordered concupiscence and violence. That is why fundamentalism – stuck thinking – breeds violence. We cannot stop the thoughts, which come into our heads, but we can stop them from lingering. We can nip the seeds of lust and vengeance in the bud by letting the aggravating thought go. This is the work of mindfulness.

Chapter 4

Making of Oneself a Stepping Stone

*A person must first be mindful of himself so that making
of himself as it were a stepping stone he may rise up
from there and be brought to God.*[1]

St Augustine's *Confessions* as Therapy

St Augustine was a slightly younger contemporary of Evagrius,
but a very different writer and thinker. Instead of short aphorisms
of condensed impact, we have with Augustine, an autobiography,
long theological treatises, innumerable sermons, and letters.
Living into the decline of the Roman Empire in the West (from
354–430) he is the big daddy of Latin theology and was the key
intellectual authority through the Middle Ages and at the time of
the Reformation. The reformers dismissed most medieval theology
but Augustine's witness was considered second only to Scripture.
Recently, to add to his accolades, he has been called 'the Father of
Christian mysticism' and the 'Prince of Mystics.'[2] But has also been
much maligned for intellectualising (and complicating) the 'simple
message of Christianity' and blamed for denigrating the human
person by introducing a doctrine of original sin.[3] At first glance, it
must be admitted, it is hard to see the parallels with contemporary
secular ideas of mindfulness. St Augustine was highly intellectual
and extremely passionate. Such things as letting go of thoughts,
not analysing, soothing one's emotions and keeping quiet doesn't

seem to be the agenda of one who engaged in reflections on the Trinity which only the most philosophically minded can follow; wrote an emotional rollercoaster of his conversion; and from whom 800 homilies survive.

Nor does Augustine immediately jump to mind when one thinks of non-judgmentalism. Augustine was convinced there was a right way to think and a wrong way to think, a right way to love and a wrong way to love. For thirty-five years, as Bishop of Hippo, he fought tooth and nail against what he thought were heretical opinions in the Church. Would not mindfulness practice with its emphasis on self-help, relaxing into the way things are, and letting go of any negative feelings about ourselves fit better with some of those Augustine criticised – say Pelagius? Pelagius believed the human will was basically unimpaired, all we needed to do was good actions and we could work our own salvation. Augustine, firebrand that he was, said no, we are deeply flawed, the world we live in provides no abiding city, we are dependent on a rescue operation of grace.

However, one cannot give an adequate account of Christian mindfulness without looking at 'the greatest mind of the Christian West.'[4] Moreover, of all the Church Fathers he is the most psychological. He explored the workings of the mind through self-analysis. 'I came to understand through my own experience,' Augustine writes in his *Confessions* (8:5). Augustine was amazed that self-awareness was not where most people started: 'People go abroad to wonder at the heights of mountains, the huge waves of the sea, the broad streams of the rivers, the vastness of the ocean, the turning of the stars – and they do not notice themselves' (10:8). Come back to yourself, Augustine advises, wonder at the mystery of your being, at the complexity of your human heart, its tug of desires, ask yourself what lies at the root of your longing? The desire for happiness. 'Whoever, indeed, desires other things, desires them for this end alone,' Augustine says, 'In whatever life one chooses, there is no one who does not wish to be happy.'[5]

Why then is there so much unhappiness? Partly, we are born into a world of hardship and vulnerability. 'There are diseases,' Augustine writes, 'for which the treatments and medicines themselves are instruments of torture.'[6] Certainly this was true in his time before the use of anaesthetic. It is still the case with chemotherapy. The unsatisfactoriness of life is the fall from paradise, the original sin that Augustine is accused of laying on us. However, far from making us feel guiltier Augustine is clear 'original sin' is not something we bring on ourselves. Nor are we completely fallen. Our innate desire for happiness shows that we have a memory of paradise, of our true homeland. There is, however, a problem that does originates from us: the apparently voluntary way we seem to dismantle our own happiness as fast as we build it. Augustine, in his *Confessions*, shows this is exactly what he did.

The early chapters of Augustine's *Confessions* record his frenzied desire for happiness, his disillusion with what he finds, and the philosophy of despair about material existence that he shared with the Manicheans. As a prize-winning public speaker and teacher of rhetoric in the imperial capital of Milan he grasped at everything that crossed his path in fear that something would be missed.

> I panted for honours, for money, for marriage [...] I found bitterness and difficulty in following these desires [...] How unhappy my soul was then! [...] I got no joy out of my learning [...] I was eaten up by anxieties. (6:6)

One might say Augustine was in dire need of mindfulness. Living in dreams and worries about the future he was quite unsatisfied with his life as it was. Augustine called this state *concupiscentia*, concupiscence. He has been criticised much for seeing this state most evident in a newborn baby. 'Who would not tremble and wish rather to die than to be an infant again.'[7] Did not Jesus take a small child and put it in front of his disciples as a model to emulate? Augustine, as Margaret Miles points out, had no romanticism about babies.

> Not content to wait to be fed, the infant screams, tries
> to grasp the breast or the bottle, exhibiting every sign of
> anxiety. As the child grows, its anxious grasping is not
> eradicated but extended, given different objects and a wider
> scope. The anxiety of infancy becomes the anxieties of
> childhood, adolescence and adulthood [...] Concupiscence
> was, for Augustine, a sickness or wound, the result of an
> ancient fall that radically debilitated human nature.[8]

For Augustine the root of our mental health problems, in other words, is our anxious pursuit of 'things', things that by their very nature are incapable of offering permanent satisfaction. It is the inability of things to fulfil us that causes anxiety and makes us redouble our efforts to get what we think we want. Augustine analysed this cycle of desire, dissatisfaction and anxiety in his own experience: 'From a disordered will came concupiscence, and serving concupiscence became a habit, and the unrestricted habit became a necessity. These were the links – so I call them a chain – holding me in hard slavery' (8:5).

So far so bad. Anxiety and a sense of dissatisfaction lie at the root of much mental health trouble addressed by contemporary Mindfulness. We are taught to let go of our worries about the future by coming back to our body, to felt sensations, to the breath. By practising thus we learn to find satisfaction in the here and now. We withdraw our attraction and aversion to what happens. We learn to be aware of 'things' without projecting onto them our desires and fears. Augustine likewise finds the only way out of his fractured state of mind is to come back to himself. Coming home for him was a last resort. This was no pleasant return to a reassuring felt sense of the body. For Augustine it was so painful that left to himself he would always run away. He had to be led there by God:

> But you, Lord, were turning me around so that I could see myself; You took me from behind my own back, which was where I had put myself during the time when I did not want to be observed by myself, and you set me in front of my own face so I could see how foul a sight I was – crooked, filthy, spotted, and ulcerous. I saw, and I was horrified, and I had nowhere to go to escape from myself. (8:7)

This seems a long stretch from the 'holding oneself in love' and 'non-judgmentalism' of mindfulness practice. But is it not a real part of what many of us experience coming back to ourselves?[9] Augustine's emphasis on the difficulty of self-knowledge may reflect his personality, which, from his own account, was an addictive type. Augustine's issue seems to have been sexual compulsion. His famous pre-conversion prayer, 'Give me chastity, but not yet,' expresses the double mind that keeps people in addiction even when they know it is a problem. Augustine's journey reflects the accounts of recovery in Alcoholics Anonymous groups. Step 4 of the AA programme – to make 'a searching and fearless moral inventory of ourselves' – would well describe Augustine's *Confessions*.[10] Augustine, like AA, challenges mindfulness practice to be real: it is often not going to be easy coming back to ourselves. Also like AA he offers a great source of encouragement for those who do find it difficult – there is a 'higher power' which can help us. Augustine calls this help 'grace', the higher power the God he found in Christian faith.

We admitted we were Powerless

Step 1 of the AA programme comes from the knowledge that we cannot control concupiscence through our willpower. Admittedly the concern is with a severe form of addiction but anything that draws us away from reality – such as continuous use of the internet – can become a compulsion that blocks self-awareness. The real psychological difficulties that can be encountered on the path of self-awareness are dealt with much more convincingly in Augustine (or even more by the Desert Fathers and Mothers) than in much self-help mindfulness literature. Some teachers of mindfulness like Kabat-Zinn do emphasise, 'while it may be simple to practice mindfulness, it is not necessarily easy.'

> Mindfulness requires effort and discipline for the simple reason that the forces that work against our being mindful, namely, our habitual unawareness and automaticity, are exceedingly tenacious. They are so strong and so much out of our consciousness that an inner commitment and a certain kind of work are necessary just to keep up our attempts to capture our moments in awareness and sustain mindfulness.[11]

Instead of emphasising effort and work, however, Augustine sees his transition to self-knowledge as the grace of God.

Mindfulness teaching like that presented by Kabat-Zinn draws on its Buddhist roots. The *Dhammapada*, the earliest record of the Buddha's teaching, says that on the path of enlightenment '*we* must make the effort [...] the awakened only point the way, those who have entered the path and who meditate, free *themselves* from the bonds of illusion.'[12] For Augustine the problem with 'do it yourself' spirituality – which he criticised in the teaching of Pelagius – is that it is easily hijacked by the ego. The sense that we are doing the practice can turn meditation into a project, achievement or desire, which keeps us from simply being aware. Ambition, pride and craving are of course undermined in Buddhist practice through insight into *anatman*, the illusory sense of the self that tries to get enlightenment on its own terms. MBSR also pre-empts 'muscular mindfulness' by a strong emphasis on 'not doing' and on the development of altruistic motives for our practice – peace benefiting others as well as ourselves.

Still, the vantage point of grace proposed by St Augustine could be helpful though, especially for those with a notional framework of a personal God. Not all start from default non-theism of MBSR, or the Buddhist tradition from which it derives. Brazilian psychotherapists Luke Vandenberghe and Fabricia Costa Prado have shown how a notion of grace has been useful in their clinical practice:

> Both the mindfulness and grace literatures promote transcendence as a better alternative to painful striving and trying to control private events. The distinction clinicians want their clients to observe between themselves and their feelings or thoughts parallels the transcendent awareness of the Teacher Within for the religious seeker. Assuming a transcendent perspective allows the mindfulness trainee and the religious client alike to be aware of their thoughts and temptations without seeing their options through the lens of these contents. Through this change of perspective, the uncertain and fleeting contents, in Augustinian terms, or the client's judgments and concepts, in mindfulness parlance, cease to be in charge. In distancing themselves from these concepts, desires and so forth, individuals cease to be subject to them and thus also dispense with the need to control them.[13]

The Buddhist notion of mindfulness refers to the original mind – not arrived at through thinking or feeling – as innate awareness. For Augustine, likewise, self-knowledge involves recognising that emotions and thoughts are unreliable, fleeting events. There is more certainty in knowing than in what is known. To become aware *that* we are aware, for Augustine, is the opening to a transcendental perspective. 'So great is the power of thought that not even the mind itself may place itself, so to speak in its own sight, except when it thinks of itself,' writes Augustine in *De Trinitate*.[14] We know the mind (as we know God who is yet further beyond) by letting go of ideas. Normally we reflect about things, not about the process of thinking. Psychologically the transcendental perspective is the innate state of the mind, inchoate while we are identified with things but increasingly conscious as thoughts and attachments are renounced. We don't need to be subject to our thoughts and feelings, neither do we need to control them or suppress them, we simply recognise they are not the whole story of who we are. And certainly not of who God is: 'If you understand, then it is not God,' Augustine says.[15] For Augustine, the movement is from being our thoughts, opinions, and desires, towards being aware of them.[16]

Augustine sees the ascent of the mind to self-awareness (and from there to God) as a gift of grace. It is something unearned, unachieved. Both Augustine and mindfulness teaching, therefore, point to a form of 'non-doing', 'non-desiring', not trying to change or stop anything. Both point out that what is going on within us and around us is passing. The right beginnings and endings, the changes we need to make in our life, will come from this awareness. Transcendent awareness can therefore be seen as 'mind-fullness'. It contains the mind's capacity to be aware of changeable things, the ability of thought to become conscious of itself, and the mind's potential to 'glance' at the imperishable. Nothing is left out. Awe at creation leads to love of the creator. In fact, while we are directing our attention towards our creator we are healed *through* our experience of temporal things.[17]

For Augustine the mind's capacity to be conscious of itself includes the full spectrum of its operations. The mind increases its awareness, beyond the processing of sense data, to reflecting on the content of thought; from there we become aware of the thinking, opinion forming, desiring activity of the mind itself, and from there, Augustine says, we open the mind to 'immutable truths'. Such mind-fullness is, in fact, innate in all thinking – without intelligible standards how could one arrive at thoughts and choices? We evaluate what our senses and imagination present through criteria of goodness, beauty and truth, which seem to be already there. This leads to a sense that there must be something beyond the mind from and by which we can be aware of the mind's activity. 'The God within is the God above.'[18] The fullness of the mind, for Augustine, must include the ascent to the immutable itself.

Peace of Mind or Mind-Fullness?

Having looked at Augustine's experience of *concupiscentia*, his sense of being saved by grace, not by effort, and his understanding of how the mind works, we are in a position to look at the joy, peace and happiness of his later life. When Augustine reached the fullness of the mind, he came to describe this as an experience of *tranquillitas*, 'the peace which passes all understanding.'[19] Kabat-Zinn agrees that mindfulness should be 'an intrinsically satisfying work because it puts us in touch with many aspects of our lives that are habitually over looked and lost to us.'[20] Augustine expresses this sense of satisfaction, completeness and peace in his mysticism. A key aspect of his mysticism is its relationality. God for Augustine is always 'Someone' who is coming to meet him. His mystical experience did not arise only from self-reflection but from conversation, with God and with others. As a philosophic type he rarely describes his mystical experiences in the first person. An exception is the account of his conversation with his mother St Monica:

> We reached forth now and in one flash of thought touched the Eternal Wisdom, which abides over all: if could this be continued, and all disturbing visions of whatever else be taken away, and this one vision were to ravish the beholder

and absorb him and plunge him in these inward joys, so
that life might ever be like that one moment of insight for
which we sighed – were not this to 'enter into the joy of the
Lord'? (*Confessions* 9:25)

This dimension of 'we' in meditative practice is still to be
properly explored. Many people in Mindfulness or Christian
Meditation groups say that the depth of silence and attention is
augmented meditating with companions. Augustine's mother was
not the only woman in his life. One of his followers to Carthage
was Anicia Faltonia Proba, the widow of the wealthiest man in the
Roman Empire. Three of her sons held the consulship in Rome,
but mother and sons were forced to leave after Alaric the Goth
sacked the city in 410. Augustine advises Anicia that real peace
does not come from privileged position. Prayer is not really about
trying to get peace of mind by hoping for favourable external
circumstances. Such peace is an image shaped by desire and not
the *tranquillitas* of mind-fullness. 'For in as much as we cannot
present peace to our minds as it really is, we do not know it,'
Augustine says, 'But whatever image of it may be presented to our
minds we reject, disown and condemn; we know it is not what we
are seeking.'[21]

Mindfulness would be very limited if it was just about trying
to experience peace. *Tranquillitas* in this sense is subtly different
from the *apatheia* of Evagrius: Peace, for Augustine, does not
come as a non-conceptual or dispassionate state, through a stilling
of the movements of the mind or by renouncing desires. Rather,
it is the fruit of self-knowledge. Peace comes when we return to
ourselves.[22] The mind reaches a state of *tranquillitas* not by giving
anything up but by finding a vantage point from which everything
can be included. The moral characteristic of *tranquillitas*, for
Augustine, is not unchangeability. (Augustine doesn't use language
of union or identification with God.) More in line with Stoic
teaching, *tranquillitas* is the peace which comes from holding firm

to the values and perspectives of intelligible things, to fortitude and a commitment to truth. Suffering, for Augustine, is not the opposite of peace. Peace must be found in suffering. Likewise strong emotions are not the opposite of peace. It is quite human to love some people more than others, feeling things strongly can help us to make clear judgments. Feelings should be in tune with reason though.

The entry point Augustine uses for discussions on the nature of the mind is to look at our capacity for making judgments as to what is beautiful or appropriate. Where animals work from instinct human beings have to think about and choose what to do. Immutable truths allow judgments and (therefore) choices to be made about mutable things. The awareness of judgment, for Augustine, leads to awareness of unchangeable consciousness:

> For, wondering how I recognised the beauty of bodies,
> whether heavenly or earthly, and by what criterion I might
> rightly judge concerning mutable and changeable things
> and say: 'This ought to be so, that ought not to be so',
> wondering therefore what was the source of my judgment
> when I did thus judge, I had discovered the unchangeable
> and true eternity of truth above my changing mind.
> (*Confessions* 7:17–23)

In his mystical ascent recorded in *Confessions* Chapter 9 Augustine moves beyond the senses and images derived from them and recognises that corporeal things are 'all changeable'. But he also reaches out – or rather for him *into* the mind – that he might know something that was permanent: '[my reason] cried aloud that the unchangeable was to be preferred to the changeable.' Augustine reflects that in order to see this, the mind must have been aware of a fixed standard by which to judge what is preferable: 'For if [reason] had not arrived at some knowledge of the unchangeable, it could in no way have preferred it with certainty to the changeable' (9:25).

This may seem a far cry for MBSR's emphasis on non-judgmentalism as the way to open awareness. However, we have to remember that for Augustine awareness starts in the mind, not in the objects perceived. Awareness does not come from not judging things but from being aware of the faculty of judgment itself. Let us follow Augustine on his journey into the mind: Augustine starts with the bodily senses but then tracks how impressions are stored as images in 'the interior power' of memory. Alongside memory, understanding – 'the reasoning power' – judges what the senses present and the memory receives as images in conjunction with what is already stored in the memory. Augustine finding that these deliberations are fluid and subject to change – because of continuous new input and new configurations – asks whether understanding can turn and look at itself; reflexively, can it 'awaken itself to its own understanding.'

So Augustine is a rather different sort of mystic than those who want to still the mind. To translate this concept into Buddhist meditative terminology he puts a greater emphasis on *vipassana* than *samatha*, on insight into the nature of things, of the mind, of God. He is a good reminder that quietening the mind may only be half the story of enlightenment.

Tasting Eternity: Food for Body and Mind

Augustine's conversation with his mother starts with the consideration of 'bodily creatures and heaven itself, whence sun and moon and stars shed their light upon the earth', from there, Augustine recalls, 'we mounted higher still by inward thought and wondering discourse on [God's] works, and we arrived at the summit of our minds; and this too we transcended to touch that land of never-failing plenty where you pasture Israel for ever with the food of life' (9:24). This 'food of life' is the 'Wisdom through whom all these things of body and mind are made.' In Wisdom, Augustine understands, 'there is no "has been" or "will be", but only "being", for she is eternal, but past and future do not belong to eternity.' In our speech 'a word has beginning and end,' but God speaks only one Word and does so eternally though its echo can be heard in all creation.

For Augustine the mind can enter into this unifying moment. The *samatha* aspect of mindfulness is expressed by Augustine in *Confessions* Chapter 11 where he says that eternity can only be found when the heart is fixed in the 'little moment' and 'fraction of time' that is Now:

> People attempt to taste eternity when their heart is still
> flitting about in the realm where things change and have
> a past and a future; it is still vain. Who can lay hold on
> the heart and give it fixity, so that for some little moment
> it may be stable, and for a fraction of time may grasp the
> splendour of a constant eternity? (11:13)

The answer of course for Augustine is God: 'You have made us for yourself and our heart is restless until it rests in you' (*Confessions* 1:1).

But 'what is time?' (11:17). This is a question that has preoccupied many a sage and mystic. For the Ancient Greek Philosopher Heraclitus, writing about 500 BC, everything was seen as transitory because of the flow of time: 'Everything changes and nothing remains the same [...] You cannot step twice into the same river, for the waters are perpetually flowing upon you.' Aristotle, writing in the fourth century BC saw time as an experience of the soul made present to understanding through the memory (*Physics* 4:14). Albert Einstein showed that movement affected time – moving clocks are slower than stationary ones. The measurement of time also dilates with increased distance from a large object for the gravitational pull on the observer is lessened. If space, time and gravity are all inter-connected then time, Augustine insists, cannot be applied to God who is by nature incorporeal and eternal and changeless. Before space, and the creation of objects, there was neither time nor any action. To ask 'What was God doing before he made heaven and earth?' is therefore a nonsensical question (11:14). From the perspective of God all is eternally present. Even from the perspective of empirical science 'The only reason for time,' Einstein said, 'is so that everything doesn't happen at once.'[23] 'The separation between past, present, and future is only an illusion, although a convincing one.'[24]

A sense of passing time is convincing, however, from the point of view of the human mind. Stephen Hawking points out that though 'the laws of science do not distinguish between past and future' psychologically we distinguish the past – which we remember, from the future – which is not in our memory. Though one thing modern science does teach, Hawking admits, is that time has become 'a more personal concept, relative to the observer who measured it.'[25] St Augustine already in the fourth century argued that time is a 'distension' (*diastasis*) of the mind. We measure time by three processes of thought which connect future, present and past: 'The mind expects and attends and remembers,' Augustine says, 'so that what "it expects" passes through "what has its attention" to "what it remembers"' (11:37). 'Past and future,' Augustine asks, 'in what sense do they have real being, if the past no longer exists and the future does not yet exist?' (11:17). In empirical terms the present moment alone exists and yet it has no duration, it passes in a flash, existing only as it slides into the past. If it endured it would not be time at all but eternity. The only part of time that has any real being, however, is the present time, but Augustine sees three tenses or times within the moment *now*: 'the present of past things' that rests now in our memory, 'the present of present things' to which we are now attentive, and 'the present of future things' which in this very moment we can expect and imagine (11:26). This is why, Augustine says, in the mind all things are present. 'Attention', he says, 'is continuous' (11:37). <u>Attention in the moment includes past, present and future things</u>.

This state of complete mind-fullness is mystical. For Augustine it is glimpsed only in a flash. It is an unselfconscious experience, a gift of pure grace that cannot be grasped. Augustine addresses God, 'Where in my consciousness, Lord, do you dwell?' (10:36). All things we experience are in our memory. Memory for Augustine, however, is more than the power to recollect as even things we forget, if they once were present to us, remain in us as unconscious impressions though we don't remember them. Augustine was writing 1500 years before psychoanalysis and yet he saw memory as containing unconscious and conscious material. He calls it 'the stomach of the mind' by which we ruminate our experience. Not everything we metaphorically swallow continues to have a taste consciously. Mind-fullness, for Augustine, is the mind's capacity to contain everything we experience. Mind-fullness is 'an awe-inspiring mystery, a power of profound and infinite multiplicity [...] utterly immeasurable' (10:26). The mind brings things to consciousness, preserving images of physical objects, impressions of emotions, abstract principles of thought, and it is capable of being present to, and aware of, consciousness itself.

Though the mind is a wonder there is, for Augustine, something even greater than the mind, which is present in the mind: God. Though dwelling in all conscious and unconscious experience, God, Augustine says, 'is not the mind itself [...] [but] Lord God of the mind' (10:36). The God we learn about dwells in our memory, our ideas and images of God change with our experience and understanding. However God in himself can never be contained in the memory. He is always more. Augustine knows he has to find God in his own experience, through his mind's presence to itself, and yet God is more than that. So Augustine is left in a dilemma: 'If I find you outside my memory, I am not mindful of you. And how shall I find you if I am not mindful of you?' (10:26). The answer for Augustine is to recognise God from what we have learnt about him but also always remember, 'If we understand it, then it is not

God.'[26] God, present to and consciously experienced in the mind, can, however, be glimpsed directly in a flash beyond the mind.

> This mind of ours seeks to find a Truth not subject to change, a substance not capable of failing. The mind itself is not of this nature: it is capable of progress and of decay, of knowledge and of ignorance, of remembering or forgetting. That mutability is not incident to God [...] For were the soul to rest in itself, it would not see anything else beyond itself: and in seeing itself, would not, for all that see God [...] I seek my God in every corporeal nature, terrestrial or celestial, and I find Him not: I seek His substance in my own soul, and I find it not; yet still have I thought on these things, and wishing to see the invisible things of my God, being understood by the things made, I have poured forth my soul above myself.[27]

To conclude: Augustine finds God in the mind's capacity to be self-present *and* in the grace of self-transcendence. The mind is not only aware of physical objects – a lesser knowledge – but is able to observe images, impressions and thoughts that amass themselves in memory. The mind's full capacity comes when we don't identify with the content of awareness but with awareness itself. We are not our thoughts. We have thoughts but there is something in us able to observe them and let them go. This point of mind-fullness is the stepping-stone by which we raise ourselves to God. God can never be contained in our thoughts and, as such, the ability to let go of our thoughts is requisite for glimpsing God in himself.

Hope, Desire and the Body

For Augustine prayer is the way to mind-fullness. Attention leads to self-awareness, desire leads to self-transcendence. In a letter to his friend Anicia Proba he presents the teaching on prayer of the Gospels and Desert Fathers adding his own characteristic conjunction of attention and desire:

> To spend a long time in prayer is not, as some think, the same thing as to pray 'with much speaking'. Multiplied words are one thing, long-continued warmth of desire is another [...] The brethren in Egypt are reported to have very frequent prayers, but these very brief, and, as it were, sudden and ejaculatory, lest the wakeful and aroused attention which is indispensable in prayer should, by protracted exercises, vanish or lose its keenness. And in this they show plainly enough, that just as attention is not to be allowed to become exhausted if it cannot continue long, so attentiveness is not to be suddenly suspended if it is sustained. Far be it from us either to use 'much speaking' in prayer, or to refrain from prolonged prayer, if fervent attention of the soul continue.[28]

Desire, for Augustine was both a problem and a resource and this had a lot to do with his views on the body. Firstly, Augustine reacted against classical anthropology – be it Platonic or Stoic – by insisting that the body was an integral and permanent part of the human person. He objected to the late classical commonplace of referring to the body as a prison for this life from which we are freed at death.

> You consider the flesh as fetters, but who loves his fetters?
> You consider the flesh a prison, but who loves his prison?
> No matter how great a master of the flesh you may be,
> and no matter how great the severity with which you are
> kindled, I am inclined to think you will close your eye if any
> blow threatens it.[29]

When Augustine speaks of the necessity of coming back to oneself this involved coming back to the body. At death the body and soul separate, but this, for Augustine, is a harsh and unnatural thing. The soul naturally loves the body and the resurrection of the body believed in by Christians was, for Augustine, the happy and natural outcome of psychosomatic love.

The place of ascetic practice, for Augustine, is not really the body but the mind's disordered desire for 'things'. The body suffers under our compulsions. 'Concupiscence is *perpetrated on,* rather than instigated by body,' as Margaret Miles puts it.[30] Such was Augustine's sexual compulsion, however, that in his case he felt he had to live a life of complete celibacy – a bit like an alcoholic having to give up alcohol completely (as is considered necessary by AA programmes). So for Augustine controlling our desires is a way of loving our bodies. Although Augustine sometimes uses the body as a foil to the soul, this is more of a rhetorical technique to emphasise the dignity of the soul or mind rather than a vestige of Manichean or dualist anthropology. He contrasts the body with the soul to highlight the spiritual nature of the latter rather than to denigrate the materiality of the former. For Augustine the moral conflict takes place essentially in the ordering of the will rather than the suppression of the flesh.

MBSR sees itself as a way of healing and integration for the whole person as a psychosomatic unity. However, for Augustine, can awareness of the body help the mind/psyche to come to stillness and peace as contemporary Mindfulness practice encourages? Can awareness of the body serve as an anchor to keep us in the present moment? For Augustine, yes and no, depending on at what stage of his thought we read him. Augustine's thought process changed not only prior to and during his conversion to Christianity, but also after. In the period after his conversion Augustine worked with a theory of sensation involving a clear distinction between the object we perceive and the sensation we have of it. Though the objects we sense are related to the body, 'sensation' was a cognitive experience. If the mind doesn't pay attention to the objects related by physical sensation then, in effect, no sensation occurs. This is why controlling the body by fasting was not, in Augustine's view at this time, a convincing way to a peaceful state of mind. Fasting may be helpful for the body, but the mind must control itself. Control of thoughts would on the other hand have a pacifying effect on the body. Augustine works with a hierarchy of influence between mind and body that proceeds only from the higher to the lower. The body apart from the mind is inanimate and cannot have desires. All bodily desires are desires of the soul experienced through the body. For the mind to give the body undue attention would imply a disorder of *concupiscentia*.

However Augustine was aware that the problem with such a monistic account of sensation is how to bridge the gap between the mind and the body. In his later thought he addresses the issue by making a distinction between *spiritus* – the part of the soul that deals with sense perception, and *mens* – dealing with cognition.[31] The lower part, *spiritus,* is orientated towards physical objects through the interior processing of sense stimuli and the images of these objects generated from the senses stored in the memory. The higher part, *mens*, works with the understanding and will. *Mens* makes sense of what is or has been experienced, and chooses what it considers best. When the mind works rightly we do not react directly from sense stimuli; instead deliberation and choice shapes our response. Thus far *spiritus* and *mens* work only on things received from below, from the data of sensation. Augustine believed that the higher faculties of the mind (*mens*) could also work in another direction, towards immutable truths. In fact *mens* is only able to process sensation when to some degree it is turned towards intelligibility.

Thus by the power of *mens* the body could be integrated and 'known' without becoming an obstacle or block to awareness. In terms of asceticism the body still needed to act rationally, but the right ordering of body and mind would enable a harmony of action. Augustine's growing sense of the active role played by the humanity of Christ in redemption meant that now he understood sensual nature as not merely subsumed and rendered quiescent by the soul but as having its own formative influence in prayer. In his later works the contrast of spirit and flesh came to be seen as a moral conflict within the soul, not as an opposition of different substances. There is a shift from an early tendency of body-soul dualism to a strong emphasis on ascetic co-operation and eschatological unity. In *City of God* – his last book – Augustine talks a lot about bodily healing and corporal resurrection at the end of time.

However there remains something of an ambiguity in Augustine's thought between his theory of sensation – which continued to emphasise a unity of predominance whereby the body could not have an effect on the soul – and his teaching on asceticism which he saw as a two way process, bodily discipline affecting the soul. Augustine wrestled in his own experience with the energies of the body that he perceived needed to be bonded to the soul and thus integrated through the practice of asceticism. This paradox of detachment from and simultaneous integration of the body in turn shapes Augustine's view of heaven. Beatitude would reach its fullness with the bodily resurrection, but resurrection was dependent on a prior separation from the body at death. Contemporary mindfulness teaching works within Augustine's earlier view in that *ascesis* is at root a way of dealing with thoughts.[32] However, like late-Augustine, mindfulness approaches sensation as an activity of the body and the mind together – the body or breath becoming an object of mental focus. MBSR meditation tells us not to try to feel or breathe differently: trying to control the body will make us think more, not less. Even physical discomfort or shortness of breath is not treated as a 'problem' but as an opportunity for awareness.

'To live in the body and to feel nothing of its being a burden is what health is,' Augustine says.[33] When the body is in a state of sickness, weakness, or distress it demands our attention: 'change this, change that, do this, stop doing that'. The sense of discomfort pushes us to action rather than repose. The soul will find it easier to be simply aware of the body in a state of health. For Augustine distraction comes from the disorder in the relation between body and the mind. In Augustinian psychology all desire originates in the will, which is part of the rational mind, not in the body. Deliberation in the mind must engage desire and lead it towards eternal things. So desire is transformed into hope. In doing so the mind orders sensate experience so that the unchangeable is preferred, intended, chosen by the senses.

The contrasts between MBSR and Augustinian paths to self-knowledge are more apparent than the parallels. MBSR uses breathing and bodily sensations as a tool for unhooking the mind from thoughts. But because nothing other is presented as an aim for contemplation body-awareness could be construed in MBSR as an end in itself. For traditional Buddhist meditation it is never more than a tool, the body is not the object of contemplation but a means to centring the mind for insight into *Dharma*. Sense awareness for Augustine doesn't even have an instrumental role for spiritual awareness. Sense awareness remains a lower capacity of the mind (facilitated by *spiritus*), it enables us to function in this world but cannot lead to knowledge or contemplation.

This World is only a Shadow

The great Indian sage and meditation teacher Sri Ramana Maharshi (1879–1950) once said that all we perceive is like film on a screen: 'God or the Self is like a cinema screen and the world like the pictures on it. You can see the picture only so long as there is a screen. But when the observer himself becomes the screen then only God or the Self remains.'[34] It is only when we are separate from the ground of being that the world arises in consciousness. Only a man standing up casts a shadow. The surrender of the 'observer', the separate sense of 'I', is the way to realise our transcendent identity as the Self, as God. Ramana has a similar anthropology to that of Augustine in understanding how desire arises not in the body but in the inter-relation of body and soul:

> The individual being which identifies its existence with that of the life in the physical body as 'I' is called the ego. The Self, which is pure Consciousness, has no ego-sense about it. Neither can the physical body, which is inert in itself, have this ego-sense. Between the two, that is between the Self or pure Consciousness and the inert physical body, there arises mysteriously the ego-sense or 'I' notion, the hybrid which is neither of them, and this flourishes as an individual being. This ego or individual being is at the root of all that is futile and undesirable in life.[35]

Like Augustine Ramana sees *ascesis* as letting go of identification with the body.

In *De Trinitate* Augustine says that *mens* when directed towards action in the world can achieve only knowledge (*scientia*) of 'things' whereas engaged in the contemplation of eternal matters it could achieve wisdom (*sapientia*) of 'the self' (12:14–15). Wisdom relies on that part of the mind (*mens*) that is able to work independently from sense perception. Body awareness is a barrier to the higher stages of contemplation. In his *Literal Commentary on Genesis* (12:15–16, 25) Augustine says that corporeal vision is quite natural when dealing with physical things but cannot grasp the supernatural. Likewise, to see spiritual realities corporeally is a form of hallucination. The first step in spiritual vision is to recognise that the object of supernatural truth is conceived in the mind through imagination and memory, not the senses. From there, Augustine says, we rise to an intellectual vision of the truth as more real than any physical and imaginary representation of it. In *Confessions* 9:25 Augustine says we can only hear God's word 'if the tumult of the flesh were hushed, hushed the sense impressions of earth, sea, sky; hushed also the heavens, yea, the very soul be hushed to herself, and by not thinking on Self to transcend Self; hushed all dreams and revelations which come by imagery; if every tongue, every symbol and all things subject to transiency were wholly hushed.'

So where does desire come into prayer? Not from the body, but rather, Augustine says, as hope, as anticipation. Living in the Now involves becoming present to the God who is always present to us. But what will be is always also Now in God. So being attentive to the present moment also involves a foretaste, a hint of the fulfilment of desire for which we long. In one of his sermons Augustine makes the parallel with the Gospel story of Mary and Martha: Martha was concerned with Christ's bodily needs, Mary with the enjoyment of his company. These are two different ways of relating to our own bodies. Martha, Augustine says, was the image of things present, Mary of things to come. Christian life involves both: patient attentiveness to the necessities of this world as they present themselves, and longing to taste even now the 'one thing' that endures to eternity.[36]

In *City of God* (completed in 426 AD) Augustine focuses on the eschatological dimension of mind-fullness. Whether it was because the Visigoths had sacked Rome in 410, or because Augustine was reaching his own old age, he became increasingly aware that in this world we have no abiding city. His eyes were fixed on heaven. Something is coming, something is to be waited for: the time when God will be all in all. The tensions in Augustine's thought – the differences between past, present and future awareness and between sensate and cognate experience – are resolved not in terms of human psychology but in the coming of God.

> It is not with God as it is with us. He does not look ahead to the future, look directly at the present, look back to the past. He sees in some other manner, utterly remote from anything we experience or could imagine. He does not see things by turning his attention from one thing to

another. He sees all without any kind of change. Things
which happen under the condition of time are in the future,
not yet being, or in the present, already existing, or in the
past, no longer in being. But God comprehends all these
in a stable and eternal present. And with him there is no
difference between seeing with the eyes and 'seeing' with
the mind, for he does not consist of mind and body. Nor is
there any difference between his present, past and future
knowledge. His knowledge is not like ours, which has three
tenses: past, present and future. God's knowledge has no
change or variation. (11:21)

Augustine is a philosopher on the move: at the end of his life
he moved his thought again. Awareness of the present moment
was now inadequate. In *City of God* the sands of time are running
out, but those with faith can look forward to a 'Last Day' when
eternity will break into time and we will see things as God sees. In
the meantime – within the city of this world – there is no complete
happiness. Here we are pilgrims and strangers, our homeland is
far off. To make our home here – to be identified with things in
this world – is to miss our citizenship in heaven. Spiritual practice
and Christian faith cannot remove us from the sufferings of
time. They can only help us deal with them. 'The good person,'
Augustine writes, 'is neither uplifted by the good things of time
nor broken by its ills' (1:8). In this life the exercise of mindfulness
is through the cardinal virtues: prudence, justice, fortitude and
temperance. Faith, love and hope are dependent on grace. 'We
are saved, we are made happy [only] by hope,'[37] he says (19:4).
Christian mindfulness must be exercised in desiring what will be,
and putting up patiently with what is:

As we do not yet possess a present, but look for a future
salvation, so it is with our happiness, and this 'with
patience'; for we are encompassed with evils, which we

ought patiently to endure, until we come to the ineffable enjoyment of unmixed good; for there shall no longer be anything to endure. Salvation, such as it shall be in the world to come, shall itself be our final happiness.

Again the sage Ramana Maharshi said something similar about the two aspects of mindfulness – awareness of this world and anticipation of heaven:

Training of the mind helps one to bear sorrows and bereavements with courage; but [...] grief only exists as long as one considers oneself in terms of this world as having a definite form; if the form is transcended, one knows the One Self to be eternal. There is neither death nor birth. What is born is only the body and this is the creation of the ego. But the ego is not ordinarily perceived without the body and so is identified with it. But it is thought which matters [...] Find out who has the thoughts. Where do they come from? They must arise from the conscious self. Apprehending this even vaguely helps towards the extinction of the ego. The realisation of the One Infinite Existence becomes possible. In that state there are no individuals but only Eternal Being. Hence there is no thought of death or grieving.[38]

Chapter 5

Letting Go, Letting God

'All things taste divinely.'[1]

Meister Eckhart and Detachment

In one manuscript of Eckhart's sermons there is a scribal prefix: 'The work of Eckhart the Master from whom God hid nothing.' This gives some indication of the admiration in which Eckhart was held. The prefix *Meister* is an academic title, like 'Professor'. Eckhart was known in many different settings: as a Scholastic who at one time occupied the Dominican Chair of Theology in Paris (a post previously held by Thomas Aquinas); as a preacher whose sermons filled churches; as a spiritual director for a whole generation of novice Dominicans, nuns, beguines and laypeople; and as a mystic revered for seeing the hidden things of God. 'What no eye has seen, no ear has heard, and what no human mind has conceived, these are the things that God has prepared for those who love him,' St Paul writes (1 Cor 2:9). These were the mysteries Eckhart expressed in language that was remarkably new. Some scholars have argued that in stretching and joining words, he did much to create the German language, which still has a unique ability to create new and exact meanings.[2] Eckhart rarely speaks of his own spiritual experiences. Only once – and then in the third person – does he hint at them: 'It appeared to a man as in a dream – it was a waking dream – that he became pregnant with Nothing, like a woman with a child, and in this Nothing God was born, He was the fruit of Nothing' (I:19:157–158).

What do we know of Meister Eckhart? Of his origin little; but on becoming famous – and in some circles notorious – his later life is better documented. One manuscript refers to him as Eckhart von Hochheim – this could mean he came from a village called Hochheim (of which there are two in the area of his early life, one near Erfurt and one near Gotha, both in Thuringia in the centre of modern Germany); or 'von' could also be part of a surname, indicating a noble status but probably also a place of origin.[3] Eckhart must have been born around 1260, as in the mid to late 1270s he entered the distinguished Dominican Priory of Erfurt as novice (it being usual to enter at the age of eighteen). He went on to study in Paris, which was the leading university for theology at the time, and then at the *studium generale* in Cologne. In both places he later held key academic posts. He also took up important administrative and pastoral duties for the Dominicans as Vicar of Thuringia, Prior of Erfurt and then Vicar General of Saxony.[4] In the latter part of his life we find him in Strasbourg and Cologne, maybe as Vicar General of the Dominican women's convents in southern Germany. It was here that he gave his famous sermons and why he is counted among the 'Rhineland mystics' when his origins were further East in Thuringia.

Alongside this active life Eckhart was a prolific writer. He wrote more than what survives. Prologues to a three-part *Summa theologica* (which as a late text may have only been in one manuscript in full version) give us an idea of what was lost in the disgrace that fell on Eckhart's final year (more on this later). But we also have Eckhartian commentaries on all the major books of Scripture. What sets him apart from other scholastic Masters is a very extensive collection of sermons. Eckhart put into practice the Dominican motto 'give to others what you receive in contemplation' – he must have received a lot, 56 sermons in Latin, 86 in German survive (some of the latter may be attributed). His use of High Middle German shows a shift towards vernacular in religious writing. Despite being a Latin scholar Eckhart was a pioneer in teaching in the 'vulgar tongue', not usually used in theology. This was probably motivated by a desire to speak to women's communities who had little Latin formation, and to the laity who flocked to his sermons.

But Eckhart is never dull, never pious, always unexpected, amusing, paradoxical, and sometimes shocking. He woke people up! He was aware of the hidden self-seeking that comes when looking for rewards and experiences from God:

> I can vouch for it that some people want to see God with their own eyes as they see a cow and to love God as they love their cow: they love the cow because it provides them with milk and cheese, and because this is to their advantage [...] Indeed, I tell you the truth, any object you have in your mind, however good, will be a barrier between you and the inmost truth.[5]

Eckhart's mysticism is centred on God, not on personal experiences or meditative practices. In that sense he could be contrasted with secular Mindfulness, which leaves God out and concentrates on personal practice. And yet, as a mystic who thinks outside the box, Eckhart offers a critique of both God-centred and practice-centred approaches. The idea of God can get in the way: 'Let us pray to God that we may be free of God that we may gain the truth' (II:87:271). God is not the product of our thought or imagination, nor is he a being in the phenomenal world. 'God is nowhere,' Eckhart says, 'God is not here or there, not in time or place' (I:33:247).

Truth for Eckhart is God 'as he is in himself,' more than any idea, and inaccessible to all methods that would try to appropriate him:

> If we think we will get more of God by meditation, by devotion, by ecstasies or by special infusion of grace than by the fireside or in the stable – that is nothing but taking

God, wrapping a cloak around his head and shoving him under a bench. For whoever seeks God in a special way gets 'the way' and misses God, who lies hidden in it. But whoever seeks God without any special way gets God as he is in himself. (I:13b:117)

In his *Talks of Instruction* to his Dominican novices he says, 'If people seek peace in outward things, whether in places or in methods of contemplation, or in people or in good works […] this is all in vain.' Restlessness comes from nothing outside us, and cannot be cured by changing externals. It comes from self-will. 'Observe yourself,' Eckhart says, 'and wherever you find yourself, leave yourself: that is the best way' (III:1:13–14). The cure of the restless ego is the recognition of God's presence:

God is closer to me than I am to myself: my being depends on God's being near me and present to me […] God is near to us but we are far from him. God is in, we are out. God is at home, we are abroad. (I:69:165,169)

Maybe the key to Eckhart's spirituality is what he calls *abgeshiedenheit*, detachment. Letting go of our normal self-centred concerns is the way to 'hold ourselves ready': 'All attachment to any work that involves the loss of freedom to wait on God in the here and now,' will cause us 'to bear no fruit' (I:8:72–3). Worrying, multitasking, spiritual ambition, all impinge on simple awareness of what is. 'To be receptive to the highest truth, and to live therein,' Eckhart says, 'a man must needs be without, before and after, untrammelled by all his acts or by any images he ever perceived, empty and free, receiving the divine gift in the eternal Now' (I:6:58). Detachment promotes a state of equanimity, similar to the *apatheia* of Evagrius. In an analogy from the writing mediums of his day Eckhart shows how thoughts must be laid aside:

If I wish to write on a wax tablet, then whatever has already been written on it, however noble it might be, prevents me from writing on it, and if I wish to do so then I must first erase whatever is on it. The tablet is never better for writing on than when it is clean. It is exactly the same with God who, if he wishes to write in the highest way on my heart, must first remove everything from my heart; whatever can be called this and that, so that he is left with a *detached* heart.[6]

'A man should be free of himself and of all things.'[7] The word Eckhart uses for 'free' is *ledig*, which means literally 'empty'. As he writes in an early treatise: 'So far as you can go out from all things, so far, neither less nor more, God will enter with all the things that are his' (III:1:14). For Eckhart, however, it is not really 'things' that get in the way, but the stickiness of our attachment. Things get stuck to our self-image. Without this grasping at them things wouldn't get in our way at all. 'Make a beginning and forget yourself, then you have left everything,' he says (I:3:13). We are the cause of our problems. Eckhart plays with German words: '*Hütte dich vor dir selber, so hast du gut gehütet.*'[8] He creates verbs out of nouns to express how that noun works. This finds a parallel in the MBSR use of the word 'selfing' which Kabat-Zinn defines as:

> that inevitable and incorrigible tendency to construct out of almost everything, and every situation, an 'I', a 'me', and a 'mine' [...] Out of virtually any and every moment and experience, our thinking mind constructs 'my' moment, 'my' experience, 'my' child, 'my' hunger, 'my' desire, 'my' opinion, 'my' way, 'my' authority, 'my' future, 'my' knowledge, 'my' body, 'my' mind, 'my' house, 'my' land, 'my' idea, 'my' feelings, 'my' car, 'my' problem.[9]

For Eckhart suffering doesn't derive from enjoying 'things' but from minding their loss, and wanting what we don't have. Sorrow is joy that has passed away, which we cling to. Everything passes. 'If I mind the loss of outward things,' Eckhart says, 'it is a sure sign that I really love sorrow and discomfort' (III:2:67). If we are immersed in God, however, then 'God shines forth in all things' and 'all things simply become God' (III:6:18, I:4:45). As Brian Pierce points out, mindfulness for Eckhart is sacramental: Taste God in all around you and then let it go, remaining only with the taste.[10] It is sacramental and apophatic: God is both present in and hidden by 'things'. 'Put aside this and that,' Eckhart says, 'and what remains is nothing but God' (II:77:220). Mindfulness for Eckhart involves letting go of afflictive thoughts, not dwelling on loss. His *Book of Divine Comfort* was written for the widowed Queen of Hungary, Agnes, who had also lost her husband and only son in the same year, and was, understandably, depressed. Eckhart's somewhat cold consolation is that the spiritual life is not a freedom from suffering, but freedom *in* suffering. Lingering in grief cannot be helpful:

> [How are people going to] take comfort and be free from care, if they [constantly] turn towards the loss and the tribulation, impressing it upon themselves and themselves upon it, so that they look at it and it looks back at them, and they talk and converse with the loss, and the loss converses with them, and they gaze each other in the face? (III:2:66–7)

Fixed thoughts are dangerous. As the *Dhammapada* says, ' "I've been insulted, I've been hurt, I've been robbed" – those who think such thoughts will not be free from hate' (Verse 3). Storing up and obsessing about things from the past cuts us off from the present and only makes us fear more for the future. Eckhart gives Agnes four pieces of advice to come out of her depression: 1) look at what you've still got – it's all a question of whether we see the glass as half full or half empty – she still had daughters! 2) Don't compare your lot to those who seem to have everything, but reflect on those who are worse off than you – one can imagine a Queen would find examples of the latter. 3) Don't love things that pass away, and 4) accept that whatever is, is God's will. Agnes must have taken this advice to heart for she retired to a convent for the rest of her life!

Simplicity and Silent Receptivity

In Sermon 53 Eckhart says that the second thing he preaches, after detachment, is 'that the human person should be formed again into that simple good which is God.' The word for 'simple' used here is *einvotatige*, 'one-willing'. But by this Eckhart does not mean 'wanting to do the will of God', that would be two wills working together – God's and ours. To be simple there must be only one will, God's. 'When I do not will anything for myself,' he writes in his *Talks of Instruction*, 'then God wills on my behalf.'[11] The human side of the will disappears. This is Eckhart's 'the poor man who wants nothing', who is not attached to anything, not even to 'the will of God'. Eckhart explains further:

> As long as someone still feels that it is his will to perform the will of Almighty God, then that person still lacks the kind of poverty of which we speak. For this person still possesses their will, with which they wish to satisfy the will of God, and that is not true poverty. For, if we are to have true poverty, then we must be as free of our created will as we were before we possessed it. I say to you in all truth: as long as you have the will to do God's will, and have a desire for God and eternity, you are not yet truly poor. For a person is only truly poor who wills nothing and desires nothing.

'Simplicity' for Eckhart firstly involves letting go of the idea of a God 'out there' whom I must will and desire. God is not another 'thing'. The goodness of God is at the centre of who we are:

> I have often said that a person who wishes to begin a
> good life should be like a man who draws a circle. Let him
> get the centre in the right place and keep it so and the
> circumference will be good. In other words let a man first
> learn to fix his heart on God and then his good deeds will
> have virtue; but if a man's heart is unsteady, even the great
> things he does will be of small advantage.[12]

Secondly, if reforming our life is not an act of the will then, for Eckhart, it is an act of acceptance, not seeking to try to change the way things are. If, when we are ill and we ask God for health, 'then health,' Eckhart says, 'is dearer to us than God.

> We wish it should be God's will for us to become well again.
> When things are going badly, then you wish that it might
> be God's will for things to improve. On the other hand, if
> God's will becomes your will and you fall ill – so be it! God's
> will be done! If your friend dies – so be it! God's will be
> done![13]

If Eckhart challenges the idea of trying to be good people from external works he is cautious of petitionary prayer if it is trying to twist God's arm. Petitionary prayer only really works, as Julian of Norwich says, if 'God is the ground of our beseeching' – if what we ask for comes from God not from ourselves. Eckhart's way of describing acceptance can seem a bit heartless, and yet being *einvotatige* with God, for Eckhart, is to live a life of compassion. 'Whatever it is that God may do – the first thing which breaks forth is always his mercy' (II:72:188–9). 'By compassion the soul is made blessed' (I:7:22). But his simple goodness comes from within, not from trying: 'We should not think that holiness is based on what we do but rather on what we are, for it is not our works which sanctify us but we who sanctify our works' (II:4:15). This is more than two centuries before Martin Luther challenged the idea of doing things in order to become holy. Goodness and righteousness for Eckhart, however, come from mindfulness and not just faith. What we are is the result of our thinking. Eckhart has parallels to the Buddha's teaching as much as to Luther:

> If a man speaks or acts with an evil thought, pain follows him, as the wheel follows the foot of the ox that draws the carriage [...] If a man speaks or acts with a pure thought, happiness follows him, like a shadow that never leaves him. (*Dhammapada* verses 1–2)

For Eckhart, however, it is not so much right thought as letting go of thought that makes us act like God: 'Love begins where thinking stops.'[14] 'We don't need to ask for the love of God,' Eckhart explains, 'we only need to hold ourselves ready for it.' The idea that we are separate from the simple goodness of God is just an idea, not reality. Eckhart uses a language of identity with God that is very different from Luther: 'There is something in the soul,' he says, 'that is so closely related to God that it is one with Him and not just united; it is a oneness and a pure union.'[15]

Detachment, receptivity to what is and being formed into simple goodness is the same thing. To act compassionately we have simultaneously to be open to the experience of others without being overwhelmed by their pain. If we are not receptive to their experience we will not know in what way we can help them, but if we are 'caught up' in what they are going through without standing our own ground as another person we will simply be of no good to them either. Real receptivity comes from equanimity, enabling us 'to respond in the same way to all things, not to be broken by adversity nor carried away by prosperity, not to rejoice more in one thing than another, not to be frightened or grieved by one thing more than another.'[16] Jon Kabat-Zinn encourages a mountain meditation whereby we 'borrow' the qualities of a mountain by holding its image in our minds, picturing its solidity.[17] Eckhart is not prone to imaginative meditations, however, rather he sees detachment as 'nothing else but a mind that stands unmoved by all accidents of joy or sorrow, honour, shame, or disgrace, as a mountain of lead stands unmoved by a breath of wind.'[18] Detachment makes for a quiet mind: 'A quiet mind,' Eckhart says, 'is one which nothing weighs on, nothing worries, which, free from ties and from all self-seeking, is wholly merged into the will of God and dead to its own [...] To the quiet mind all things are possible' (I:1:7).

Such equanimity involves living without imposing our own agenda on life, accepting it as it comes, empty of expectations of how this moment should be. To be open to God's presence in what is, that is life in its fullness. As Eckhart says:

> If you asked life, 'Why do you live?' if it could answer, it would only say, 'I live because I live'. That is because life lives from its own ground, and gushes forth from its own. Therefore it lives without a *Why*, because it lives for itself. (I:13b:118).

To be 'simply good' involves not expecting anything in return (whether in gratitude, sense of self-worth, or heavenly reward), we are good for the sake of goodness itself.

If Eckhart is iconoclastic about practices, does he teach any specific 'way'? The way he teaches is the way of the present moment. Eckhart says emphatically, 'There is but one Now' (I:8:74). 'There is no becoming', only being (II:93:319). God's 'is-ness' is always a present tense verb (II:49:38–9). 'God is a God of the present' (III:1:29). When we are mindful then the Now of eternity breaks through into time: 'That which happened on the first day and [...]

the last day,' Eckhart says, 'is there all in the present' (I:25:198). For Eckhart this is not just a theory but part of his experience: 'The soul knows all things in God new and fresh and present and joyous as I have them now present' (I:29:216).

The Training of Effortless Attention

For Eckhart, however, freedom from 'ways and whys' comes at a cost: it involves discipline, determination, right intention. His first bit of advice is to cultivate interior silence: 'Hide from the turmoil of inward thoughts, for they but create discord' (I:2:20–21). 'We must learn to acquire an inward desert, wherever and with whomever we are,' he says (I:6:19). In silence we are able to hear the echo of God's Word in creation: 'We must learn to break through things and seize our God in them' (Ibid). 'We should receive God in all things,' he says, 'and train our mind to keep God ever present in our mind, in our aims and in our love' (I:6:17). Eckhart compares this insight into God's presence to the hard training of learning to write:

> If we are prepared to practise diligently and often, we will learn and master the art. Of course, at first we have to remember every letter and fix it firmly in our mind. Later on, when we have acquired the art, we will be completely free of the images [of the letters] and will not have to stop and think, but will write fluently and freely – and the same with playing the fiddle or any other task that requires skill. All we need is to want to learn this skill, and even if we are not paying full attention and our thoughts wander, still in time we will learn. Thus persevering [in mindful attention] God's presence will shine forth for us without any effort.

For Eckhart this effortless attention comes through turning the whole person – mind and senses – towards God. In his *Talks of Instruction* he explains how this starts inwardly by receiving whatever life presents, and yet also works outwardly through the body:

> In all things we should consciously use our mind, having in all things a perceptive awareness of ourselves, and our inward being, and in all things seize God in the highest possible way. We should be as our Lord said, 'Like people on the watch, always expecting the Lord' (Luke 12:36). For indeed people who are expectant like that are watchful, they look around them to see where he whom they expect is coming from, and they look out for him in whatever comes along, however strange it may be, just in case he should be in it. In this way we should consciously [mindfully] discover our Lord in all things. This requires much diligence, demanding a total effort of our senses and powers of mind. (III:7:20)

For Eckhart 'the spark of the intellect' is a tiny spark of the Divine nature (I:31:229). 'The divine light rises in the soul and makes morning' (I:32b:241). It enlightens the senses as well as the mind, 'welling over [from the soul] into the body, which is filled with radiance' (I:2:16). The light comes from within but floods outward things. Meanwhile the watchman waits patiently for the dawn. 'It is a little difficult in the beginning in becoming detached,' Eckhart admits, 'but when one has got into it, no life is easier, more delightful or lovelier' (II:69:169). For it leads to a quiet mind and a relaxed body. The one 'who is in full control of his mind and uses it [in his sense life] alone knows true peace' (III:7:20).

Effortless attention comes through living each day wakefully. 'What is today?' asks Eckhart, and answers, 'Eternity' (II:50:46). 'God is ever at work in the eternal now, and his work is the begetting of his Son' (II:79:230). The Son is the seed of God in us. In *Of the Nobleman* Eckhart writes:

> God's seed is in us, if it were tended by a good, wise, industrious gardener, it would then flourish all the better, and would grow up to God, whose seed it is, and its fruits would be like God's own nature. The seed of a pear tree grows up into a pear tree, the seed of a nut tree grows up to be a nut tree, the seed of god grows to be God.[19]

Using another image, in *The Book of Divine Comfort* Eckhart says God gives birth to his son in us as fire gives birth to fire in wood. As the wood is turned into fire so we – body and soul – are turned into God. The Word of God, 'through whom all things were made', expresses God in all things (Jn 1:3, Col 1:16). It continues to create the world 'now and in this day' (II:66:144). God makes all things new but he does so in silence – 'there is nothing so much like God's action as silence,' Eckhart writes, 'God is a word, a word unspoken.'[20] In terms of mindfulness, for Eckhart, this involves 'a forgetting and an unknowing; there must be a stillness and a silence for this Word [the voice of God] to make itself heard' (I:2:20–21).

The sensate imagery Eckhart uses for mindfulness involves sight and hearing (he prefers the latter – 'We learn more wisdom by hearing than by seeing' (Ibid). However, the Word is also the hand of God, reaching out (like Michelangelo's God in the Sistine Chapel), quickening our physical life. It is also the breath. When we turn our whole being towards God we are touched by the Word and we receive the Holy Spirit as breath. Our breath is our lifeline to God both in our original creation and in every moment. Eckhart plays with Psalm 104:30: 'When you [God] send forth your spirit [*ruah, breath*] all things are created; and you renew the face of the earth.' The Hebrew and the Latin for breath is the same as spirit. The Divine breath 'in the beginning' gives us life; 'God breathed the breath of life into the man [Adam]'s nostrils and he became a living soul' (Gen 2:7). At Pentecost creation is renewed, Jesus breathes the Spirit into his disciples. In this breath we are given more than life, we are given the fire of love: 'The love with which we love, is the Holy Spirit,' Eckhart says (I:12:103). 'The greater the love that is in the soul, and the more the Holy Spirit breathes on it, the more perfect the flame' (II:62:113). Our appropriation of this gift does not happen all at once, 'the Holy Spirit breathes gradually on the flame,' Eckhart says, one breath at a time (Ibid). Transformation takes time, but the breath that God has given us nudges us on. The Spirit 'reminds' us, brings us to mindfulness, reconnecting us to the teachings and to the peace of Jesus (Jn 14:26–27).

At the time of his preaching, despite the popularity of Eckhart's sermons, they were sometimes misconstrued and maligned in certain quarters. By preaching such mystical things openly he provoked those who considered themselves guardians of Orthodoxy. 'People would be misled.' The boldness of Eckhart's language and his use of paradox meant that a particular saying when taken out of context could sound a little 'dangerous'. Eckhart's close association with women's groups like the Beguines which did not have, nor want, canonical status as a religious order meant he was under the gaze of ecclesiastical authorities. The Archbishop of Cologne opened proceedings against Eckhart for heresy. The Dominicans came to their Meister's defence. The Archbishop was a Franciscan so this was seen as part of the usual intellectual sparring between the orders – but the Archbishop was not to leave it at the level of debate. Eckhart was summoned to face the Inquisition. He responded by insisting on being heard by the Pope – to whom the Dominicans vowed general obedience rather than being under the jurisdiction of local Bishops. In 1328, at the age of 68 Eckhart started his journey to the exiled Pope in Avignon, southern France. The journey of some 1,800 km on horseback and foot must have exhausted him for he died soon after arrival while the trial was unconcluded. Many of his sayings – taken individually – were declared heretical, though he himself was not. Eckhart's many followers were left to salvage his teaching and it has been passed on as an inspiration to Christian mysticism up to today. Eckhart's personal reputation as an authentic Christian mystic has now been restored. He is again recognised as a *Meister* who knew the secrets of God.

The Cloud of Unknowing

At the end of the fourteenth century (some seventy years after Eckhart's death) four epistles and a free translation of a classic mystical text were written in English by an anonymous author.[21] *The Cloud of Unknowing* (the longest of his epistles) jumps in at the deep end of Christian mysticism. The author's concern is how 'a soul is oned with God' (1:2);[22] similar to Eckhart. However, unlike the German mystic the *Cloud*-author tries to give some methods or practices for 'letting go and letting God'. This may be a contrast between the German and English temperament: one more speculative and philosophical, the other practical and pastoral. The *Cloud*-author is keen to offer 'ways' that make letting go easier, ways of getting ourselves out of the way and becoming aware of God's presence at the centre of our soul. I will look at three he offers: attentiveness to time, use of a prayer word, and the felt sense of ourself. These have parallels in contemporary Mindfulness practice: cultivating acceptance, the capacity to observe and the discovery of embodiment.

Ideas as to the *Cloud*-author's identity range from Carthusian monk to Adam Easton (1330–1397), the Benedictine Cardinal Vicar of England.[23] The dialect of his Middle English shows him to be from the East Midlands. He was a priest: a priestly blessing is given at the end of the *Cloud*, and well educated in Latin and the scholastic theology of the Universities – both (given the medieval context) confirm the gender. The author wrote epistles for the benefit of a young man aged twenty-four seeking the solitary life but intended them for a wider readership.

These Epistles were written in a very different era from today, at a time when renunciation of the world was seen as requisite for

contemplation. Fourteenth-century England saw a flowering of
the hermit and anchorite life, the *Cloud* is part of that movement;
contemplation is praised above active life, prayer above study,
absorption in God is the ideal. Our approach may be different
today. Preserved in the monastic culture of post-Reformation
England these treatises were regarded as specialist teaching
on prayer. It is only in the last century through the work of
William Johnston and teachers of Centring Prayer and Christian
Meditation that its value for non-monastics has been recognised.
As Laurence Freeman writes: 'The *Cloud*'s description of the stages
of spiritual growth from the active to the highest contemplative
life in a cloister has been replaced by a modern awareness of the
contemplative dimension of every life style and the unique process
of the complexities of individual growth.'[24] Still, the *Cloud* reminds
us that to be contemplative in the world we need at intervals to
take time out from our everyday concerns. In that 'quiet time' we
have to do the work of detachment and transcendence the Spirit
inspires in us.

For the *Cloud*-author the heights of contemplation may be the
preserve of solitaries but this doesn't narrow his assessment of
those who are called. 'God often brings about this work in those
who have been habitual sinners' (38:13–14). This may seem a
surprising statement from one who previously said that various
levels of perfection must be reached before contemplation is
possible, however, the *Cloud*-author works within an Augustinian
theology of grace. Contemplation in the end is a gift from God,
not something we achieve, and God gives as he pleases. The more
conscious we are of sin, the more aware we are of our need of God,
the more open we are to the workings of grace. Also this 'work' of
contemplation, the *Cloud*-author says, is the one thing in which
no moderation need be kept. The abandonment and letting go
that make a good sinner find here their proper direction. Those
who are temperamentally self-sufficient and restrained may be at
the disadvantage. It must be remembered, however, that the *Cloud*
does urge moderation in all things but this.

The author's main concern is perennially relevant to meditative practice: leaving behind images and thoughts, the step from discursive to contemplative prayer. 'Live at the deep solitary core of your being,' he encourages his twenty-four year old disciple (8:15). There is only one of us in the world and so to be ourselves is to be solitary. The premise of solitude is interiority: its fruit, the *Cloud*-author says, is the ability to be 'attentive to time and the way we spend it.'

> There is nothing more precious than time [...] God, the master of time, never gives the future. We will not be able to excuse ourselves at the last judgment, saying to God, 'You overwhelmed me with the future when I was only capable of living in the present.' He gives only the present, moment by moment, for this is the law of the created order, and God will not contradict himself in his creation. Time is for man and woman, not man and woman for time. (11:18–29)

We shouldn't be ruled by our agenda and timetables to the point where we cannot dwell in the moment. In Alexander Technique keeping our mind and actions focused on results while losing sight of the means whereby those results are achieved is called 'end gaining'. When I am sitting on the bus I am thinking about where I have to get to, annoyed at the slowness of the bus, looking at my watch, instead of simply enjoying being on the bus and experiencing what is going on. In this scenario I am ruled by time.

Being mindful of time, for the *Cloud*-author, doesn't mean being anxious about being 'on time' – we would then be ruled by something in the future – our appointment, agenda, timetable. Rather the opposite, it is to be attentive to each moment as it passes. The *Cloud* is written in parts in a dialogue form where the author imagines the response of his reader. The intimacy of the epistle is in this conversational quality. His reader asks, 'How long will this contemplative work take?' It takes 'only an instant' – the shortest possible time imaginable, literally 'an atom of time.' In medieval understanding there were 22,560 'atoms' in an hour so we should be aware of the present moment six times every second! In other words, always! The author imagines the response of the young man:

> What am I to do? If all he says is true how am I to justify my past? I am twenty-four years old and until this moment I have scarcely noticed time at all […] Besides I know very well that in the future, either through frailty or laziness, I will probably not be any more attentive to the present moment than I have been in my past. I am completely discouraged. Please help me for the love of Jesus. (11:30–40)

The *Cloud*-author gives two responses: one more theological, one practical. The *Cloud*-author's faith response is 'Stay close to Jesus'. Jesus is always in the present moment.

> In love all things are shared and so if you love Jesus, everything of his is yours. As God he is creator and dispenser of time; as man he consciously mastered time; as God and man he is the rightful judge of humanity's use of time. Bind yourself to Jesus, therefore, in faith and love so that belonging to him you may share all he has and enter the fellowship of those who love him. (12:2–3)

We can 'put on the mind[fulness] of Christ' (1Cor 2:16). This is echoed in John Main's re-presentation of the *Cloud*'s teaching in *The Way of Unknowing*. 'The journey of prayer,' he says, 'is simply to find a way to open our human consciousness to [Christ's] human consciousness, and to become, on that way, fully conscious ourselves.'[25] In becoming human Christ makes present the eternal moment of salvation within time. Becoming attentive to God's presence, therefore, becomes a human possibility. The eternal moment is no longer an ideal outside human experience but can be accessed in Christ-centred meditation. The *Cloud*-author says that, in the present moment all the saints and the angels are in fact there to help us: 'Mary, who was full of grace at every moment; the angels who are unable to waste time; and all the blessed in heaven and on earth, who through the grace of Jesus employ every moment in love' (12:18). But we have to play our part as well 'with the help of grace to be mindful of time' (14:32–34).

The second, more meditation-based is to let go of thoughts and desires which drag us away from being content with the present moment: 'It is inevitable,' the *Cloud*-author says, 'that ideas will arise in your mind and try to distract you in a thousand ways. They will question you saying, 'What are you looking for, what do you want?' His advice, taken up also by contemporary teachers of Christian Meditation and Centring Prayer, is to take a short word, of one syllable, which expresses the intention of our heart. The *Cloud*-author recommends the word 'God' or 'Love': 'fix it in your mind so that it will remain there come what may [...] To all of [your thoughts] you must reply, "God alone I seek and desire, only him." If they ask, "Who is this God?" tell them he is the God who created you, redeemed you and brought you to this work. Say to your thoughts, "you are powerless to grasp him. Be still"' (14:34–38). No more theology is needed than that. We know God in the stillness.

The prayer word – or mantra as we might call it today – plays two roles: it puts down and suppresses all manner of thoughts under 'a cloud of forgetting', and it gathers all the energy of our heart to reach out to God in 'a cloud of unknowing.' To persevere in the 'nothing' and 'nowhere' of contemplation, sandwiched between two clouds, can be frustrating to the body and the mind. Like demanding children thoughts and sensations are used to being the centre of attention. However if we persevere the *Cloud*-author is confident 'God in his goodness will give you a deep experience of himself' (9:37–39). The word should not be analysed, for that would take us back into thought. Take the word whole, the

Cloud-author says, 'If your mind begins to intellectualise over the meaning and connotations of this little word, remind yourself that its value lies in its simplicity' (16:5). All thoughts must be let go of, those about worldly things and spiritual things. Knowledge of all created things and their works (i.e. science and the social sciences) must be put beneath 'a cloud of forgetting,' but God also must be approached 'nakedly', 'blindly', in 'a cloud of unknowing', not through reflection. We cannot know God with our thoughts the *Cloud*-author insists. God-logic, theo-logy, has its scope, it can know how God works (creation, incarnation, redemption, etc.) but it cannot know God's self. In contemplation we reach out to God without images, not looking for any of his gifts or manifestations in history. There must be 'a naked intent' (9:30–31).

> For I tell you everything that you dwell on in this work becomes an obstacle to union with God. For if your mind is cluttered with these concerns there is no room for God. Yes, and with due reverence I go so far as to say it is equally useless to think that you can nourish your contemplative work by thinking of God's attributes. (14:1–5)

However, although God cannot be thought he can be loved. In fact this is the meaning of creation: 'Human beings were created to love and all other things were created in order to make love possible' (11:11–12). Love can grasp and comprehend God because 'God is love' (1Jn 4:8). 'Truly this is the unending miracle of love: that one loving person, through their love, can embrace God, whose being fills and transcends the entire creation' (10:37–39). 'A sharp dart of longing love' will pierce heaven. This act of the will can be 'wrapped and enfolded in one word,' the *Cloud*-author says, 'so that you can hold on to it better' (15:30–31). Like an arrow, which is very focussed at its point, so a short word passes through the cloud. If you were standing at the window in a house on fire, you would not call out a long sentence, 'There is a fire, I don't know how it started but I need to get out, can you help me please?' you would cry 'Fire! Help!' Short words carry energy. The immediate intensity of the words will get the attention of another. So it is with God.

The *Cloud*-author is aware of the unruliness of the mind. If we are distracted he gives three bits of advice: First try ignoring thoughts: 'Look beyond them – over their shoulder, as it were – as if you were looking for something else, which of course you are' (37:2–3). Here the prayer word helps 'unhook' one's attention from a set thought and fix it on God who is 'beyond'. The mind needs something to do and won't just be quiet on demand. If thoughts still continue, he says, maybe we are trying too hard to fight them off. Resistance gives them power. The *Cloud*-author's advice is to relax our effort, accept that our minds are powerless, surrender to God and He will help you. God may be using precisely our feeling of weakness in prayer to keep us humble. If thoughts still continue then keep trying to keep your mind on God but accept and put up with what comes. 'Distractions may be our purgatory on earth' (37:29–30).

Mindfulness practice, as we have seen, combines *samatha* as one pointed attention on the breath, with *vipassana* or general awareness using the body scan or a sensation like taste. The mysticism promoted by the *Cloud* recommends one pointed focus on a word. Obviously different from the breath this does, however, serve the same function: centring attention and letting go of extraneous thoughts. The theocentric nature of the *Cloud*, like all Christian mysticism, means the aim is not personal wellbeing but God-centredness. For the *Cloud* the word expresses the intention of the heart, gathering the energy of the heart to unite it to God. This is a subtle difference between the *Cloud* and Evagrius. The Desert teachers emphasised stilling the *logismoi*, or thoughts, so as to arrive at a state of *apatheia*, or dispassion. The emphasis is on 'attention' to God's presence rather than desire for God. Meister Eckhart as we have seen takes this even further by saying that the will itself should be silent at the time of prayer;

the contemplative should will nothing. For the *Cloud*-author, as for Augustine, desire and the will are much more engaged. Unlike Augustine the *vipassana* aspect of meditation is not emphasised in the *Cloud*. 'Do not be curious to know more,' he says, 'only become increasingly faithful to the work of love until it becomes your whole life' (38:38–39).

Body, or not Body: that is the Question

Vipassana can be cognitive, as with Augustine, or can emphasise physical awareness, as in MBSR. The *Cloud*-author at first sight seems to conclude (like Augustine) that, in prayer, attention must be taken away from the body. The soul is closer to God than the body and therefore to focus on bodily things renders the vision of God opaque.

> God is spirit and whoever would be one with him must
> be, in truth and in depth of spirit, far removed from
> any misleading bodily thing [...] For by its nature every
> physical thing is farther removed from God than any
> spiritual [...] Whenever you find 'yourself' spoken of
> in spiritual writing understand that it is your soul that
> is referred to, not your body [...] For in contemplative
> praying we should forget all about time and place and body.
> (49:14–16, 20–21; 64:10–11; 61:38)

However, even in his seemingly dualistic statements, the body is only 'further from' never 'removed' from God. To God all things are equally present. So the *Cloud*-author exclaims,

> God forbid that I should part what God has joined, the
> body and the spirit. For God wants to be served with
> body and soul, both together, as is right, and to give us his
> heavenly reward in body as well as in soul. (50:15–17)

This understated 'holistic' side of the *Cloud*-author's teaching is rooted in the scholastic commonplace that if the body is alive it must be linked to the soul. The soul is the life of the body. As the soul ceases to give attention to external things but finds its own centre within, so the body also orientates inward and finds its own poise and self-awareness. Meditation, the *Cloud*-author says, 'will provide spiritual food and inner strength to body as well as to soul; for since all sickness and corruption took hold of the flesh when the soul ceased this exercise, so all health will return when the soul bestirs itself to start again.'[26] Meditation renders the body peaceful and pleasing to behold, it 'has a good effect on the body as well as the soul.' (55: 25–27)

For the *Cloud*-author good health helps with meditation. A calm mind and body doesn't interfere with contemplation. However, we don't meditate *in order* to be healthy: psychophysical health is not an end in itself. In fact inordinate concern with the state of the body, as with business in the world, can be a distraction. But more than fearing that spirituality could hijacked for health benefits the *Cloud*-author's real worry is it would be unnatural to try to 'feel inwardly' with the 'outer' physical senses. Touch, taste, sight, hearing, smelling are naturally oriented to external objects. To try to sense inwardly would be a delusionary form of spiritual sensation. True, he says, 'the subjection of the body to the spirit can be seen after a fashion' but that 'manner' is external observation (of others, or ourselves in a mirror), not an inner sensation (63:10–11).

There is a critique here of the emphasis of some contemporary teachers on 'feeling the inner body', transforming the soul through the body, or finding the spiritual body.[27] For the *Cloud*-author in meditation the body does not *become* spiritual but *behaves* spiritually. The body becomes naturally more upright following in a physical way the 'uprightness' of the soul. For the *Cloud*-author the effects of prayer on the body are physical not spiritual and should not become an object of mental focus. Awareness of physical sensations cannot lead to soul transformation for, reversely, it is the soul that leads and integrates the body. From the spiritual perspective Mindfulness practices of the body-scan could be seen as putting the cart before the horse. Some teachers of Mindfulness from a spiritual perspective know this. Eckhart Tolle admits that 'the body that you can see and touch cannot take you into Being [for] that visible and tangible body is only an outer shell, or rather a limited and distorted perception of a deeper reality.'[28] However, in order to take attention off 'Mind-thinking' awareness of the body is still proposed, by Tolle, as a 'portal' to 'the unmanifested.' We come to know that we are ourselves beyond outward form if we learn to feel the body from within, feel the life inside the body, not any particularised object of sensation. 'In your natural state of connectedness with Being,' Tolle says, 'this deeper reality can be felt every moment as the invisible inner body, the animating presence within you.'

What then is the object of focus the *Cloud*-author proposes? It is to contemplate 'God in himself', unmanifested, stripped of attributes and images. The simple awareness 'that God is', not 'what God is.' He calls this 'a naked awareness of God's being' (39:9–10). The means is not self-awareness but love: Love reaches where thought cannot go. But, the *Cloud*-author says, we must learn to love God not *because* of anything but for God's own sake: 'A blind stirring of love' (18:38). However, there are stages to this blind or naked awareness. His *Epistle of Privy Counselling* (written after *The Cloud*) makes allowances for body awareness as a tool for centring the mind: 'Because of your crude uncultured natural state and your spiritual immaturity I ask you in the beginning to cover and clothe the feeling of God in the feeling of yourself' (89:3–4, 8–10). To know 'that God is' we can first know 'that we are', not thinking about or analysing ourselves, but feeling.

The Felt Sense of Self

In what sense is the felt sense of self an embodied experience? Expressions of the 'outer' and 'inner' in spiritual writing do not necessarily distinguish between body and the soul but more between two ways of being body: that which is orientated externally in relation to the world and body as experienced internally in the mind.[29] The senses work outwards towards objects, through them we understand ourselves as an object in relation to others. For medieval writers like the *Cloud* sensual extroversion created 'the world and the flesh'. The body is only an intermediary for knowledge outside ourselves. However, the body can also be felt interiorly and directly. Such a felt sense of the body seems to encourage the 'body-scan' taught in Mindfulness. For the *Cloud*-author also we prepare for contemplation by drawing the senses inward, redirecting the body into the mind. The body then shares the mind's capacity for self-awareness. Such sensation is not 'clothed' by any external objects but is 'a naked awareness and a blind feeling of *our* own being' (*Epistle* 75:23).

Eckhart Tolle gives a similar teaching, and similar ambiguity, in different ways of being body:

> You *are* your body. The body that you can see and touch is only a thin and illusory veil. Underneath it lies the invisible inner body, the doorway into Being, into Life Unmanifested. Through the inner body, you are inseparably connected to this unmanifested One Life – birthless, deathless, eternally present. Through the inner body, you are forever one with God.[30]

It may be a way to God but the *Cloud*-author would balk when Tolle goes on to say that, 'in its deepest aspect [the inner body] *is* the Unmanifested, the Source from which consciousness emanates [...] If you take your attention deep into the inner body, you may reach this point, this singularity, where the world dissolves into the Unmanifested.'[31] The *Cloud*-author is at pains to show that felt sense of self can only apply to God by analogy, in itself it is no spiritual or esoteric teaching. The consciousness it gives rise to is sensitive not intellectual: 'This is plainly proper to the most uneducated cow or to the most irrational beast [...] that is to *feel* their own proper being' (*Epistle* 76:39–77:1).

Medieval anthropology believed that humans differed from animals in their ability to think abstractly, the 'intellective soul' worked beyond the data provided by sensation. Yet, the *Cloud*-author says, the capacity to 'know oneself' is shared by animals as much as humans, in fact they may have it better! To know ourselves is a sensitive capacity. However, the *Cloud*-author wants to confirm that God – as pure consciousness – is no sense object. Bodily senses are naturally occupied only with physical things. God cannot even be arrived at through turning the physical senses inward for consciousness is incorporeal. The felt sense of self can only help in knowing God by analogy. As in sensation we know 'we are' irrespective of attributes ('we are this or that...) so us know the 'we are', so contemplation of God should aim at knowing that God is, stripped of attributes, unmanifested as this or that.

The Epistle of Privy Counselling favours meditations that come by 'naked feeling' than those arrived at by 'work of the intelligence' (78:1–10). The mind is occupied with 'qualities of our being' but awareness of the body enables 'whole worship, offering up to [God] simply and completely our own self' (78:15–16, 32–33). To offer ourselves 'generally and not specially' it is better to go through the body, which takes us as a whole person, than through mental analysis, which leaves out direct feeling (78:34). The mind when it is linked to the body is more whole than when it acts separately. 'God will be served with body and with soul, both together, as is seemly,' the *Cloud*-author says (*Cloud* 50:15–16).

The imagery of nakedness and stripping used to describe a felt sense is reminiscent of Christ in his Passion. In the late Middle Ages there was a popular use of carnal affections and imagination in relation to the humanity of Christ. The *Cloud*-author insists, however, that as an exterior object of meditation 'it is necessary that [Christ] go bodily from you' (*Epistle* 90:5–7, 98:18–19). His humanity is the door to heaven, but doors have to be passed through, and we have to do so 'in no bodily manner' (*Cloud* 61:21–24). The *Cloud*-author uses the body dialectically, even paradoxically. A position held at one point is counterbalanced at another. He is clearly worried about a one-sided reading of his work: 'If a man saw one matter and not another, in this way he might easily be led into error' (*Cloud* 1:28–29). The tension is held between the felt sense as a way to wholeness and the body as something we pass through and beyond. In contemplation there is an alternation of the felt sense of God in the body and its absence. Sensual consolations 'nourish and feed our spirit to persevere,' absence of the felt sense 'exercises our patience' (*Epistle* 97:5, 96:37). This alternation makes the contemplative 'flexible' to God.[32] Despite being an introductory stage of spiritual practice the *Cloud*-author does conclude that the body is capable of God and part of the process of mystical transformation.

Chapter 6

Yoga and Loving-Kindness Meditation

'It is very important for any soul that prays, whether little or much, that it doesn't tighten up or squeeze itself into a corner.'[1]

Stillness of Body, Stillness of Mind

Alongside sitting meditation (following the breath) and the body scan, a third practice encouraged by therapeutic Mindfulness is *hatha* yoga. When 're-minding' ourselves we have to 're-body' ourselves. *Hatha* yoga is derived from Indian meditation techniques – more closely associated with Hindu than Buddhist practice. The classic text the *Yoga Sutras of Patanjali* was composed around 400 BC. *Asanas* or postures are one of the 'Eight Limbs' of ascetic practice. For Patanjali the physical regimen is placed within a life of restraint and withdrawal of attachments aiming at 'the cessation of the movements of the mind.' As therapeutic and educational Mindfulness can be seen to take one aspect of Buddhism and leave many others, so much yoga taught in the West leaves out the original meditative and devotional context.[2] Jon Kabat-Zinn believes that *hatha* yoga is not just exercise, nor is it simply preparation for meditation, but *is* meditation itself. There is no need to add spirituality to yoga. Giving attention to the body, letting go of our stiffness in our thoughts and limbs, is a 'consciousness discipline' that leads to healing and wholeness.

Yoga is a Sanskrit word meaning 'yoke'. In fact the words have the same etymological root in the Proto-Indo-European verb *yewg* – 'to join'. Yoga is understood as the practice of unifying body and mind as two oxen are yoked to pull a cart. For Patanjali the cart was the *atman* or spirit within the human person. Yoking of body and mind brought about the most favourable conditions for the exploration of who we really are. Paradoxically, considering the emphasis that the body is given regarding *hatha* yoga in the West, Patanjali's aim was the realisation that we are neither our body nor our mind! The *atman* had to be extracted from the body-mind as one draws out the inner blade of grass from its sheath.[3] It is one of the paradoxes of religion that Buddhism and Hinduism, who put the least emphasis on our identity as body, have the most physical practices. Islam also uses postures in prayer. While Christianity, which believes that we are our bodies and that they have an eternal destiny has a tendency to neglect the body in prayer and denigrate 'fleshly' desires.

In theory at least there has always been a place for the body within Christianity. The early Church Fathers defended a literal understanding that God became flesh in Jesus of Nazareth. God reveals himself ultimately not through wise sages or the theophany of nature, not through his relationship with a particular people or the inspired words of a book. God reveals himself through a body. To characterise other religions in these ways is no doubt reductionist but Christianity can nearly be reduced to one mystery, 'the Word [of God] became flesh and dwelt amongst us' (Jn 1:14). In fact the central and specific mysteries of Christianity are bodily: the incarnation, which elevates Mary as 'Mother of God'; Christ's very physical death, whereby we can say that 'God died in the flesh'; the resurrection of his body (and ours at the end of time). The extreme physicality of Christianity is evidenced in the sacraments: Baptism – with water; Communion – through bread and wine making present the body and blood of Christ; Reconciliation – by confessing our sins vocally and receiving the words of absolution' Confirmation and (for some) Ordination –

in both the Spirit is transmitted through the laying on of hands; Marriage – where the couple create the sacrament through vows heard by witnesses, and through the intimacy of their sexual relation; Anointing of the Sick – through oil and invocation of the names of God in the Trinity.

Then there is the liturgy – the use of gesture in different ways across different traditions: kneeling, standing, signing ourselves with the cross, raising our hands in prayer, bowing with the 'Glory be', genuflecting to the tabernacle, kissing icons or the wood of the Cross, giving the sign of peace, prayers for bodily healing, processions, etc. Outside of liturgy the act of pilgrimage is a Christian equivalent to walking meditation. Fasting could be a way of mindful eating. Going on retreat parallels the regular 'day of no busy-ness' recommended in Mindfulness.

Lastly, the use of the body in private prayer: St Dominic (1170–1221) founder of the Dominicans (of which Meister Eckhart was a brother) was remembered for using nine postures or corporal practices for prayer. A treatise written a half century after St Dominic's death remembers him 'bowing humbly [...] his head right down'; 'throwing himself flat on the ground'; 'whipping himself'; 'kneeling down and standing up again' alternately; 'holding his hands before him', 'joining them on his heart' and then 'opening them to his shoulders'; 'stretching out his arms as far as they could go, in the form of a cross'; 'stretching his whole body up to heaven, like an arrow being shot up in the air, hand stretched right above his head, either held together or open as if to receive something from heaven'; 'sitting quietly'; 'walking by himself and praying as he walked'.[4] Dominic repeated certain lines of scripture or prayers with each posture 'recollecting himself in himself, and fixing himself in the presence of God.' At times he seems to follow a form of *Ashtanga* yoga, 'his movements rapid, yet always sure and orderly.'

Louis Hughes, an Irish Dominican, continues the tradition of his founder in showing how classic hatha yoga *asanas* can express corporally some attitude of Christian faith.[5] The forward bend –

'Bend my heart to obey your law, O God' (Ps 119:36); Spinal twist – 'Turn to me now and be saved' (Isaiah 45:22); Child's pose – 'At the name of Jesus, every knee shall bend' (Phil 2:10); Corpse pose – 'Into thy hands, O Lord, I commend my Spirit' (Ps 31:5). Nancy Roth, an Episcopal priest, maps the ten classic *asanas* of the 'Sun Salutation' to the prayers contained in the 'Our Father', meditating on each line with the pose that expresses it: Inhale and raising the arms – 'Our Father who art in heaven'; bowing down, hands to the ground – 'Hallowed be thy name'; right forward lunge – 'Thy Kingdom come'; plank – 'Thy will be done'; low and then fully stretched cobra – 'On earth, as it is in heaven'; dog – (appropriately) 'Give us our daily bread'; left forward lunge – 'as we forgive those who trespass against us'; bowing down, hands to the ground – 'And lead us not into temptation'; inhale and raising the arms – 'But deliver us from evil, For thine, etc.; palms together – 'Amen'.[6]

The Christian mystics also advise on posture for meditation. John Main in teaching Christian Meditation always gives a simple rule of posture: 'Sit still, sit upright – on a chair or cushion whatever is most comfortable – with your spine upright. Sit relaxed but alert, with your hands resting in your lap or on your knees. Lightly close your eyes.' He was not the first to give this advice on posture for prayer. Richard Rolle, a hermit mystic living in England in the first half of the fourteenth century, says that contemplation is made easier when we 'take great rest in mind and body.'[7] We must learn this psychophysical repose by taking time out. For, 'in much bodily business as in unsteadiness of mind, high rest is neither attained nor held.'[8] 'When the body is tired, then the heart is not able to be quiet.'[9]

Rolle records how he tries various postures for prayer and finally decides that sitting is the best. The reason he gives is the psycho-physical unity of the human person: 'I am aware there is an underlying reason for this, for if a man or woman does much standing or walking their body gets tired, and thus their soul too is hindered, wearied and burdened.'[10] This is echoed in Rolle's late Middle-English work, *The Form of Living*:

> All who love contemplative life, they seek rest in body and in soul [...] And I have loved to sit still, for no penance [...] but only because I knew that I loved God more, and the comfort of love lasted with me longer, than if I was walking or standing or kneeling. For while sitting I am in most rest.[11]

The endeavour of Rolle to present a role for the body in prayer has parallels with a group of writers living at the same time on Mount Athos in Greece. *Hesychia* (stillness, rest and silence) had a corporeal aspect and, as an aid to concentration, the 'Hesychasts' evolved a 'physical technique' which has parallels with other 'limbs' of Patanjali's yoga: *pranayama* (breathing exercises), *dharana* (control of the senses) and *dyana* (concentration through cultivating inner perceptual awareness).

Kallistos Ware explains that for the Hesychasts 'each alteration in our physical condition reacts adversely or positively on our psychic activity. If, then, we can learn to control and regulate certain of our physical processes, this can be used to strengthen our inner concentration in prayer.'[12] In terms of the body the 'Hesychast method' has three aspects: 1) External posture: often sitting on a low stool, about nine inches high, head and shoulders bowed, eyes fixed on the place of the heart. Not, you might think, very comfortable. 2) Control of the breathing: slowing the breath, co-ordinating it with the rhythm of the Jesus Prayer. Often the first part, 'Lord Jesus Christ, Son of God', is said while drawing in the breath, and the second part, 'have mercy on me a sinner', while breathing out. The recitation of the Prayer may also be synchronised with the beating of the heart. 3) Inward exploration: just as the aspirant in yoga is taught to concentrate their thought in specific parts of their body, so, under careful guidance, Hesychasts concentrate their thought in the cardiac centre. Along with inhaling through the nose and propelling the breath down into the lungs, the intellect 'descends' with the breath while the Hesychast 'searches' inwardly for the place of the heart.

The main spokesman for Hesychasm was St Gregory Palamas (1296–1359), a direct contemporary of Rolle. Palamas' treatise 'In Defense of Those who Devoutly Practice a Life of Stillness' encourages novice meditators to focus awareness inward with the aid of the breath:

> The mind, of all things, is the most difficult to observe
> and the most mobile. It darts away as soon as it has been
> concentrated. They must continually bring it back. That is
> why some teachers recommend them to pay attention to the
> exhalation and inhalation of their breath, and to restrain it a
> little, so that while they are watching it the mind too may be
> held in check.[13]

The culmination of this practice, Palamas says, is 'unified concentration.' In this treatise for beginners, concentration is described as taking attention away from the body. However, *Triads* – written for those further on the path of contemplation – explains that once we are no longer identified with bodily experience then the body finds its real place, becoming an active partner in prayer:

> What pain or pleasure or movement is not a common
> activity of both body and soul? [...] There are indeed blessed
> passions and common activities of body and soul, which far
> from nailing the spirit to the flesh, serve to draw the flesh
> to a dignity close to that of the spirit, and persuade it too
> to tend toward what is above [...] In spiritual people, the
> grace of the spirit, transmitted to the body through the soul,
> grants to the body also the experience of things divine, and
> allows it the same blessed experiences as the soul undergoes

[...] When the soul pursues this blessed activity, it deifies the body also; which, being no longer driven by corporeal and material passions [...] returns to itself and rejects all contact with evil things. Indeed, the body then inspires its own sanctification and inalienable divinisation.[14]

It is another mystic of the fourteenth century who had a very physical experience of God in prayer – Dame Julian of Norwich – to whom we can turn to see how our bodies can be a catalyst for contemplation. Awareness of the body for her was the best way to awaken compassion. Compassion is Divine, but it is awakened through awareness of human fragility. When we love someone we love with our body and heart together. Loving-kindness has its roots in the passion and tenderness of what it is to be human.

Quietening our Conscience

In various mindfulness approaches there are befriending or compassion meditations. These have their roots in the Buddhist tradition of *metta*, or loving-kindness meditations and involve awakening compassion for oneself, for a stranger and for those we find difficult. This practice has strong parallels in Christian teaching on forgiveness, on loving our neighbour as ourselves and loving our enemy. By meditating on our common humanity, our vulnerability and inability to judge ourselves, let alone others, we learn to shift the centre of our consciousness towards God's unconditional love. Being non-judgmental, free from self-expectations or the expectations others have for us, sets us free to accept the gift of our being. St Paul writes to the Corinthians, 'I care very little if I am judged by you or by any human court; indeed, I do not even judge myself [...] It is the Lord who judges me' (1Cor 4:3). Being compassionate to ourselves is what St John calls the ability to 'quieten our conscience in God's presence': 'Whatever accusations our conscience may raise against us, God is greater than our conscience and he knows everything'(1Jn 3:19–20). St John goes on to say that we need not be afraid in this all-knowing presence for 'God is love' (1Jn 4:8). By loving in turn we become children of God who 'make(s) the sun to rise on the evil and on the good, and sends rain on the just and on the unjust alike' (Mt 5:45). Laurence Freeman, contemporary teacher of Christian meditation, puts it like this:

> We cannot learn to be still without learning to love ourselves. We learn through the stillness of meditation, to treat our own anger with compassion, our own irritability with compassion, our own judgmentalism with compassion and tolerance and non-violence. We come dimly to understand, as we enter into the school of love, that this love of self leads to love of others and to love of God, and that this is one love. It is the same reality.[15]

St Augustine puts it starkly in *City of God* (10:3), 'First see whether you have learned to love yourself [...] If you have not learned how to love yourself, I am afraid that you will cheat your neighbour as yourself.'

God's unconditional love is expressed very beautifully in a medieval treatise *A Showing of Love* written by Dame Julian of Norwich, an exact contemporary of the *Cloud*-author. Julian received a series of revelations; the meaning of all of them was love. Julian refers to herself as 'a simple creature unlettered' meaning 'not knowing Latin and not trained in the universities' but this in no way minimises her theological expertise. It is clear from her treatise that she was well educated for a woman of her time and may have been educated with the Benedictine nuns at Carrow to which the anchoritic cell at St Julian's Church was linked.[16] Surmises about Julian's life remain hypotheses, but her genius, her ability to think creatively and original use of the spirituality of her time are clear.

Most of our knowledge of Julian comes from the autobiographical details in the two versions of her vision. Her *Showings* were given in May 1373 when she was thirty-and-a-half years old; she was, therefore, born towards the end of 1342. Evidence from wills naming her as a beneficiary show her still alive in 1416. From childhood through to adulthood she lived through the great plague or Black Death, which, in 1349 and, episodically, again in 1361 and 1369, decimated the population of Europe, killing close to half the people in big cities, such as Norwich, and leaving the rest mourning and traumatised. In comparison to some religious preaching of the time, which showed the plague as a punishment sent by God for sin, and that God was angry, Julian's perspective in her *Showings* reassure us that there is no wrath in God.[17] Moreover faced with the trauma of an uncontrollable illness and the precariousness of human life the *Showings* give consolation that 'all will be well, all will be well and all manner of things will be well' (211:28–29).[18] Instead of blaming ourselves for the bad things which happen in our life Julian points out our inherent innocence: there is a part of us, in fact the deepest part of us, which never consents to sin. Sin is something we fall into against our deepest inclination, which is always towards the good. And it is this underlying good intention that God sees. When we fall, God looks at us with pity not with blame, so we should not blame ourselves: 'It is not God's intention that we should go to great lengths in our self-accusation, nor that we should feel too wretched about ourselves. He means us to look at once to him' (371:29–31).

Learning to love ourselves, realising that we are not blamed for our mistakes, leads us, in Julian's vision, to 'charity towards our even-Christian' 145:58). We share the same human nature. Julian makes a play on the Middle-English word for 'nature' (preserved in modern English in such words as 'humankind'): 'It is kind to be kind.' For Julian, this link we have with all humanity is expressed in courtesy, even towards those who sin against us and against others. This has its exemplar in God's love, which, she says, 'endlessly surpasses what our weak loving and our bitter labour deserve, spreads abroad and shows the noble, abundant largesse of God's royal lordship in his marvellous courtesy' (267/9:27–29).

Julian has a realistic approach to our and others' failings. Sin is the opposite of goodness and is the cause of 'all the pains and passions of all [God's] creatures' (209:12). She wonders 'why, by the great foreseeing wisdom of God, the beginning of sin was not stopped' (5–6). She sees, however, that the root of all this suffering 'has no manner of substance', for sin is known only in the pain it causes (22). Like a hole in one's shoe which lets in water and makes one's feet soggy, so sin is a lack, an absence of being and goodness, which lets in suffering. Examining our conscience so as to pinpoint why we act in unhelpful ways is, therefore, of limited value because it is caused by something that is not there. This lack can only be made good by turning to the fullness of God. For Julian the fount of goodness was shown in Christ on the cross. Though we may feel sinful, if we turn to him we will find that he always 'beholds us with compassion and pity, as children, innocent and not loathsome' (213:30).

If God doesn't blame us for sin, it would be unkind for us to blame God for sin. As God believes in our goodness so we can return the favour and put faith in Him. In fact, Julian comes to see that the hole in the shoe that lets in the water is '*behovely*' – the Middle-English word can be translated as 'useful', 'necessary', even as 'advantageous'. Compassion which comes from suffering has such profound value that it outweighs the terrible pain brought into the world by our lack of goodness. Not only 'all will be well' despite sin, but also more dramatically, all will be mysteriously much *better* because of sin. Our sins, Julian says, will be our trophies in heaven. Why? Because our wrongdoings, our meanness, our unkindness, when brought into consciousness, make us realise our lack and need. Such awareness makes us compassionate rather than judgmental to others. Even in the pain it causes, our sinful nature is not acting wilfully, but only out of a lack of awareness. All people have leaky boots and it is no wonder that at times they kick out in frustration.

Where does Love come from?

In the loving-kindness meditations of MBSR and Buddhism there is, of course, much less of a stress on God but they do emphasise a source of kindness and compassion within ourselves which we can tap into by recognising our common humanity. The Four Noble Truths of Buddha recognise the fact of suffering (*dukkha*): nothing in itself can be fully satisfying, there is a lack in all things. The cause of personal suffering is the illusory path of seeking fulfilment in what cannot fulfil. All things are impermanent; our neediness cannot be satisfied by possessing what, like us, is incomplete and passing away. To overcome this, Buddhism teaches the *Dharma*, the Noble Eightfold path, as a way of life based on non-possessiveness and realisation of the inter-dependence of everything.[19] Like in Julian's vision, Buddhist wisdom teaches that the inherent lack in all things – the fact that nothing exists fully in itself – is a way of realising how everything in the world depends on, and is in relationship with, all other things. This realisation is the seed that awakens the heart of Buddhist practice: compassion. The suffering of another – of any sentient being – is our own suffering because we are all deeply inter-connected. The best way to happiness, as the Dalai Lama says, is to ease the pain of others and of ourselves. Or, as Jesus put it, 'love thy neighbour as thyself' (Mk 12:31).

Buddha teaches us to be a resource to ourselves, a lamp unto ourselves, not to look for security in what others say. Mindfulness is the way of accessing this resource. As Thich Nhat Hanh writes:

> The Buddha said that there is an island in each of us, and when we go home to ourselves, we are on that safe island. There, we touch the energy of the Buddha, which sheds its light on any situation, enabling us to see near and far and to know what to do. We touch the living Dharma on that island by practising mindful breathing. Mindful breathing and mindfulness practice are the living Dharma.[20]

Kabat-Zinn evokes the expansiveness of this practice once the resource of love has been tapped in our hearts:

> Once you have established yourself as a centre of love and kindness radiating throughout your being, which amounts to a cradling of yourself in loving kindness and acceptance, you can dwell here indefinitely, drinking at this fount, bathing in it, renewing yourself, nourishing yourself, enlivening yourself. This can be a profoundly healing practice for body and soul. You can also take the practice further. Having established a radiant centre in your being, you can let loving kindness radiate outwardly and direct it wherever you like [...] There is really no natural limit to the practice of loving kindness in meditation or in one's life. It is an on-going, ever-expanding realisation of interconnectedness.[21]

It may be argued that in this teaching the self rather than God is the source of love. However, in Julian of Norwich's vision this may not be as marked a difference as at first may appear. 'The substance of who we are' she says, 'dwells in God' (299:19). She goes as far as to say that 'I saw no difference between God and our substance, but saw it as if it were all God' (297:13). 'God is never out of the soul' (299:24). She qualifies these statements by recognising that we are creatures in God. Love is in us, but that is only because we are immersed in love – God's love. When Julian speaks of the soul she emphasises God's presence in it, when she speaks of sensuality she speaks of us being 'clothed and wrapped' in God.

Julian has such a high opinion of the human soul that she subtly subverts traditional teaching of *creatio ex nihilo*, that human beings are created out of nothing. She identifies the soul as 'created but of nothing that is made' (295:35). It is, in other words, 'made of God' (33). 'God is also in our sensuality', she says (299:20). By sensuality she means the aspect of the soul that enables perception of physical things, i.e. our body and the world around us. Mindfulness practices like 'scanning the sensations of the body' or focusing on a particular sense experience like eating, listening, touching, seeing, or smelling, would be, for Julian, ways of encountering God. However, for Julian, it is the motherhood of God, which enfolds our sensuality. This aspect of God is expressed in Jesus' life. What Kabat-Zinn calls 'cradling, drinking, bathing, renewing, nourishing and enlivening yourself in loving kindness' evokes the sense of being held by love, another key attribute of Dame Julian's teaching. She identifies the maternal aspect of God in Christ's taking on human flesh, and thereby meeting us in our humblest physical needs. We experience God through our bodies because of Jesus' natural motherhood – in that through him all things were made, his gracious motherhood – in himself becoming flesh and restoring all things, and his active motherhood – keeping us through the sacraments, Christian community and the teaching of the Church. Through all these Christ helps us to grow as a mother raises her child: 'As the child grows in age and size, she changes what she does, but not her love' (315:45–47).

Becoming like a child is a gospel imperative. For Julian it is the mildness and meekness of this grace-given state of childhood that make it so 'precious and lovely in the sight of our heavenly mother' (321:29–30). It is 'in feebleness and failing of might and of wit' that the superlative stature of childhood is revealed 'until the time that our gracious mother has brought us up to our father's bliss [in heaven]' (37–38). Julian sees the prototype of fatherhood and motherhood in God. They are not human images transposed onto God. In fact to say that we have a human mother and father is true only by analogy, through their participation in God's Motherhood and Fatherhood.

> We know that all our [human] mother's bearing of us is to pain and to dying; and what is that unless our true mother Jesus, he, all love, bears us to joy and endless living [...]

A mother may give her child her milk to suck. But our precious mother Jesus, he may feed us with himself, and he does this most courteously and most tenderly with the blessed sacrament that is the precious food of true life. (313:15–17, 25–27).

Julian like a good psychologist realised that however good our parents were, however much they shared in the qualities of Divine parenting, there is a lack we experience at a natural level as children. Not all our needs were met; our parents could never give us the full attention we felt we needed. Julian believes that by finding the fullness of a mother and father's love in God we can be healed of this inevitable wound. Kabat-Zinn uses a similar image to describe the acceptance of loving kindness:

Allow yourself to be cradled by your own awareness as if you were as deserving of loving kindness as any child. Let your awareness embody both benevolent mother energy and benevolent father energy, making available for you in this moment a recognition and an honouring of your being, and a kindness you perhaps did not receive enough of as a child. Let yourself bask in this energy of loving kindness, breathing it in and breathing it out, as if it were a lifeline, long in disrepair but finally passing along a nourishment you were starving for.[22]

Wrapping Everything in Love

The practice of mindfulness involves coming to our senses. Our breathing is always in the present moment, our sense of taste, touch, sight, hearing and smell tell us of what is happening now around us. Kabat-Zinn's advice on loving-kindness meditation is to 'start by centring yourself in your posture and in your breathing, then, from your heart or from your belly, invite feelings or images of kindness and love to radiate until they fill your whole being.' Julian's visions also started with what she called 'bodily vision'; her showings were fully somatic experiences. One of Julian's earliest prayers, long before she had her illness and visionary experience, was that she might 'feel more of Christ's passion' through bodily sickness. She also 'desired a bodily sight, wherein [she] might have more knowledge of the bodily pains of our saviour' (125:6–7). This form of devotion was to awaken compassion more strongly by engaging the body in the experience so that what she reads about becomes real to her in the moment. Julian's friend Margery Kempe experienced aspects of Christ's life so intensely in the present moment that she wept boisterously in her meditations. One day in a church, probably fed up with the noise of weeping, 'The priest came to her, saying, "Woman, why criest thou so, Jesus is long since dead." When her crying ceased, she said to the priest, "Sir, his death is as fresh to me as if he had died this same day, and so, I think, it ought to be to you and to all Christian people." '23

Awareness of bodily sensations puts us in the present moment. For Julian, however, the focus is not on the body but on the empathic revelation that embodiment brings. Julian means to put her body in the place of Jesus', to share his experience. Her body is as such merely a vehicle for revelation; Julian's experience is more heart based than body based, as the active element is empathy. Yet, compassion becomes more real as it becomes physical, even to the extent of tears – which will always be the most physical of responses to the suffering of another. In contrast to a tendency to split from the body after a traumatic experience (like that of the Black Death) Julian reaffirms God's action and grace within sensuality. Spirituality is never a way of dis-identifying with bodily experience but rather, for Julian, an acting out of holistic body-spirit anthropology. She not only tries to root her spirituality in physical experience – to the extremity of seeing illness as a way of participating in Christ's sufferings – but also looks for God through created things. She sees in 'bodily vision' that 'God is everything which is good, and that the goodness which is in everything is God' (151:16–17). From this bodily vision of God in all things Julian says she 'was greatly moved in love towards my fellow Christians' (22). Being aware of one's own body in its vulnerability, and the value of all creation in its fragility, leads to a deepening sense of love in the present moment. This is again paralleled by Kabat-Zinn, 'When you can love one tree or one flower or one dog or one place, or one person or yourself for one moment, you can find all people, all places, all suffering, all harmony in that one moment.'

Julian sees that God loves every *body* literally; 'He serves us in our humblest needs [...] in the simplest task that belongs by nature to our bodies' (143/5:32–34). Breathing, for example, or the even more humble example Julian uses – our need for the toilet!

> For the food we have eaten is closed as in a beautiful
> drawstring purse. And when it is time for nature's necessity,
> the purse is opened up and then closed again very cleanly.
> And it is God who does this. (30–32)

Julian is not embarrassed about embodiment, it is through the body that we come to realise God's care of us. 'For as the body is clad in the cloth, and the flesh in the skin, and the bones in the flesh, and the heart in the chest, so,' Julian writes, 'are we, soul and body, clad in the goodness of God and enclosed in it' (35–37).

It may seem strange; therefore, that Julian as a young woman had what she calls 'a wilful desire to have of God's gift a bodily sickness' that would bring her close to death (127:18–19). This does not seem to be a sign of loving herself or especially her body. Kabat-Zinn, without positing a God to pray to, says that we should 'invite feelings of peacefulness' to be present to us, and that one can even evoke 'feelings of loving kindness' by wishing ourselves well, saying to ourselves from time to time, 'May I not suffer. May I be happy.' Julian seems to be inviting a very traumatic experience.

Moreover, by a 'wilful desire' she seems to be trying very hard to get some experience – hoping for sickness so that she might be 'purged' in a penitential way, and prepared – as in a dress rehearsal – for her actual death. Kabat-Zinn's teaching on mindfulness is couched much more as an acceptance of what is and 'not trying to improve or to get anywhere else [...] not even running after special insights or visions.'[24] Far from cultivating pain and suffering, he hopes mindfulness meditation would be 'a profoundly healing practice for body and soul.'

Certainly Julian with all her creative thought was also a woman of her time and the fourteenth century, which, partly because of the experience of the Black Death, tended to encourage a spirituality that focused on the mystery of suffering. One could say there was enough suffering around without wishing it on oneself! However, when Julian prays for this gift of sickness Julian says she does so 'freely and without any seeking.' She does so not through any attachment to suffering. To ask for suffering she recognises 'was not the common use of prayer,' nor advisable, unless, as in her case, it is something inspired by grace. The unusualness of visions and divinely induced sickness means Julian prays for them only if they are according to God's will. She does not, therefore, cultivate sickness or a visionary state through maltreating or neglecting her body. Quite the opposite, 'It is God's will that we hold ourselves in comfort with all our might.' Suffering is never the aim, 'For bliss lasts forever, and pain passes [...] Therefore it is not God's will that we pay attention to the feeling of pain in sorrow and mourning, but quickly pass over it and hold ourselves in the endless happiness that is God' (177:24–28).

Julian in her everyday life is so far from cultivating a state of sickness that when she does get ill she has quite forgotten about the prayer she made as a young woman and, when ill, she 'at no time desired a bodily sight nor any manner of vision of God' (133/5:36–41). The illness and the visions – bodily and spiritual – are therefore given without her seeking them. And the illness in fact ends in healing. It is revealed to her, 'All things will be made well' (221:1–3). This includes sin – which is the worst scourge, but also bodily sickness. Julian is healed from her illness (in her thirtieth year) and lives on to a very old age by medieval standards.[25] Not only is her body restored to health but 'sensuality' is embellished by her near-death experience. She has a foretaste of heaven as sensual bliss! All the senses will be fulfilled: 'We shall all be unendingly held in God, seeing him truly, feeling him fully, hearing him spiritually, smelling him delectably and swallowing him sweetly' (259:41–46).

Giving and Receiving Peace and Love

So Julian in her own experience and visions of Christ not only focuses on the problem of suffering but also comes to a great sense of peace, wellbeing and God's providential care in all that happens. Peace is terribly important in the spiritual life: 'We cannot be blessedly saved until we are truly in peace and in love,' she writes, 'for [peace and love] is our salvation' (271:24–25). God is never angry with us, for anger is a lack of love and there is no lack in God. Rather, she says, 'It is because of the anger and contrariness in us that we find ourselves in tribulation, distress, and sorrow' (25–26). The key to realising divine peace, therefore, is peace with ourselves. 'The soul is "oned" to God when it is truly peaceful in itself,' she writes, 'And thus I saw, when we are all at peace and in love, we do not find opposition in any kind of obstacle [in life]' (22,35). But it is 'God who nurtures peace in us [...] God is our true peace, and our sure keeper when we are ourselves unpeaceful, and he continually works to bring us into endless peace' (33–34).

This 'givenness' of peace and love has an echo in contemporary mindfulness practice, which according to Kabat-Zinn, is not trying to change anything but 'uncovers what is always present':

> Love and kindness are here all the time, somewhere, in fact, everywhere. Usually our ability to touch them and be

touched by them lies buried below our own fears and hurts, below our greed and our hatreds, below our desperate clinging to the illusion that we are truly separate and alone.

In fact the 'somewhere' and 'everywhere' Kabat-Zinn speaks of here is, in the Buddhist tradition, the mind itself. The opening verse of the *Dhammapada* declares, 'All phenomena are preceded by the mind, issue forth from the mind, and consist of the mind.' Mindfullness is complete awareness. A slightly later Buddhist text the *Anguttara Nikaya* speaks of loving-kindness as the quality of the brightly shining mind. The process of meditative development, it says, is like refining gold, removing impurities to reveal the beauty of what is already there. At this level of awareness all things are perceived as interconnected, no phenomena exists in itself, all is dependent on its relation with everything else. It is, therefore, as Julian says, 'natural to be kind.'

Wellbeing is not just for ourselves. It is common in Buddhism and secular Mindfulness to dedicate one's practice to the wellbeing of others. This insures that our motivation is not selfish, and opens us up to a love that reaches much more than the ego. 'We are all one in love,' Julian reminds us, 'for truly it was not shown me that God loves me better than the least soul' (153:4–5). Julian makes no claim to possess what she has received in her visions but offers it up for the benefit of others:

> In all this I was much stirred in charity to my fellow
> Christians, that they might all see and know the same as I
> saw, for I wanted it to be a comfort to them [...] For God's
> courteous love and endless goodness would show this
> generally to the comfort of us all; for it is God's will that you
> take it with great joy and liking as if Jesus had shown it to
> you. (151:22–24, 153:35–37)

Accepting the gift of peace and love in Julian's vision comes from God's reassurance, 'I keep you completely secure' (235:8–9). This is the message of 'ease and comfort' she knows God wants to communicate through her (153:3). Cultivating wellbeing is the root of learning to love ourselves and others. This is why mindfulness is therapeutic. We have to give time to the practice though. It is not a quick fix. Difficult things continue to happen in life but the way we react to them changes. We need, as the famous prayer says, serenity to accept the things we cannot change, courage to change those we can, and wisdom to know the difference.[26] For Julian suffering is the test point for peacefulness. To be in a state of peace and love, she says, involves 'being completely pleased with God and with all his works and all his judgments, and loving and content with ourselves and with our fellow Christians and with everything God loves' (271:29–31).

But should we really love and accept everything? In the Middle Ages when European culture was often nominally but near universally Christian, 'loving and being content with our fellow Christians' was just about synonymous with 'everyone'. Julian's expression may also be an appeal to include those Christians known as the Lollards who were out of favour with the Church and state in early fifteenth-century England. In 1401 Archbishop Arundel of Canterbury arranged the passing of a parliamentary statute *De Haeretico Comburendo* against 'Christians who do not accept the Latin Bible, and the offices and teachings of the Church.' After fines and imprisonment, if those convicted did not recant they could be burnt. It was the first such law against religious offenders in England's history. In the same year, under King Henry IV's personal command, William Sawtre, the vicar of St Margaret's Parish in Bishop's Lynn – forty-four miles west of Norwich – was the first Lollard burned alive for his views. This was about the time Julian was writing her long text. Being 'loving and being content with our fellow Christians' was more than a vague sentiment but an appeal for tolerance, and peace.

Not only the Lollards – Julian had lived through the Peasant Revolt of 1381. Increasing Royal taxation after the death of Edward III in 1377 had put many under strain. An army of discontents was led by a veteran soldier Wat Tyler and by a renegade Priest and preacher John Bull. After taking London, the rebellion was appeased by the personal intervention of King Richard II, but his promises were not kept. In the aftermath the rebel leaders and many of the peasants themselves were mercilessly executed. Julian's teaching on mildness, mercy, forgiveness and love certainly would have covered these rebels who saw themselves as motivated by Christian ideals though their violence showed they did not always act out of peace and love. Julian's term '*evencristen*' does try to heal the divisions between people through their common membership of Christian society. It also appeals to the values of peace and love that such a society *should* live out.

However by speaking of 'loving and being content with our fellow Christians' is not Julian ruling out non-Christian sub cultures, which existed even in Europe in the Middle Ages, notably in Jewish communities? There had been extensive killing of Jews in Norwich in 1190 and 1230. In 1290 King Edward I expelled Jewish communities en masse from England. Most fled, though some converted to Christianity as a way of placating their persecutors. There were intermittent investigations of Jews who had become Christian. It was only in the seventeenth century that Jews began returning to England. So when Julian was writing at the beginning of the fifteenth century there were no non-Christian Jews in England. So Julian's term '*evencristen*' did in fact cover everyone. It may, as with the Lollards, have also been an implicit appeal to accept those Jews who had nominally converted a century before but continued to marry only among themselves and to keep what some considered 'suspicious privacies.'[27]

So Julian, in effect, was including everyone. Although she herself says she accepts all that is taught by the Church she sees that there is room within that teaching for it to be tolerant of differences and include all. There is room among '*evencristen*' for 'the anonymous or "natural" Christian' identified by Karl Rahner. These are those who live the life of Christ though their own good nature without necessarily adhering to, or even hearing, the teaching of the Church. Julian would agree. For her 'Every natural feeling of compassion that someone has for his *evencristen* with charity, it is Christ in him' (213:18). Julian sees all people in herself because she sees our common humanity. She speaks for all, maybe especially for those 'outside' the Church but are yet '*evencristens*' to us (153:31).

The unity of the charity – what she calls the '*onehead*' – covers not only the human world but all creation. She moves out in ever-expanding circles, from herself to her *evencristen,* to 'all mankind that shall be saved', to 'all that God hath made' (155:8–10). Julian explains how these levels are all interwoven:

> He that generally loves all his evencristen for God, he loves all that is. For in mankind that shall be saved is included all: that is to say, all that is made and the maker of all. For in man is God, and in God is all. And he that loves in this way, loves everything. (11–14)

This is the most expansive stage of loving-kindness meditation. MBSR teaching presents it thus:

> You can direct loving kindness toward anybody, toward people you know and people you don't. It may benefit them, but it will certainly benefit you by refining and extending your emotional being. This extension matures as you purposefully direct loving kindness toward people you have a hard time with, toward those you dislike or are repulsed by, toward those who threaten you or have hurt you. You can also practice directing loving kindness toward whole groups of people – toward all those who are oppressed, or who suffer, or whose lives are caught up in war or violence

or hatred, understanding that they are not different from you – that they too have loved ones, hopes and aspirations, and needs for shelter, food, and peace.

The Worshipful Medley of Life

But if 'everyone' is accepted, what about 'everything'? Certainly Julian sees that there is something that causes the suffering, injustice, and lack of peace and love in the world, this she calls 'sin'. So, on the one side she is the patron saint of the anxious – 'all will be well, all will be well and all manner of things will be well', even sin is turned to our good. On the other, this is no naive optimism or pious complacency. Of all theologians – except maybe Augustine – she does the most to probe the mystery of sin and the suffering it causes. In the face of the sin and suffering of the world she continues to question in anxiety, sorrow and dread how this can be: 'In this I stood [my ground], contemplating generally anxiously, mournfully, saying thus to our lord in my meaning with the greatest dread: 'Ah, good lord, how might all be well, for the great harm that has come by sin to your creatures?" (213:1–3).

At first Julian is invited to trust that God not only has the power to make things well but the wisdom, will and intention to do so, and that she will see that it is so. There will be a great act, which will make all things well into which Julian cannot pry. However Julian continues to question, for alongside accepting that 'all will be well' she feels impelled to discern between good and evil. She recognises that we have to let go of judgments and striving because the truth is more than we can understand or control. However, in life there are ethical issues and we need to choose. This quality of discrimination is key to Buddhism, as it is in Christianity though somewhat neglected in secular mindfulness.

Julian for her part continues to question and receives her most remarkable theological showing. She sees a Lord sitting richly apparelled in a desert place; on his left a servant in threadbare clothes. The servant runs off to do a task for his master, in his enthusiasm to serve his master he falls into a hole. The hole is deep, he is injured and can't get out or see over the edge. He feels the heaviness of his body weighing him down. He feels he's completely on his own, in pain and, as time passes, guilty that he has not done the task he was asked to do. His master whom he loves will think he has run away. The servant blames himself for his lack of mindfulness; he thinks he will be angry that he was so foolish as to fall into a pit. We spend our time 'wallowing and writhing, groaning and mourning' in our pain (275:13).

Well, Julian says, reflecting on this, that is the way we see the bad things that happen in life and from the human perspective it has a relative truth – if we had walked mindfully we wouldn't have fallen in the pit. But it is not true for God's view. There are two parts to truth: 'It is appropriate for a man or woman to meekly accuse themselves, but it belongs to the proper goodness of our Lord God courteously the excuse each of us,' Julian says (213:27–28). She sees that if the servant could have seen over the edge of his pit he would have seen that his master's love for him had never changed. In fact the Lord looks at his servant with pity and compassion, he realises that it was only because of his good will in wanting to do the task that he ran into the pit. We will never be blamed for not living our lives mindfully.

Julian goes on to reflect that the servant is both 'us' and at one and the same time God's Son. Jesus takes on the threadbare clothing of humanity, participates fully in the perilous human condition, and, falling by his own will into the womb of Mary, becomes what we are. Julian realises that God loves us in our troubles and weaknesses in life as much as He loved Jesus; it is the same love, our good will *is* Christ and we are one with him also in our sufferings. We will be rewarded for all our troubles because although we think we have brought them on ourselves that is not God's way of seeing it. He sees only our good will; our lack of mindfulness only makes him love us more. For Julian mindfulness is not doing everything cautiously, rather it is about raising ourselves up, even our pain, so that we can see over the edge of the pit of our life. Our blindness comes not from what we do, but from not seeing we are loved whatever we do.

If there is a real unmindfulness, it comes from giving too much attention to our feeling of pain, and adding to it with a sense of guilt. 'If only I hadn't done that', 'I am so stupid to have been so inattentive' – is the way we see it and, with a wrong image of God, religion can compound this sense. Or we can think, 'Why didn't God help me? Why couldn't he have prevented this?' Julian encourages us to 'turn our face [away from ourselves] and look up on [our] loving Lord, who is really near and in whom there is real and full comfort' (275:16–17). From God's perspective our sins exist only as crowns or trophies because our fall brings us greater humility, greater compassion and greater wisdom. In our falling we find Christ.

The story of the Lord and the servant ends with Christ's Resurrection and ours from out of the pit. The servant back at the Lord's side (this time the right side). His old tunic, which was 'tight, bare, ragged and short', is changed into one that is 'fair, new, white and bright, of endless cleanness, roomy and ample' (287:59–61). Unlike the Lord's robe, which is blue (as signifies heaven), the servant's robe is made of what Julian calls a 'medley cloth'. This was a cloth made of wools, dyed often with different colours or shades, and mingled before they were spun. She says she cannot describe this robe for it is so worshipful and yet it is woven from all the different feelings and experiences we have in life. Nothing we pass through in this life is wasted. In this visual story of the Lord and the servant 'not only our good Lord showed our excusing', Julian writes 'but also the worshipful nobility that he shall bring to us, turning all our blame into endless worship' (293:81–83). Mindfulness is living with the awareness that the robe of our future glory is made from the texture, colours and shades of our experience now. Don't worry if the stitching seems strange, or the medley a little baffling, the hand that weaves it is love.

Chapter 7

God among the Pots and Pans

While washing the dishes, you might be thinking about the tea afterwards, and so try to get them out of the way as quickly as possible in order to sit and drink tea. But that means you are incapable of living during the time you are washing the dishes. When you are washing the dishes, washing the dishes must be the most important thing in your life. Just as when you are drinking tea, drinking tea must be the most important thing in your life.[1]

Mindfulness and the Spanish Mystics

Leaving behind the Middle Ages, this chapter will glance briefly at the Spanish mystics of the sixteenth century and move on to French mysticism of the seventeenth, eighteenth and nineteenth century as guides to mindfulness.

St Teresa of Avila (1515–1582) is well known for her flights of ecstasy, not something particularly promoted or expected in contemporary mindfulness practice. However, she was also remarkably down to earth. She founded seventeen new convents on top of being Abbess in her own in Avila. She had to deal bravely and cautiously with all the political and ecclesiastical chicanery of the time. Her main concern was the revival of contemplation and prayer and poverty of lifestyle within her Carmelite Order. God meets us not only in prayer, Teresa says, but in our work. Those who taste contemplation would prefer to be with God without interruption, but if obligations call them to fulfil everyday duties then, Teresa says, God will be more present in those duties than in the highest ecstasy of prayer. 'If obedience demands of you to be employed in external things, then understand that if these are in the kitchen then the Lord walks among the pots and He helps you there both externally and internally.'[2]

Teresa herself was an excellent cook (as she was with most of the things she set about). On great feasts she herself cooked for her friends and guests, and emphasised that whoever is in the kitchen she must cook just as if she cooked for Christ himself. When she met for the very last time her master Saint Peter of Alcantara (they both knew it would be the last time), she cooked a dinner of five delicious courses for him. All the monastery was watching what would Peter, the famous faster do. Peter ate all the courses without a word.[3]

Complicated programmes of prayer were impossible for Teresa. She recognised herself as one of those whose 'souls and minds are so scattered that they are like wild horses no one can stop.' Instead Teresa recommends the practice of 'recollection' whereby, 'the soul collects its faculties together and enters within itself to be with its God' (WP 28:4).[4] She goes on to say that the soul is 'centred there within itself.' Recollection leads to a second stage of 'representing Christ interiorly.'[5] This was a sort of visual mantra, an inner icon which opened Teresa to an awareness of the real – not imagined – presence of Christ in her soul: 'Settle yourself in solitude and you will come upon Him in yourself,' she writes, 'Don't imagine that we need wings to go in search of Him. We have only to find a place where we can be alone – and look upon Him present within us.' (WP 28:2)

With a practice of recollection the wild horses of the mind are tamed but thoughts will still pester like 'unquiet little gnats, which buzz and whizz at night, here and there, for just so our thoughts whizz from one to another' (L 17:6). Teresa proposes *advertencia* in prayer, which has been translated as 'attention' or 'clear awareness'.[6] Close to Buddhist ideas of *vipassana*, *advertencia* involved seeing into the heart of things. Even as a young woman Teresa had practised this in the presence of nature: 'Fields or water or flowers: in these things I found a memory of the Creator – I mean that the sight of these things was a book unto me; it roused me and made me recollected' (L 9:5). The transition from recollection to what Teresa calls the prayer of quiet could be paralleled with the transition from mindfulness to meditation. For Teresa what leads this deepening is a sense of love's presence in all things, not any effort to stop our thoughts. Better to be mindful in daily life than discouraged in sitting meditation when we are not ready for it. 'If we have no sense of love's presence there is no need to sit inert like a dolt,' she writes her *Interior Castle* (4/8:5). 'When we are dry and distracted Our Lord wishes us to return to prayer and to actively placing ourselves in God's presence.' But mindful living does prepare for meditation. 'Although in this prayer of active attentiveness the soul makes no effort towards letting go of thought, yet often,' Teresa says, 'for a very short time, the mind ceases to think at all.' From the Prayer of Quiet we are led on to that of Inebriation and of Union. This is where Meditation moves into Mysticism as God progressively takes over. No one has worked out with such insight the relation of what we might call the three M's: Mindfulness, Meditation and Mysticism, as St Teresa.

We may think, 'Oh! if only I had more time to practise recollection, I have so many things to do.' So did Teresa – managing seventeen new convents! Busyness is no excuse. In fact, she says, if we are busy all the more we need to practise recollection. Small regular moments of mindfulness during the day are enough however: 'Don't think that if you had a great deal of time you would spend more of it in prayer. Get rid of that idea! God gives more in a moment than in a long period of time, for His actions are not measured by time at all.'[7] Even in the seventh and last mansion of the *Interior Castle* deep prayer involves no other-worldliness, but 'in all that belongs to the active service of God [the contemplative] is more alert than before' (7/1:8).

Teresa's fellow worker in the Carmelite reform, St John of the Cross (1542–1591), also saw prayer as a process of simplification. It should be practised as 'a general loving awareness of God, without particular considerations, in interior peace and quiet and repose, and without discursive acts and exercises in which one progresses from one point to another.'[8] He encouraged, in other words, what Mindfulness calls 'the beginner's mind' – not cultivating 'advanced' states of mind or extraordinary experiences but remaining aware and alert in ordinary life until we experience how extraordinary it is! Kabat-Zinn calls this 'a mind that is willing to see everything as if for the first time.'[9] For John this happens 'in a person who opens his eyes with loving attention.'[10] John's mysticism scales the heights though, to areas well beyond the more 'practical' approach of mindfulness. He does retain the idea of following the breath, though, even in descriptions of mystical marriage: "The soul that is united and transformed in God breathes God in God with the same divine breathing with which God, while in the soul, breathes the soul in himself.'[11]

Where would John have learnt a practice of following the breath? Before joining the Carmelites John was educated by the new religious Order, 'The Society of Jesus'. The founder of these 'Jesuits' was another Spanish mystic from the Sixteenth century, St Ignatius of Loyola (1491–1556). He put together a highly influential programme of *Spiritual Exercises.* These can seem like the sort of complicated programme of prayer that Teresa found difficult – certainly his recommendation of imaginative meditation on Gospel passages was hard for Teresa. However he offers also 'the Third Way of Praying' in the section of 'Additional Material' at the end of the *Exercises.*[12] This meditative practice is called variously 'by rhythm' or 'of the breath.' It used to be regularly overlooked in Ignatian retreats (maybe because it is an appendix to the *Exercises,* but also because strictly contemplative practice was not seen as fruitful to the mission-orientated early modern Christianity). The practice itself is simple. Take a well-known prayer, for example, the Our Father, and link each word rhythmically to your breathing. Each word in succession is interiorly pronounced between each breath while the mind focuses quietly on the presence of God. Ignatius seems to have come to this practice through his own experience.

Another 'mindful' aspect of Ignatius' *Exercises* is his invitation to 'see' or 'find' God in all things, without exception, and conversely to see all things as flowing directly from God. Part of 'The Contemplation of Divine Love' (which is seen by many as the crowning synthesis of the *Exercises*) is to 'consider how God dwells in creation: in the elements, giving them being; in the plants, giving them life; in the animals giving them sensation; in human beings, giving them understanding. So He dwells in me, giving me being, life, sensation, and intelligence.'[13] There are echoes of this ideal in Ignatius' letter to Fr Brandao concerning younger Jesuit students:

> Scholastics should seek God's presence in all things, in their conversations, their walks, in all they see, taste, hear, understand, in all their actions, since his divine Majesty is truly in all things by his presence, power and essence. This kind of meditation which finds God our Lord in all things is easier than raising oneself to the consideration of divine truths which are more abstract and which demand something of an effort if we are to keep our attention on them. But this method is an excellent exercise to prepare for great visitations of our Lord, even in prayers that are rather short.[14]

The Practice of the Presence of God

Those trained by St Ignatius went all over the world so we can be justified for jumping from sixteenth century Spain to seventeenth century France. The main influence on French spirituality during this time was, however, Teresa's Carmelite reform. St Jeanne-Françoise de Chantal (1572–1641), a Carmelite who went on to found the Visitation sisters summed up the spirituality she had learnt and wanted to pass on as 'a very simple practice of the presence of God, by an entire self-abandonment to His holy providence.'[15] St Jeanne-Françoise's friend and spiritual guide St Francis de Sales (1567–1622) believed this ideal should be lived out in as practical a way as possible: 'Just as before the day's dinner you prepare a spiritual repast by means of a time of meditation, so before supper you must prepare a light spiritual supper of recollection.'[16] Outside these times of prayer St Francis de Sales encourages the one who wishes to lead a devout life to practise mindfulness and patience in the ordinary activities and troubles of life: 'These little daily acts of charity, this headache, toothache, or cold, this bad humour in a husband or wife, this broken glass, this contempt or that scorn, this loss of a pair of gloves, ring or handkerchief [...] humbly turning the spit, kindling fires, dressing meat, kneading bread, and doing the meanest household chores cheerfully,' are for de Sales the context in which we live out our love of God.[17]

The practice Chantal and Sales encouraged is now most famous through the brief writings of Brother Lawrence who entered the reformed Carmelite monastery in Paris. Born into a poor family in Lorraine in the eastern side of France, his baptismal name was Nicholas Herman. His family was so poor that he had to leave home as a teenager and serve in the army in order to eat. During the thirty years war he was injured and continued working as a footman in Paris. It was there, one winter that Herman looked at a barren tree, stripped of leaves and fruit. It reminded him of himself. But gazing at the tree he suddenly realised that it would come back to life. God's continual grace and unfailing providence would always lead to spring and the abundance of summer. God had life waiting for him, and the turn of seasons would bring fullness. At that moment, he said, that leafless tree 'first flashed in upon my soul the fact of God,' and a love for God that never ceased. In *The Practice of the Presence of God,* a book put together after his death from his short writings and the reminiscences of his followers it was said, 'this vision was so great and sublime that after forty years it was as clear as when he first received it.' His admirers commentated, 'This was his practice throughout his life, using things he saw to lead him up to the eternal [...] In all the events of life, whenever they happened, he would instantly arise and seek the presence of God.'[18]

After this conversion experience Herman joined the Carmelites and became Brother Lawrence. Having no education he remained all his life a lay brother doing practical work; in charge of the kitchen, arranging the provisions for the monastery and in his old age repairing the friars' sandals. He was on his own account a clumsy person though (maybe because of his wartime injury), he found walking so difficult that at times he used the old barrels of monastery wine as a wheelchair and rolled around his work. Far from being a dab hand in the kitchen Lawrence, from the beginning, knew he was not a practical man, he chose such work as a penance. It was noted that when he entered the monastery 'he had a natural and great aversion' to kitchen business (47). It was a real trial for him to be sent on trips to Burgundy and Auvergne, for example, to buy wine. Alongside difficult mobility went a lack of confidence in dealing with commercial transactions. He soon found though that what he had taken on as penance could be transformed into a joy by learning to trust completely in God's providence. He was not disappointed in that trust and, he says, remarkably his business transactions as Cellarer always seemed to go well.

Lawrence's competence – which he attributed to relying on God's help at every moment – soon was noticed and 'it was also observed that in the greatest hurry of the business in the kitchen he still preserved his recollection and heavenly-mindedness' (61). People were attracted to him. They noted the conversations they had with him. The Vicar General to the Archbishop of Paris, Joseph de Beaufort (who later collated the material about Lawrence) began to visit him. He was struck that 'very far from distracting him from his communion Brother Lawrence's work aided him in it.'

> This is what he once told me: 'My time of business is no
> different from the time of prayer, and in the noise and
> clatter of my kitchen, while several persons are calling
> together for as many different things, I possess God in as
> great tranquillity as when I kneel in silent prayer. (14)

The humble friar had become something of a celebrity. He was asked to write something about his amazing power to remain mindful. He wrote about three things: keeping the mind centred, relying on God and doing things with love:

> We must do our business faithfully, without being troubled
> or uneasy, recalling our mind to God mildly and with
> tranquillity as often as we find it wandering from Him. It
> is however necessary to put our whole trust in God, laying
> aside all other cares. (84)

We can do little things for God. I turn the cake that is frying in the pan for the love of him. (15)

This simple, threefold practice was taken on by others. In his *Letters* he often narrows it down to two: 'My most useful method is this simple attention, and a general passionate regard for God' (78). That is, living the ordinary mindfully and prayerfully. Those who follow this practice 'pray in every place, at every time,' Lawrence writes, 'not using many words or thinking to be heard for their much speaking, but in secret in the depths of their soul while walking, conversing with others, reading, eating or working' (18).

When asked more about what prayer was Lawrence told them what it was *not*. It was not introspection: 'In reality introspection is but the remnant of unexpelled self-love, which under the guise of zeal for our own perfection, keeps our eyes down to self instead of up to God' (17–18). It was not the following of reflective devotions: 'At times we must also lay aside certain forms of devotion, which though very good in themselves, are ones that we often continue to engage in unreasonably, for these devotions were only intended as a means to an end. So when by this exercise of the presence of God we are with Him who is our end, it is then useless to return to the means, which we used to arrive at this state' (14). It does not involve saying prayers: 'I do not advise that you use many words in prayer, for many words and long discourses are often the reason why our mind wanders. Hold yourself in prayer before God like a dumb or paralytic beggar at a rich man's gate' (89). Neither is it thinking (but in this saying Lawrence reveals his answer): 'In the way of God thoughts count for little, love is everything' (15). Well, love and mindfulness – what some contemporary teachers have called 'heartfulness'. Mindfulness must be practised both in formal meditation times and during the rest of the day, as he wrote to a friend:

> Let it be your business to keep your mind in the presence of the Lord. If your mind sometimes wanders and withdraws from Him, do not upset yourself about it. Troubled thoughts and uneasiness serve to distract the mind rather than to recall it – the will must bring it back into tranquillity. One way to recall the mind easily in the time of prayer, and preserve it more in tranquillity, is not to let it wander too far at other times. You should keep it strictly in the presence of God. (89)

While Lawrence was still alive a controversy broke out in French mysticism over what was known as the practice of 'Quietism' proposed by (among others) Madame Guyon (1648–1717). Both sides appealed to Brother Lawrence as a witness to their cause but he seemed to be quite uninterested. Language of 'not striving', 'keeping still', 'letting go' of 'external' religious practices, was taken out of the practical context of Bother Lawrence and used to discuss inner states of prayer. One sometimes hears people accusing modern mindfulness practices as being 'quietist', normally meaning that it is not concerned with changing the world and neglects the more socially or religiously engaged aspects of faith. Such criticisms are quite easy to counter: Thich Nhat Hanh has always been concerned to live out mindfulness within a context of promoting peace in the world. Kabat-Zinn applies the practice to helping people with difficult struggles in their minds and in their lives but never encourages the avoidance of external activity as a way to peace. In its rather practical, down to earth bent, mindfulness, as it is taught today, has more in common with Brother Lawrence than 'Quietism'.

There may be more justification for the parallel, however, if one looks at how Mindfulness teachers rarely address how the practice can be integrated with religious belief and forms of prayer. This I believe is something that Mindfulness has to address if the practice is to tap into deeper motivational resources. When we realise that there are real difficulties in our life, being mindful for our own benefit can get us going, but can it really keep us going? 'Mindfulness' in its contemporary secular form is quite a recent phenomenon; and has had a large take up. We are yet to measure how many keep it up. To keep on the way we need to access a deeper motivation; being mindful for the sake of helping others, or, being mindful for the sake of living in the presence of God. Here is where religions can give resources for the on-going journey, the deepening of mindfulness into love. In turn mindfulness practice can help religions to find their contemplative centre again, to bring religion back to its senses, to stop being divided from each other and in conflict. When he died in 1691 Brother Lawrence was regarded as a man of deep peace as well as an excellent mender of shoes. His faith had become totally real to him in the ordinary experiences of the day: in what he saw and touched, in what he tasted and heard. In his last letter he writes, 'I believe no more, but I see. I feel what faith teaches us' (98). It is the transition religion has to make: from the idea to the reality. Only that is the antidote to fundamentalism. 'God,' Brother Lawrence says, 'is only love' (76).

Pay no Attention to Distractions

Jean Pierre de Caussade was born in Cahors in the south of France in 1675. He entered the Jesuit novitiate in 1693 and followed an academic career of teaching and study within that order. In the latter half of his life he was primarily engaged in spiritual direction, for ten years serving in that role for the Visitation sisters at Nancy. It is to them that we owe most of his writings: his letters, and the spiritual treatise *Self-Abandonment to Divine Providence*. Caussade lived well into the eighteenth century, dying in 1751. He was never famous in his lifetime beyond being known as a skilled spiritual director. In fact it was not until 1861 that his treatise was published by the Jesuits. It became a religious bestseller, and is still so today. *Self-Abandonment* is as much the work of the nuns at Nancy as of Caussade, the manuscript is a collation of 'advice' he gave to the community. The nun copying these notes added an introductory warning that the doctrine was not suitable for general distribution. This was the aftermath of the 'Quietist controversy'. So matters remained for a hundred years. Such was the stigma of 'Quietism' – and Jesuits had been the main opponents of Madame Guyon & Co. – that even after its publication in 1861 the Jesuits turned on it, challenging both its orthodoxy and Caussade's authorship of it. Scholarship today accepts the doctrine of the treatise to be that of Caussade but in great openness to the Carmelite-based spirituality of Chantal who had founded the Visitation some hundred years before his involvement in it.[19]

Forwards and backwards, Jesuits and Carmelites, all very complicated, but the remarkable thing about Caussade's teaching is its simplicity. He and the nuns of the Visitation were true heirs of Brother Lawrence and, without knowing it, of Julian of Norwich three and a half centuries before. The message is: Let go! Let go! Things are okay. You don't have to always be at the driving wheel. Hand over trying to control things. Sit back, breathe. Take your place in the passenger seat of God's providence. Caussade, as you might expect, puts it slightly, but not very differently. (I will draw first on his letters and later on the treatise that has come down to us.) 'Let us not make 'providence' for ourselves,' he writes to one of the nuns, his great friend Sister Marie-Thérèse de Vioménil, 'Our own hard work and our own anxious foresight simply can't do it.'[20] 'Remember our great principles,' he says (notice 'our' and 'us' – his teaching was a collaboration with the nuns he lived with): '1) There is nothing so small or apparently trifling, even the fall of a leaf, that is not ordained or permitted by God; 2) God is sufficiently wise, good, powerful and merciful to turn the most seemingly disastrous events to the good and profit' (10:123).

Caussade's letters illustrate his teaching from his own experience. In 1740 he was asked by his Order to leave his role as chaplain to the Visitation in Nancy and take up an official administration role for the diocese at Perpignan. He was devastated, both to leave his beloved nuns and, as a retiring contemplative man, to take on the work he was asked. He writes back to Marie-Thérèse (to whom all of his more personal letters are addressed):

> On my arrival at Perpignan, I found a quantity of business
> of which I understand nothing, and many people to see and
> conciliate: the Bishop, the Intendant, the King's Lieutenant,
> Parliament, and Army Staff. You know my horror of all
> sorts of formal visits and above all of visiting the great,
> yet I find that none of this frightens me; I hope God will
> supply for everything and I feel a confidence in his divine
> providence, which keeps me above all these troubles. So
> I remain calm and in peace in the midst of a thousand

worries and complications in which I should have expected, naturally speaking, to be overwhelmed. (3:112)

In the same letter he says that dealing with the vicissitudes of life and people we may not necessarily like, begins with the way we see things:

> You ought to know my habit of always looking at the good side and most favourable aspect of everything. This fortunate habit keeps me out of danger and, in a certain way, prevents me thinking, judging, or speaking ill of anyone. I strongly advise you to adopt this method. It will contribute greatly to the preservation of the peace of your soul. (113–114).

The on-going correspondence with Sister Marie-Thérèse shows a form of spiritual friendship common among mystical writers:

> My dear Sister, – I am touched by your sympathy in my trials, but I am glad to be able to reassure you. It is true that at first I suffered acutely on seeing myself burdened with a quantity of business and anxieties contrary to my liking for solitude and silence, but see how divine Providence has come to my aid. God gives me grace to remain unattached to all these affairs, even while I do them, so my spirit always remains free and unburdened. I leave their successful issue to his paternal care, so that nothing distresses me. (4:114)

A letter some years later to Marie-Thérèse opens up the theme of living in the present moment that is the subject of the treatise the nuns collated after his death:

> Dear Sister, – So you want to know when I am coming back? That I do not know myself. I cannot know it nor do I

wish to know it. Each day and every day I surrender myself
utterly and in all things to divine providence [...] God
forbid me to take even the slightest step to emerge from
my present utter ignorance of my future [...] In this self-
abandonment I find peace and a profound tranquillity –
both of heart and mind that rids me alike of vain thoughts,
restless cravings and all anxiety for the future. (29:183–184).

Caussade sums up his practice of mindfulness in a letter to
Marie-Thérèse: 'One acts gently, without trouble or hurry, without
disquiet about the future or regret for the past, abandoning oneself
to God's fatherly providence' (5:116). Caussade's letters to the
other nuns are less personal but he shows himself as a concerned
spiritual director, helping them with their prayer, particularly
how to deal with thoughts that pester the mind. Caussade's
advice here is very similar to that of contemporary meditation
and mindfulness teachers. To Sister Mary-Antoinette de Mahuet
he advises, 'The best way to drive off useless thoughts is not to
combat them openly and still less to allow oneself to be troubled
and disquieted by them, but just to let them drop, like a stone into
the sea; little by little the habit of letting them drop makes this
salutary practice easy' (1:127). To Sister Marie-Anne-Thérèse de
Rosen: 'You should pay no attention to distractions, but when you
become aware of them, recall very gently your mind and above
all your heart to faith in the presence of God and to enjoyment
of reposing in that presence' (8:140). Mindfulness in the Brother
Lawrence tradition.

The Sacrament of the Present Moment

When we turn to the treatise put together by the nuns from
Caussade's conferences what is distinctive and new is the emphasis
given to the present moment as the 'sacrament' of God's presence:
'O bread of angels, heavenly manna, the pearl of the Gospels, the

sacrament of the present moment.'[21] Sacrament is a strong word – it may be why the nuns did not think it was safe to distribute the treatise widely. According to Catholic understanding following the Council of Trent a sacrament 'contains the grace which it signifies and confers that grace on those who place no obstacles in its way.'[22] Not only adding an extra sacrament during the contentious post-Reformation debate over how many sacraments there were, *Self-Abandonment* proposes a sacrament that depended on no priestly mediation. The treatise goes so far as to propose a meta-sacrament containing the Eucharist (nourishment), Confirmation (strengthening), Confession (purification), Orders of matrimony or priesthood (enrichment), and Extreme Unction (sanctification): 'A soul can be truly nourished, strengthened, purified, enriched and sanctified *only* by the divine plenitude of the present moment. What more do you want? Since all that is good is here now, why seek it elsewhere' (1/7:13). There is no evidence that Caussade envisioned leaving traditional sacramental life behind – as was evident among some of the 'Quietists' – but, as a mystic of mindfulness, he does offer a way to God mediated by the present moment.

How does this sacrament make itself present? Trent had defined sacraments as being efficacious '*ex opere operato*', intrinsically, not through the merit of those enacting or receiving them. So in Caussade's view it is not we who make the present moment holy, it is our awareness of the present moment that makes us holy. The present moment doesn't become a sacrament by 'doing holy things' – going to Church, saying prayers, practising mindfulness – it is intrinsically sanctifying whatever we do, if we could but be present to it. 'Holy people,' the treatise says, 'do not seek out holy things and circumstances but holiness in all their circumstances' (8:16). If we try to do too much, 'pursuing a multitude of means to perfection', we may interfere with 'the soul's simple union with God.' The essence of the sacrament of the present moment is its simplicity and efficacy as 'constantly present to us' impressing on everything which happens to us 'its unique incomparable action' (2/11:35–36). As the treatise says:

> There is no moment at which God does not present himself
> under the guise of some suffering, some consolation
> or some duty [...] Could we pierce the veil and were
> we vigilant and attentive, God would reveal himself
> continuously to us and we should rejoice in his action in
> everything that happens to us. (1:18–19)

How do we pierce the veil? The treatise gives two pieces of advice. Firstly, the 'outer' part consists in doing what we have to do. We don't have to do anything special. 'Each moment,' it says, 'brings with it a duty to be faithfully fulfilled' (1:3). When time to get up, get up; when we have to get the children ready, get them ready; breakfast time, have breakfast. The experience of the Visitation nuns rings out: 'On that duty the whole of our attention was fixed at each successive moment, like the hand of a clock which marks each moment of the hour.' Caussade had taught them that holiness consisted in doing what life presented: 'The passive part of holiness is easy, it consists merely in accepting what most frequently cannot be avoided' (3:7). The 'inner' or active part involves giving our whole heart to living in the flow of the moment. Living freshly means letting go even of the wisdom we have gained from life experience. 'What was best for the moment which has just passed, is so no longer,' the treatise says, 'for what is past is no longer the will of God; this now presents itself under other appearances, and forms the duty of the present moment' (6:10). Humility is the Christian equivalent of the 'beginners mind' encouraged in mindfulness practice. 'Do not let me hear of the wisdom of old men, but rather of their folly,' T.S. Eliot writes in *The Four Quartets* (2:2), 'The only wisdom we can hope to acquire is the wisdom of humility.' Humility makes us look in the right direction: 'God reveals himself to the humble in the humblest things,' Caussade says (2:5).

Self-Abandonment advises against any spiritual practice that tries to get something for, 'We shall find in the present moment all that our heart can desire' (2/3:23). The present moment 'instructs us', it says, and 'forms in us that experimental knowledge' which is the essence of mysticism (8:31). We have to let go of second-hand, or accumulated learning. Referring to the Gospel story of Mary and Martha, Caussade says 'the 'one thing necessary' is always to be found by the soul in the present moment [and in] everything that happens' (10:33–34). The difficult part is accepting the present moment in all its forms. God's presence comes disguised in the traffic jam, in the parking ticket, in the sickness, and even the terrible things of life. When things go well God's presence is close enough to taste, but when all seems to go wrong we hold onto God's presence through faith: 'The more our senses are deceived, revolted, uncertain and in despair, the more surely faith says: "This is God; all is well"' (2:23).

Accepting everything – not trying to avoid or block out unpleasant experiences – is no mean task. But the humble know where to look for the hidden manna, 'What you suffer, and the mundane tasks you have to do, from moment to moment, does this not deserve attention from you?' (4:26). To believe there is a bigger plan than what our partial experience can make clear is faith. We might not find any sense, or feel any value, in what is happening to us but we can still be open to it. If we might see all then all might seem good. 'Everything is significant,' Caussade says, 'there is a perfect meaning everywhere' (5:28). But with our limited perspectives we have to take this on faith. 'The present moment is always full of infinite treasures, it contains far more than you have the capacity to hold,' but, Caussade says, 'Faith is the measure; what you find in the present moment will be according to the measure of your faith' (3:23).

What does Caussade really mean by faith? Moreover, if something that happens is downright wrong should we accept it?

Isn't Caussade's advice passive and naive in the face of the terrible things which happen to us and those around us? As if in response to these questions Book Two of the treatise asks: How does a statue feel while it is being carved?

> It would feel nothing but the cruel edge of the chisel cutting it away and destroying it, for the stone which is being chipped by repeated blows is totally unaware of the figure which is being carved out of it by these blows. It feels only the chisel which is reducing it in size, is beating it, cutting it and changing its shape [...] Suppose you ask a poor piece of stone, 'What is happening to you?' If it had faith and was abandoned as to itself it might answer, 'Don't ask me. As far as I'm concerned there is nothing for me to know or to do except to remain steady under the hand of my master, to love this master and to put up with his treatment. As for what I am destined to be, it is his business, not mine. I do not know what he is doing or what I am being turned into by his work; I only know that whatever he is doing is best and most perfect, and I accept each blow of the chisel as the most excellent thing for me, although to speak the truth every blow makes me feel that I am being ruined, defaced and destroyed. But I leave all this to him and content myself with the present moment, thinking only of my duty; and I accept this skilful master's treatment of me without knowing or troubling myself about it.' (2/6:66–67)

In terms of practice, *Self-Abandonment* advises 'from time to time to hold yourself back a little in peace and silence, attentive before God.'[23] But like non-religious mindfulness teachers the treatise avoids setting up 'spiritual' life as a prerogative: 'In the state of self-abandonment the sole rule,' it says, 'is the present moment.' (2/6:66)

When God gives himself in this way, the ordinary becomes extraordinary, and this is why nothing seems extraordinary. For the path in itself is extraordinary and it is quite unnecessary to adorn it with irrelevant marvels [...] It is a miracle which, while it renders marvellous all our everyday life of the senses, has nothing in itself that is marvellous *to* the senses. (4/11:104)

The grace of the present moment is given through the ordinary experience of our body and of other natural things:

People go on seeking God in corners, no wonder they cannot find him! What folly on their part not to breathe the open air, not to walk about the countryside, not to find water where it abounds, not to take hold of God and taste him and find his action present in everything [...] All you have to do is accept everything and let God act. Everything directs you, keeps you straight and carries you along. Everything is in the hand of God. Earth, air, water are God's. [... God's presence] enters us by all our senses [...] There is no atom, which, in penetrating us, does not make the divine action penetrate us to the marrow of our bones. The vital liquids which pour through our veins do so only by the movement which divine action gives them; all the variations to be found in our movements during the day, their strength and weaknesses, languor or vivacity, are divine instruments. All the states of our body are the operation of God and the working of grace. All our feelings, all our thoughts, however they arise, all come from the invisible hand of God [...] All you have to do is ever to love and esteem as best what is present to you.[24]

Returning where we started in Caussade's letters to his close friend Marie-Thérèse de Vioménil. In the *Spiritual Councels* he gave to her in 1731 (when she was twenty-eight years old) he sums up his teaching:

> To avoid the anxieties which may be caused by either regret for the past or fear of the future, here in a few words is the rule to follow: the past must be left to God's measureless mercy, the future to his loving providence; and the present must be given wholly to his love through fidelity to his grace. *Amen.*[25]

That this marvellous simplicity of Caussade's message blossomed in such life-affirming mysticism is a model for mindfulness practice and teaching today. In 1750, a year before Caussade died, he wrote to Marie-Thérèse – they had now been separated for ten years since he left his role as Chaplain to the Visitation. Caussade shows no regret at their parting and no expectation of their meeting again. Why? Because in the present moment they had always been together. Could it have been Marie-Thérèse who compiled – even wrote – *Self-Abandonment*? We don't know. The one(s) who made Caussade famous to posterity remains hidden. Marie-Thérèse's side of the correspondence is not extant, but her reflections may well have gone into the treatise collated after Caussade's death. Passages of this treatise do read like a love letter between two separated in body but united in spirit:

> What is the secret of finding this treasure we share? There is no secret at all. The treasure is everywhere; God, being God, offers himself to us the whole time, wherever we are. All creatures, whether they are our friends or our foes, pour out this treasure without stint, making it flow through all the faculties of our bodies and our soul to the very centre of our hearts. Let us open our mouths, they will be filled. The action of God inundates the universe, penetrates all creatures, swims above all creatures; wherever they are, it is

going ahead of them, accompanying them, following them. All we have to do is let ourselves be carried away in its waves. (1/3:7)

The Little Way of St Thérèse

Caussade's *Self-Abandonment to Divine Providence,* as we have said, was not published until 1861. Marie-Françoise-Thérèse Martin was born in Alençon in northern France in 1873. On joining the Carmelites at Lisieux at the precocious age of 15 (for which she had to get special Episcopal permission) she became Thérèse of the Child Jesus. There is no direct evidence that Thérèse read Caussade's work though it is quite likely: the book was a religious bestseller while Thérèse was growing up and Monsieur Martin, her pious father, allowed little Thérèse to browse in his upstairs study at the family home in Lisieux. Caussade's doctrine was being taught from the pulpit and the confessional at this time with all the enthusiasm of a new discovery, little Thérèse was a regular at both. The writings of St Thérèse are in the lineage we have been tracing in this chapter. Loved by many, some people find her influential writings a little too pious, but there is no doubt that she is in many ways a perfect example of mindfulness. Ida Görres in her masterly 1944 study of Thérèse says, 'Thérèse accomplished the apparently impossible feat of being, every moment, in a state of sharply focused, intensely controlled alertness, and at the same time completely unselfconscious and spontaneous in all that she did.'[26] Monica Furlong notes how Thérèse gave up fantasies and impossible religious dreams in favour of living in the present moment her little acts of love and acceptance.[27] This Thérèse called her 'Little Way'.

Thérèse, on all accounts, was larger than life. Her novice mistress at Carmel said that she was 'mystic, comic, everything [...] She could make you weep with devotion and just as easily split your sides with laughter during recreation.'[28] And yet she always wanted to be smaller than life, 'as little as a drop of dew' she wrote to her sister Céline.[29] Thérèse wanted to follow the way of the child, totally dependent on the providence of God at each moment. The theologian Hans Urs von Balthasar in a study of Thérèse writes:

> At each moment, her sole concern is to carry out the will of God as it was revealed to her second to second [...] Thérèse never tries to dominate the course of events. In a very womanly fashion, she simply tries to receive everything, and to receive it lovingly. For her, every moment comes so fresh and immediately from the hand of God.[30]

Thérèse described her 'Little Way' as 'the way of spiritual childhood, the way of trust and absolute self-surrender.'[31] Her way was new, direct and quick, like a recent invention she had once travelled in:

> We are now living in the age of inventions, and we no longer have to take the trouble of climbing stairs, for, in the homes of the rich an elevator has replaced these very successfully. I wanted to find an elevator to raise me to Jesus for I am too small to climb the rough stairway to perfection [...] The elevator which must raise me to heaven is your arms, O Jesus! And for this I had no need to grow up, but rather I had to remain little and become this more and more.[32]

It was the way of childlikeness but not of childishness. 'It is possible to remain *little* even in the most responsible position,' she writes.[33] In fact as Novice mistress at Carmel she was far from naive but was astute in dealing with people.

Spiritual childhood for Thérèse involved three things: Firstly, not being judgmental. 'I want to be charitable in my thoughts towards others at all times,' she writes in her autobiography (10:222). She berated her novices on this score:

> You do wrong to find fault, and to try to make everyone see things from your point of view. We desire to be as *little children*. Now, little children do not know what is best. Everything is right in their eyes. Let us imitate them.[34]

Secondly, it involved learning from everything, not just learned and complex books (for which Thérèse had little taste), but most especially from nature. Remembering when she was five or six she writes in her autobiography:

> I shall never forget the impression made on me by my first sight of the sea. I couldn't take my eyes off it, its vastness, the ceaseless roaring of the waves, they spoke to me of the greatness and the power of God [...] In the evening at that moment when the sun seems to bathe itself in the immensity of the waves, leaving a luminous trail behind, I went and sat down on the huge rock with Pauline. I contemplated this luminous trail for a long time. It was to me the image of God's grace shedding its light across the path [I] had to travel. (2:48–49)

By being mindful of natural things we could learn about God's providence: 'If a wild flower could talk, I imagine it would tell us quite candidly about all God has done for it' (1:15). Thirdly spiritual childhood for Thérèse meant living in the present moment. Just before her death in 1897 she said, 'I resemble a very little child [...] I am without a thought of anything; I suffer simply from minute to minute, without even being able to preoccupy myself concerning what is to follow.'[35]

Looking at these three in turn: Not being judgmental for Thérèse meant accepting with patience whatever life presented, even, and maybe especially, if it is irksome. Thérèse tells a story about how it is better to try to enjoy everything, rather than grit your teeth and put up with it:

> For a long time at evening prayers, my place was just in front of a sister who had an odd nervous affectation; she would rub her rosary beads together to make a grinding sound. Perhaps none heard it but myself, for my hearing is extremely acute, but I cannot say how much it tormented me. How I longed to turn my head and give one sharp glance to make her stop the tiresome rattling. But my heart told me to bear it patiently, for love of the good God, in the first place, and also to avoid giving her pain. So stayed still, and tried to get closer to God; perhaps I could forget it altogether, this tiny noise [...] Absolutely useless; there was I with the sweat pouring down me, in the attempt to make my prayer into a prayer of pure endurance! At last I sought for means of suffering with peace and joy. I hit on the idea of trying to *like* this exasperating noise. Instead of trying not to hear it – a thing impossible – I listened with fixed attention, as if the sound were of some delightful music, and all my prayer – it was certainly not the prayer of quiet our mother Teresa [of Avila] recommended – consisted in offering this music to our Lord. (11:249–250)

In a similar vein Thérèse tells how she was regularly splashed with dirty water while doing laundry by a vigorously working but rather inattentive nun. Instead of complaining she decided she would try to like it: 'At the end of a half-hour of this practice, I had really acquired quite a taste for this novel sort of aspersion.' (250)

Secondly, learning from everything: Thérèse on her own account wasn't particularly good at private silent prayer. She either felt distracted with her thoughts, or often fell asleep. When her novices asked her for advice on prayer she said, 'Don't bother about thoughts, accept whatever comes along, even outlandish ones!'[36] The worse your thoughts were, the better, for that would make you turn to God. Prayer, for Thérèse, was simply turning to God. 'As for me, prayer is a lifting up of the heart,' she writes, 'It is a simple glance towards heaven, a cry of gratitude and love in the midst of trials as well as joys.'[37] Be open to whatever life presents, for everything gives an opportunity to learn, and turn towards the truth. 'No book, no theologian taught this Way to me,' she writes, 'and yet I feel in the depths of my heart that I possess the truth.'[38] Even falling asleep at prayer contained an important lesson: 'You think that I ought to feel sad because I fall asleep (a thing that has been going on for seven years) during my meditation? Well, I don't grieve over that! Little children please their parents as much while they sleep as when they are awake' (8:165). Besides, she says, 'doctors put patients to sleep when they operate on them.' Why not God?

Thirdly, living in the present moment: Thérèse took to her heart the Gospel saying, 'Sufficient unto the day is the evil thereof,' tomorrow will have worry of its own (Mt. 6:34). 'God gives grace only for the present moment,' she advised her novices, 'The future will never happen as we imagine it anyway. We lose our peace when we leave the present.'[39] Like De Caussade Thérèse believed the best way to practice 'abandonment' is to enclose oneself in the present moment. When facing her diagnosis of tuberculosis and asked whether she feared it, she told her novices:

> Imagining what painful things might happen to me in the future is like interfering with God's work of creation. He doesn't give the future. Running in the way of love we must never worry about anything. If I did not accept my suffering from one minute to another, it would be impossible for me to remain patient. But I see only the present moment, forget

the past and take good care not to visualise the future.
When we become discouraged and despair it is because we
think of the past and the future.[40]

An Instant is a Treasure

Mindfulness, for Thérèse, involved using well the one moment we
have. 'Let us see each instant as if there were no other,' she writes
to her sister Céline in 1888, 'An instant is a treasure.'[41] On 1st June
1894 she wrote a poem called *My Song of Today*:

> My life's a jot of time,
> an hour that comes and goes;
> My life – this moment; *now* –
> escapes and runs away.
> To give You while on earth,
> O God, the love one owes,
> I've got … only today!
> What does it matter to me
> If the future may somber be?
> To pray to God for tomorrow –
> Ah no, that is not my way:
> O give to me Thy love,
> And wrap me in Thy grace
> Just for this one day![42]

Thérèse, despite her devotional language, could well be the patron
saint of secular forms of mindfulness. 'There will be something [in
my Little Way] for all tastes,' she said, 'except for extraordinary
ways.'[43] 'Holiness, does not consist in saying beautiful things; it
does not consist in even thinking them, or feeling them.'[44] 'On the
path of spiritual childhood, nothing departs from the ordinary.'[45]
Holiness comes though 'fidelity to the smallest things' (4:74). She

was very suspicious of visions, as being liable to illusion. 'In my little way only the most ordinary things find place.'[46] 'Imaginations do not help me, I can draw no sustenance except from the truth as it is.'[47] All her religiosity was stripped from her as she grew older until, in her final illness she had no sense of God's presence at all. She identified herself with those who did not believe in God because that was what she experienced. In 1896 a year before her death she struck a deal with God: 'I tell Him that I am happy not to enjoy heaven on earth in order that He may open heaven for ever to all those who don't believe' (10:214). (On this ground alone we may be confident that atheists may well have heaven opened to them.) It seems God took Thérèse up on this deal. For the last eighteen months of her life Thérèse was in acute physical pain and in complete spiritual desolation. As regards her body she was dying slowly from respiratory and intestinal tuberculosis: finding it harder and harder to breath and living with intense abdominal pain. As regards her mind Thérèse says she was 'overrun by impenetrable darkness, the thought of heaven was nothing but conflict and torment' (213). Therapeutic mindfulness has helped many people suffering from depression. Thérèse entered into this herself. Lying on her bed in the infirmary her trial of faith made it very difficult to pray, her practice was to look through the window. On seeing Thérèse gazing out at the sky one of the Sisters said she was rapt in mystical contemplation, Thérèse smiled but later said to Mother Agnes, 'Looking at the blue sky I meditate only on the beauty of the material heavens; the other is more and more closed to me.'[48]

Thérèse came back to her childhood experience of contemplating nature. She looked out at the trees in the garden, focusing her whole attention on the play of sunlight in them but also the darkness where the sunlight didn't reach. One day pointing at a 'black hole' among the trees she told Mother Agnes: 'I am in a black hole just like that, body and soul. Ah! What darkness! However, I am still at peace' (Epilogue: 266). Stripped of all religious imagination she who had longed for heaven through her life now found an afterlife impossible to imagine. She was stripped to her senses: 'I know only what I see and feel!' she tells Mother Agnes (267). Like in mindfulness practice but from the harsh reality of her illness she became aware of the gift and blessing of the breath: She said to Mother Agnes, 'If you but realised what it is to suffocate!' (270)

What Thérèse had learnt in life she practised in death. On the 19th August five weeks before she died she told the nuns, 'I suffer only for the present moment; it is through thinking of the future and the past that we become discouraged and despair.'[49] In her final weeks she spoke of her continuing desire to believe. Her own resources of faith had come to an end, 'I am like a tired and harassed traveller, who reaches the end of his journey and falls over. Yes,' she says, 'but I'll be falling into God's arms.'[50] Outwardly she seemed cheerful but warned her sisters not to leave anything poisonous near her: 'If I had not had any faith, I would have committed suicide without a moment's hesitation.' At the end of her life she felt she couldn't pray, but continued to look at the trees and the statue of the Our Lady by the window. Her prayer simplified itself down to the practice of the Desert Fathers and Mothers, taking one word. 'I can no longer pray,' she tells Mother Agnes, 'I can only look at the Blessed Virgin and say "Jesus!"' In the end even the intimacy of that name dissolved into love: 'I can't sleep,' [Thérèse told her sister Céline], 'I'm suffering too much, so I am praying.' 'And what,' [her sister asked], 'are you saying to Jesus?' 'I say nothing to him, I love him.'

Thérèse's last words were pronounced very distinctly, while gazing at the crucifix held before her; 'Oh! I love Him!' And a moment later: 'My God, I love you!' Suddenly her eyes came to life, she looked at the window to the statue and the trees. The nuns remembered that for those moments she seemed completely well and happy. Then she closed her eyes. Some months before she had written some words to the Chaplain, Père Bellière, 'I am not dying; I am entering into life.' (Epilogue: 271)

Chapter 8

The Way of Attention

*If we could see only the present and lived wholly in
the present moment we would achieve goodness
here and now.*[1]

Walking Mindfully on Water

The philosopher, a complicated man, prone to melancholy, carried
his genius like a sentence of strangerhood. He had wanted to be
normal, to fit in with married life, with society, with the Church,
but his critical intelligence turned in upon himself. Playing any
role (including that of the outsider) became a caricature. Even that
which was closest to him – his writing – was not him: he wrote
using pseudonyms. He was considered a master of irony, yet for
him it was inevitable that all truth was subjective and therefore
partial. No personal experience could take in the whole picture. It
was his calling, however, as a philosopher to search and speak for
truth. He could only do that by taking many perspectives, writing
as different people, contradicting himself, exaggerating the one-
sidedness of a particular view. This is what set him apart from
the crowd, which, he felt, had a general unexamined consensus
on things. He would always be on the side of the viewpoint left
out. That was the way of the individual: a narrow way, quite often
wrong, but the only way to come to anything from one's own
experience. Truth, he said, had to be naked: 'In order to swim
one takes off all one's clothes – in order to aspire to the truth one
must undress in a far more inward sense, divest oneself of all one's

inward clothes, of thoughts, conceptions, selfishness etc. before one is sufficiently naked.'[2]

One part of his writings he did give his own name to, his *Edifying Discourses* on Scripture and Christian faith. These were written each year for Church newsletters and pamphlets, and even when collected in books they sold much less than his literary work. Here, however, he could speak for himself, for earlier in his life he made 'a leap of faith.' Not because he saw that Christianity was true in an objective sense – doctrines meant nearly nothing to him – but because he chose for himself this path, choosing it with all the passion of one-sidedness. His religious faith was not a way of fitting in to a belief structure, a Church, or society, but came from a sense of being summoned. Like Peter on the Sea of Galilee he felt called to leave the boat of companionship and relative safety and walk on the stormy water with no securities, with nothing to hold him up but faith. He knew he could not do this, but he never doubted the calling.

Walking mindfully on water is not easy. In his religious writings he called himself by his real name – Søren Kierkegaard – but he could not see himself as a teacher or preacher. His *Edifying Discourses* were not sermons. He dreaded comparing himself with anyone else 'as if he were superior by virtue of being the speaker.'[3] To be in any position of authority would immediately make him doubt himself. To speak objectively about truth would set him like Peter looking at the stormy weather and rough waves of his self-doubt. His sharp irony about everything 'external', everything supposedly rational, would tear his faith apart and he would sink. The only way was 'the way of inwardness', knowing himself as fallible and yet trusting. His *Edifying Discourses* are attempts to put one step ahead of another on stormy waves. To think he had arrived in the arms of his master and speak as one with wisdom would make faith redundant when for him it was the only thing that enabled him to take the next step ahead. Faith, for him, was to trust despite all self-doubt and evasive ratiocinations.

'Faith expresses itself not in belief but in unbelievable action,' he said.[4] Inwardness, self-awareness, holding back from identifying with anything, was paradoxically the only way to free action. But this, our philosopher said, comes from a radical sense of dependence on another. Not on the confident self-acting individual as Nietzsche and Sartre would later take existentialism. Realising the vulnerability of job, marriage, health, social position, letting go of external props, means we have to act from faith. He criticised religion if was meant to guarantee a calm and settled way of life in the world – what he called an 'undecided life'. Religion as a motivation for transcendence, however, as a leap of faith, would help us walk on water. Even amid the wild waves thrown up by life if we could take a step – one step at a time responding to Christ we would hear, 'Take heart, it is I; do not be afraid.' (Mt 14:27)

It has been said that Kierkegaard is a prophet of the twentieth century living in the nineteenth. Certainly his 'existentialist' approach – the value of subjectivity – had enormous influence on philosophers a century afterwards. But he himself lived through a time of peace in a religiously settled world. Born in 1813 in Copenhagen, he died in 1855 without travelling far beyond his hometown. People could not understand why he was making such a fuss. He became something of a joke to the settled society of his time. *Either/Or, Fear and Trembling, The Concept of Anxiety, Sickness unto Death* – his books spoke of drama and choice, knife-edge decisions, leaps of faith, suspensions of the ethical. His words fit the traumas of the twentieth century. Mindfulness practice likewise is a response to unprecedented levels of anxiety in the modern world. Kierkegaard foresaw the collapse of religion as a collective influence within society. From now on faith would have to be a personal choice, not something we inherit outside ourselves – which gives security in relation to the world – but something we have to discover – which sets us apart from the world by having our only security in God. In a world without belief we need faith.

Anxiety; lack of self-esteem; loss of belief that things that happen have any meaning or direction; stress; believing everything depends on us alone; all these doubts are symptoms of the modern world that Kierkegaard lived and wrote about. In his *Discourses* Kierkegaard not only reflects on the meaning of these experiences, but tries to help counteract such painful states of mind. These discourses (there are 80 of them) are much gentler and more pastoral in tone than his literary works. In them he shows how the wisdom of Christianity can heal. Despite the strong faith perspective, the practical advice Kierkegaard offers shows common ground with Mindfulness teaching in four ways: 1) His emphasis on 'considering things', 2) the need to leave self-consciousness behind, 3) not comparing ourselves with others, and 4) living in the moment.

Kierkegaard would not have liked to be called a mystic. His journals show he had a dislike for the term and the type of spirituality that boasted extra-ordinary experiences. God had to be found in ordinary life, amid the people and things we see: 'The most dangerous of all escapes is wanting to love only the unseen or that which one has not seen.'[5] 'Mysticism has not the patience to wait for God's revelation.'[6] He was writing at a time when mysticism in Catholic Europe had gone in for otherworldliness and a concern with super-natural phenomena. As in many ways a deeply Lutheran thinker he would have been a critic of mysticism anyway. A 'direct' or 'unmediated' experience of God would bypass faith, and it was, in his mind, only through faith we are justified. Also, like Luther, Kierkegaard was a critic of the organised religion of his time and placed the emphasis on personal response to a calling rather than security in external practices.

One could call Kierkegaard a protesting mystic. His concern for 'inwardness', though couched as a protest against religiosity, came from a personal experience. This is clearer where he speaks as himself in *Edifying Discourses*. Kierkegaard is otherworldly in his critique of comfortable conformity and complacency but is not so in the way he encounters God. In his *Discourses* he revels in the natural world as 'divinely appointed teachers.' Kierkegaard was an exact contemporary of the Danish storyteller Hans Christian

Andersen (1805–1875) and like Andersen he delights in tales and comparisons drawn from nature where plants and animals speak. Nature lifted his spirits. His mysticism was to pay attention, listen, look and learn.

Kierkegaard among the Lilies

One day our philosopher is taking a day out to walk in the fields around Copenhagen. Life in the city has made him anxious, lonely, sad. He was vexed both by temperament and circumstance: his pious father had put the fear of God into him; he had broken off his engagement to the woman he loved as he felt happiness was not his lot in life; he had backed out of ordination within the Church, silently; and later, vocally, he fulminated against the mediocrity of Christianity in his time; he did not fit in with the concerns of people around him. Indeed! No, others could not help him, he 'does not want to hear what others have to say about comfort and hope.' Neither the happy nor the sad could be of help to his existence:

> The happy do not understand. When those who are
> strong and wise offer comfort they seem precisely to place
> themselves far above by doing so. What other anxiety
> sufferers have to offer only depresses one further. (86–87)

At least nature keeps silent out of respect for one who is anxious. The kindest thing we can do for someone who is troubled, he says, 'is to take them somewhere where there is nothing to remind them of their trouble, not even sympathy.' (113)

One could say that our philosopher has signs of depression. But out there 'in the field, with the lilies, where the sky is arched high above' he finds 'it is like breathing properly, where the great thoughts of the clouds dispel all pettiness' (93). Out there he does not stare ahead in the fixed gaze of one going about his city business. He looks about him. Langer's research shows we move from one-track thinking by being open to new things.[7] Our philosopher agrees; 'If anxiety has a firm grip on someone then it will be necessary for them to do something to look away from it and stop thinking about it' (114). He recommends two *asanas*: looking down at the wild flowers at our feet and up into heaven at the birds flitting joyfully in the air. To look at the heavens alone may put the fear of God into one. No, our philosopher says, best to keep one's eyes on natural things where in our loneliness we have a 'divine distraction' (115). The lilies and the birds are not the sort of spectacle that tries to grab our attention through appealing to our desires. They seem insignificant and yet 'are so infinitely rich' (116). 'If you seek comfort where the lily flowers in loveliness – in the field – and where the bird is free and at home – in the air – there you will find uninterrupted silence: no one is present, yet everything constantly speaks to you.' (88)

Awareness of nature takes us out of our fixed thoughts. Before long our lonely philosopher finds himself 'woven as a part into the great common life […] the great fellowship of existence.' (114)

> Imagine yourself hurrying on your way on some important errand and along the path that runs by the edge of the wide sea and then think of how the sea affects you. Of course, no one is calling to you, no invitation is issued, no one is screaming out, and no cannons are roaring to advertise some human entertainment – but think of how it affects you: if you stand still for just a moment, won't the movement of the waves, even in their monotony, win you over? (116–117)

The divine distractions that nature provides 'are [also] meant to give us something to think about' (118). To get what nature is saying we have to pay attention. Looking at the lilies and the birds, the sorrowful 'forget about themselves in thinking about *them* and *their* life' (88). The Gospel says we have to 'consider' them (Lk 12:27, Mt 6:28). For Kierkegaard this means 'observing them closely, making them the object not of a quick glance as you pass by, but of observation' (88). 'Consider' is a mixture of focus and inquisitiveness key to educational and therapeutic mindfulness today. For Kierkegaard this is not an esoteric practice:

> It is what the fisherman does when he comes in the morning and looks at the nets that have been set all night. It is how the doctor looks at the invalid. It is how the child looks when its elders are doing something it has never seen before. That is how – and not with divided attention or distracted thoughts, but with focused attention and reflection – one is to carefully consider the lilies and birds. (100)

What do we learn that will soften our anxiety? The beauty of wild flowers is unselfconscious. It is not that of cultivated roses, which T.S. Eliot noted, 'had the look of flowers that were looked at'[8] Though sometimes in groups, wild flowers don't compare themselves to each other as we do. They don't worry about what they look like, they don't 'toil and spin' to be well dressed and 'yet even Solomon in all his glory was not arrayed like one of these.' If that is the case with the wild lily, why not with us? 'Learn to be content with being human,' our philosopher concludes, 'Don't become anxious about the differences between one human being and another' (98). 'All *worldly* anxiety has its basis in human beings being unwilling to be content with being human and, under the influence of comparison, becoming anxiously desirous of being different in some way' (99). And, if we consider the birds, what do we learn? To let go of earthbound worries! The birds 'neither sow, nor reap nor gather into barns' – how could they, they belong in the heavens. Our philosopher reflects: sowing, reaping, storing up, belong respectively to past, present and future. These birds have no care for any of them! Why? Because they are cared for. 'Your heavenly Father feeds them.' *My* heavenly Father? Then he cares for me.

'Let us consider this more closely,' Kierkegaard says, 'Why does the bird not worry about what to eat? It is because he lives only in the moment' (127). 'No matter how high up in the sky he flew to look down on the world, and no matter what else he saw, he never saw 'the next day".[9] Can I likewise be blind to futurity? No, Kierkegaard says,

> Because human beings are conscious of eternity, they are conscious of 'tomorrow'. Consciousness reveals a world that the most well-travelled bird doesn't know – the future, or what is to come – and it is when we take this consciousness of 'what is to come' back into the present moment that we discover an anxiety that the bird does not know. (127)

This is both a blessing and a curse that sets us apart from nature. We have a sense of eternity, which is different from the present moment for it includes past and the future. We 'have a dangerous enemy that the bird does not know: Time.' Through consciousness 'time and eternity come into contact [...] the eternal breaks into time.' And yet 'as God lifted human beings high above the bird by means of the eternal element in consciousness, so He pushed them back down below the bird, if one can put it like this, by virtue of their knowledge of care, of temporal care of which the bird knows nothing' (128). We can, therefore, learn from the bird as our teacher and exemplar in not worrying about what tomorrow's food. And yet as God's 'co-workers' human beings are given their food normally through work: to see our work as a sharing in God's providence is a yet higher perfection than the birds.

Oh but our philosopher has outstripped his experience of looking at the birds and is already reflecting again on human life. His mind is already back in the city where he knows he has to live.

Out here in the fields he is called simply to learn from the birds of the air. The bird flitting above him may have troubles some days, he may find food scarce when it snows (as it does in Denmark), he may even one day be swooped down on by an eagle and killed, but he never has tomorrow's troubles. He lives only in the day, in the moment. We have invented troubles for ourselves by worrying about 'the next day'. *We* have to get rid of 'the next day' – the bird never had it. How hard to get rid of it for it always slips away as 'the next day'. How do we let it go? By getting on with this day. 'Each day has enough troubles of its own.' (Mt 6:34)

> Take rowers in a boat: their backs are turned to the direction of travel – and that is how it should be regarding the next day. When, helped by the eternal, we are immersed in today, this very day, we turn our backs to the next day, and the more deeply, the more eternally, we immerse ourselves in today, the more decisively we turn our backs on the next day, until we reach the point at which we don't see it at all. If we were to turn around then the eternal would take on a confused form and transform itself into the next day. But when we work our way towards our destination (eternity) by turning our backs to it, then not only do we not see the next day, but the eternal helps us to see this very day and its tasks all the more clearly.[10]

The bird is entirely free from anxiety. Christians have a blessing – the consciousness of eternity, which enables them to live each day wholly, mindfully, which enables them to be, as Kierkegaard says, truly 'contemporary with themselves'. The opposite is the state of mind of Mr James Duffy described by James Joyce in his short story *A Painful Case*:

> He lived at a little distance from his body, regarding his own acts with doubtful side-glances. He had an odd

autobiographical habit, which led him to compose in his mind from time to time a short sentence about himself containing a subject in the third person and a verb in the past tense. He never gave alms to beggars but walked firmly, fixedly down the street.

For Kierkegaard to live whole-heartedly in the Now involves letting go of thinking about ourselves. It is to come back to our bodies as more lovely than even the flowers, and it is to realise that God cares for all people whether they work or not. It involves opening our eyes to what is around us. We are saved from our own anxieties when we realise that, even more than the birds, we can be co-providers with God for others.

The *Via Negativa* of Simone Weil

Simone Weil was born in Paris on 3 February 1909 into a highly cultured secular Jewish family. Her father Bernard was a respected medical doctor and her older brother André was to be a famous mathematician. Simone herself was something of a prodigy. Precocious to the extent of never having a childhood, at the age of six she spent her time reading *Le Monde* and following her brother's enthusiasm for mathematical quandaries. At the age of twelve she started to experience violent and chronic headaches that were to plague her for the rest of her life. These episodes were not only painful but made it difficult to eat, as chewing only aggravated the pain and caused nausea. Matters got even worse at fourteen when she fell into a depression so severe that she considered taking her life. Typically for Simone this adolescent crisis came from a sense of intellectual inadequacy *vis-à-vis* her brother's mathematical genius: 'What grieved me was the idea of being excluded from that transcendental kingdom to which I believed only the truly great have access.'[11] She did her own cognitive therapy in the end through realising it was not intelligence that created genius but longing for truth and the ability to apply one's attention. This experience was later to propel her interest in school studies. To rate intelligence by performance was superficial. Real intelligence was cultivated when interest was motivated alongside patient attentiveness.

Despite this bout of self-depreciation (a characteristic which continues in Weil's writing) the young Simone's intelligence did show outwardly. In 1928 she was admitted to the *École Normale Supérieure*, the top college of the University of Paris. It was only the second year that this elite group admitted women. In the entrance examination Weil came first, followed by Simone de Beauvoir, topping a list of thirty men. Motivated by the search for truth she studied philosophy and roughly fell in line with the existentialism popular in Paris in the late 1920s. It was while at college that Weil developed her political proposal of a non-violent revolution championing the rights of manual workers. She leaned temporally towards Marxism. Dishevelled in her appearance, she was quite uninterested in any amorous pursuit. Her existentialist friends nicknamed her 'the Red Virgin'. After graduation, at a time when women couldn't teach in Universities, she taught in various Lycées, where she put her views on education into practice; downplaying exam results so students could explore their own interests. She also offered evening classes to industrial workers and continued to campaign for trade union causes.

Weil's strong sense of identity with those doing manual work motivated her to work in the holidays in vineyards giving the money she earned to building up a library for working men and women. It was at this time she had her first mystical experience of silence: she noted that there was 'a silence which is not the absence of sound but which is something we can actually sense in itself'. This was more real to her than any sound: instead silence being the background to sound she said: 'If there are any noises they only reach me after crossing the silence' (WG 24). In October 1934 she got a year's unpaid leave from school teaching for 'personal studies', but her real intention was to gain first-hand experience of factory work. She worked for four months at three factories in Paris, drilling, operating a power-press and turning crank handles. For one trained in academic life and fascinated by silence the experience was crushing. With constant headaches and humiliation from fellow workers she was unable to think and was left physically exhausted. But the experience shaped her mysticism of the present moment – she found that she forgot past and future in what seemed like the eternity of the working day! The French (and English) word *monotonie* comes from the Latin *monos* – single, and *tonos*, tone. Weil's characteristically negative take on the eternal Now should not deter us from the positive value she gleaned from 'monotony as the most beautiful or the most atrocious thing.'[12] The experience left an indelible mark on her later reflection on affliction and 'the spirituality of work.' In extreme suffering we are stripped of past and future. To do the necessary tasks of the day is the best way to be in the moment because it involves coming back to our bodies.

> In manual work time enters into our bodies [...] If we are worn out it means we are becoming submissive to time as matter is. Thought is forced to pass from one instant to the next without laying hold of past or the future. That is what it means to obey. (GG 181)

Obedience, for Weil, found its only real expression in response to necessity. Doing what must be done, not something we think about and then decide is a good action, but what the moment demands *now*. Weil's work with machinery meant she had to give full attention to what she was doing: any distraction would be dangerous. Attentiveness meant responding to what life presents: no more, that would be pride – no less, that would be sloth. 'We have to consent to be subject to the necessities of life, and to act only in handling those' (43). Weil is in the tradition of French mysticism in her stress on attention and the absoluteness of God's presence. She writes in her letter to her confidant Père Perrin, 'All things which come about are according to the will of God, without any exception' (WG 1). Weil gives a little practice of mindfulness in how to go about discerning that will in the moment: 'If we make a quietness within ourselves, if we silence all desires and opinions and if with love, without formulating any words, we bind our whole soul to think 'Thy will be done', the thing which after that we feel sure we should do (even though in certain respects we may be mistaken) is the will of God' (GG 47).

Manual work freed Weil from the tendency, derived from her upbringing, to always think about things, training her to be attentive to one thing. Learning was more a matter of depth, she realised, than accumulation of information. This depth could be practised. She repeated a poem she loved, 'saying it over all the time', savouring every word (WG 21, 23). She also 'made a practice of saying the Greek Our Father through once each morning with absolute attention. If during the recitation my attention wanders or goes to sleep, in the minutest degree, I begin again until I have once succeeded in going through it with absolute pure attention' (24). Manual work freed her from worrying or imagining the future and made her compassionate for others, especially those who lived doing mechanical tasks the end result of which was meaningless to them. If affliction pins us down in the present we are still able to make a choice in that moment to keep our hearts open. The positive side of suffering is the ability to make 'a vow of love, inwardly renewed each second of each day, each time eternal and each time wholly complete and new.' (35)

Living in the past and future and not being in the present Weil compares with the plight of the miser who, from avarice (of the past) and fear (of the future) stores up money rather than spending it. Affliction is the experience of loss, where all our reserves are spent. After a day's work in the factory Weil felt drained of any sense of 'I used to be' or 'shall be'. 'Renunciation of past and future is the first of all renunciations' (19). The tendency, however, when we are tired is to turn the television on, escape into images, so

'Imagination, the sole consolation of the afflicted,' is the second renunciation (GG 16). When our sense of personal story and our escape into the imaginary stories of others are reduced to nothing then we pass through the eye of the needle into the present moment. In the moment our sense life is invigorated:

> We live in a world of unreality and dreams. To give up our imaginary position as the centre, to renounce it, not only intellectually but in the imaginative part of our soul, that means to awaken to what is real and eternal, to see the true light and hear the true silence. A transformation then takes place at the very roots of our sensibility, in our immediate reception of sense and psychological impressions [...] We see the same colours, we hear the same sounds, but not in the same way. (WG 98–99)

Welcoming all Opinions

We have seen that for Ellen Langer mindfulness is the capacity to notice things without preconceived ideas. Weil is one Christian mystic who believed that multiple perspectives were more conducive to attentiveness than fixed conclusions. She saw her vocation not as an apologist of Christianity but as one who 'serves God and the Christian faith in the realm of intelligence.' Faith, she felt, not only demanded intellectual honesty but impartiality. 'My thought should be indifferent to all ideas without exception, including for instance materialism and atheism,' she wrote to Père Perrin, 'it must be equally welcoming and equally reserved with regard to every one of them' (WG 35). This is the 'mental flexibility', which Langer encourages. For Weil the impartial mind should be like water, not weighing what falls into it but allowing each object to find its own buoyancy. To be attentive without imposing our opinions demands, she says, an 'indifference of thought on the level of the intelligence.' The ability to enquire is short-circuited by any belief that 'we're right.' To be mindful is to be open to and inquisitive about what others think. The path, Weil says, is 'to empty ourselves of our false divinity, to deny ourselves, to give up being the centre of the world, to discern that all points in the world are equally centres.'

Weil's sense of vocation as a critical observer was one reason why she couldn't accept baptism into the Church despite her deep sense of connection and identity with it. She was worried about the one perspective mentality she found so often there. Her sense of God's presence in Classical literature and in religions like Buddhism meant she could never believe truth could be wholly contained in one system of thought.[13] Openness to truth in all its forms, like the vulnerability to each moment that suffering imposes, is in no way incompatible with the love of God. For Weil love is best expressed in intimacy rather than enthusiastic group events. Social enthusiasm, she says, is a poor substitute for religious faith. Because love of Christ is different from communal loyalty she felt called to remain outside the fold of any national, ecclesial or political group. 'The children of God should have no other country here below but the universe itself,' she wrote, 'That is the native city to which we owe our love' (44). Faith is not for her an affirmation but a denial of everything that is not God.

> This refusal does not presuppose any belief. It is enough to recognise, what is obvious to any mind, that all the goods of this world, past, present or future, real or imaginary, are finite and limited and radically incapable of satisfying the desire which burns perpetually within us for an infinite and perfect good.[14]

With liberty of thought Weil also defends the rights of the individual to think differently from the group. The shadow side of social religion is the mind-police of the inquisition, which Weil felt reached its worst in the irreligion of Nazism. Belief as group opinion requires the counterbalance of contemplation. Letting go of our ideas fosters the ability to take in views different from our own. Contemplation doesn't involve having no views oneself – Weil had strong views on politics, religion and her own French identity – but she never saw her viewpoint as the whole truth. If we think we are our thoughts then anyone who thinks differently jeopardises our sense of self. We begin to defend our opinions trenchantly. No, 'We must welcome all opinions,' Weil writes in her notebook. But this does not mean levelling or relativising all ideas, 'they must be arranged vertically and kept on suitable levels' (GG xiv). For Weil this hierarchy is in inverse proportion to collective (and therefore unconscious) opinions. Justice involves leaning towards the least represented, most outcast viewpoint. Because the crowd is so influential being aware of what is most often ignored in and around us is the key to impartiality: 'Our love should stretch as widely across all space, and should be as equally distributed in every portion of it, as is the very light of the sun.' (WG 44)

Weil argues that developing the faculty of attention is 'the real object and almost the sole interest of studies' paralleling again Langer's use of mindfulness in education (54). Langer has never referred to Weil as an influence in her writings and yet Langer identifies attention as the remedy to 'mindless learning' – learning by rote and without personal interest: 'Attending to the world, doesn't mean that we need to become hyper-vigilant. Our attention naturally goes to what is different and out of balance.'[15] Attention involves noticing small, unexpected things, which are outside or on the periphery of our usual cognisance. Weil is similarly concerned that attention is not 'confused with a kind of muscular effort': 'If one says to one's pupils: 'Now you must pay attention,' one sees them contracting their brows, holding their breath, stiffening their muscles. If after two minutes they are asked what they have been paying attention to, they cannot reply. They have been concentrating on nothing' (54). Attention, 'the greatest of all efforts perhaps', should, she says, rather be a 'negative effort', watching, waiting, not seeking anything. Like mindfulness practice it shouldn't make us tired. Relaxed alertness, like breathing in and breathing out, Weil says, is the best way to apply ourselves to any task or life situation.

> When we become tired, attention is scarcely possible any more, unless we have already had a good deal of practice. It is better to stop the endeavour altogether, to seek some relaxation, and then a little later to return again; we have to press on and loosen up alternately, just as we breathe in and out. Twenty minutes of concentrated un-tired attention is infinitely better than three hours of frowning application [...] Attention consists of suspending our thought, leaving it detached, empty and ready to be penetrated by the object. (55–56)

Objectivity is the state of mind necessary for learning about things in themselves rather than our views of them. It necessitates even-mindedness, not being attached to any pre-conceived notions but while focusing being inquisitive also about the space around and above our thoughts. Weil compares this to 'a man on a mountain who, as he looks forward, sees also below him, without actually looking at them, a great many forests and plains. So attentiveness should be in relation to all particular and already formulated thoughts' (56). This is very similar to the Buddhist notion of *upeksha,* sometimes translated as 'equanimity', which, as Thich Nhat Hanh explains, derives from the Sanskrit *Upe* – 'over', and *ksh* – 'to look'. 'We climb the mountain top', Hanh says, 'to be able to look over the whole situation, not bound by one side or the other.'[16] Pre-set ideas have to constantly be revised in the face of new experience: 'What is true here', Langer says, 'need not be true over there [...] A psychology of possibility' involves 'try[ing] out different things without evaluating ourselves as we go along.'[17]

'The soul empties itself of all its own contents,' Weil says, 'in order to receive into itself the being it is looking at, just as he is, in all his truth' (59). Mindfulness involves unsticking any thoughts to which we have become fixated, freeing the mind from its own internal monologue. 'The capacity to drive a thought away once and for all is the gateway to eternity,' Weil says, 'The infinite in an instant.' (GG 118)

To love without imagining and without imposing our interpretation on things is attention, it is to be aware of the reality of what is different to us, it is Weil says, 'the rarest and purest form of generosity' (WG 54). It leads to love of God and neighbour: 'Prayer consists of attention, warmth of heart cannot make up for it' (51). 'Those who are unhappy have no need for anything in this world but people capable of giving them their attention.'[18] It also involves acceptance of ourselves: 'If we consider what we are at a definite moment – the present moment, cut off from past and future – we are innocent,' Weil says, 'We cannot at that instant be anything but what we are.' (GG 37)

Forgiving our Existence in Time

'To live in the present moment, isolated from past and future, implies pardon,' Weil says, 'But such isolation is detachment' (GG 37). What is forgiven is our existence in time. For Weil 'time does not exist (except within the limit of the present), yet we have to submit to it. Such is our condition' (52). Physically and emotionally we are linked to memories (of what has happened) and fears or expectations (of what will happen). We organise our lives with diaries, timetables, deadlines, but 'that to which we are subject does not exist,' Weil says, 'We are bound by unreal chains. Time which is unreal casts over all things including ourselves a veil of unreality.' Forgiveness for Weil means accepting that a large aspect of our and others' lives will always and necessarily be under this veil. 'Necessity is God's veil' (104). To live mindfully within time implies pardon but requires detachment. Anything that has duration must be carried lightly for it is not our true identity. Thoughts have duration. They arise in our mind and play themselves out as long as we follow them. If we take our attention off them, however, following some other sensation like the breath, or body awareness or the repetition of a poem or sacred word we are able to let them pass.

The illusion of past and future alienates us from our innocence in the present moment but as necessity freely accepted it becomes a way of living in the present. The fact that our thoughts are bound up with time is actually our salvation, for no thought is eternal. There is nothing more dangerous than stuck thought. It is at the root of fundamentalism and neurosis. The healthy mind realises that 'all things are impermanent'. Thoughts pass and so do actions. What is done in time as a response to necessity is also a way to self-transcendence. The sense of 'me' as doer is removed when we do simply what life presents. Living within time mindfully is also the key to love: to love someone eternally only God can do, the scope of human love is the changing circumstances of time – for better and for worse, for richer and for poorer, in sickness and in health, until death – the ending of time – brings the human mode of love to an end. If our love for others is not under the condition of contingency then, Weil says, it is imaginary.

But we have to live within the contingent with attention. We have to function in time – our life story is part of who we are – but it is not the whole story. We have to think, but our thoughts cannot tell us who we are. It is necessary, Weil says, that we live at the intersection of time and eternity, of thought and silence. For Weil this is the cross. The cross is the furthest distance from God in that it expresses the extreme consequences of necessity: being locked into our thoughts. 'God is crucified from the fact that finite beings, subject to necessity, to space and to time, think' (89). To loosen our thinking is to live in the present moment. This is the vertical stake of the cross, cutting across the extension of time. Weil rarely states the positive side of contemplation, fearing that it would encourage imagination rather than attention. One could say, however, that God is raised from the dead in the fact that finite human beings, subject to necessity, to space and time, let go of their thinking. Describing her practice of repeating the Greek 'Our Father' every morning and while working she does hint at this experience of bodily resurrection: 'At times the very words tear my thoughts from my body and transport my *body* to a place outside time and space where there is neither perspective nor point of view' (WG 38).

Simone Weil died in 1943 in England, in exile from Nazi occupied France. T.S. Eliot recognised her genius and produced with Faber & Faber the first edition of her writings in English in 1951. Much of her concerns are strongly echoed in Eliot's later poetry: how we must simultaneously live beyond time and within it, beyond thought and yet using it:

> Time past and time future
> Allow but a little consciousness.
> To be conscious is not to be in time
> But only in time can the moment in the rose-garden,
> The moment in the arbour where the rain beat,
> The moment in the draughty church at smokefall
> Be remembered; involved with past and future
> Only through time, time is conquered.
> [...] Words move, music moves
> Only in time; but that which is only living
> Can only die. Words, after speech, reach
> Into the silence.[19]

The journey of John Main

Before he became a Benedictine monk, while serving in the British Colonial Service in Malaya from 1955–1956, John Main (then Douglas Main) met a Hindu monk, Swami Satyananda, who taught him how to pray with a mantra. Sent on an apparently routine assignment to deliver a goodwill message John Main was deeply impressed by the holiness of Swami Satyananda. Neil McKenty in his biography of John Main comments that 'initially the teacher was more important than the teaching.'[20] Main asked the Swami to discuss the spiritual base of the many good works carried out at the orphanage and school he had set up. Many years later John Main remembered,

> I was deeply impressed by his peacefulness and calm wisdom. He asked me if I meditated. I told him I tried to and, at his bidding, described briefly what we have come to know as the Ignatian method of meditation. He was silent for a short time and then gently remarked that his own tradition of meditation was quite different. For the Swami, the aim of meditation was the coming to awareness of the Spirit of the Universe who dwells in our hearts in silence.[21]

John Main asked whether as a Christian he could practise prayer as simple awareness of God's presence. 'Yes,' the Swami agreed, 'it will make you a better Christian.' Main was invited to meditate with him once a week. On his first visit the swami spoke about how to meditate:

> To meditate you must become silent. You must be still and you must concentrate. In our tradition we know only one way in which you can arrive at that stillness – that is concentration. We use a word that we call a mantra. To meditate, what you must do is to choose this word and then repeat it, faithfully, lovingly, and continually. That is all there is to meditation. I really have nothing else to tell you. And now we will meditate. (GT 12)

This was at a time before Transcendental Meditation and the Beatles had made meditation well known in the west. Swami Satyananda pointed out that since the young western visitor was a Christian, he must meditate as a Christian and he gave him a Christian mantra. He also insisted it was necessary to meditate twice a day, morning and evening. For eighteen months Main meditated with Swami Satyananda. This encounter led him to the pilgrimage of meditation discovering eventually the tradition of using a prayer phrase of John Cassian. Main's confident openness to the religions of Asia is directly attributable to this Hindu monk who had accepted him as a Christian disciple. In 1959 Main himself became a monk and, when, many years later in 1976, he started teaching meditation, he said that he had little more to add to the simplicity of Swami Satyananda's advice: 'Say your mantra.'

> I learnt to meditate from a man who was not a Christian but he certainly believed in God – knew God – and had a deeply vital sense of God dwelling within him. Now it may be significant that it was not until 15 years after I learned to meditate with him that I began dimly to understand what my master had taught me and to understand the incredible richness of its full exposition in the Christian vision. (11)

This delay was due to being told, as a novice in the monastery in 1959, to give up the practice of mantra meditation as non-Christian. He was urged to return to a more discursive and active form of prayer. Later, through his reading of the early desert monks (particularly Cassian) John Main recognised the Christian tradition of meditation using a prayer-word.

Though the source of the contemplative renewal Main proposed came from the Christian tradition, the catalyst was an inter-religious encounter. As contemporary Mindfulness practice (though non-religious in form) developed through an encounter with Buddhism, so John Main's recovery of a Christian tradition of mantra meditation was prompted by a meeting with Hindu spirituality.[22] Main emphasised not so much the meaning of the prayer-word as its sound and vibration as important in the practice. Swami Satyananda had taught him,

> The mantra is like a harmonic. And as we sound this harmonic within ourselves we begin to build up a resonance. That resonance then leads us forward to our own wholeness [...] And then the harmonic begins to build up a resonance between you and all creatures and all creation and a unity between you and your creator. (GT 14)

John Main may well have recommended *Maranatha* because of its open vowel sounds, which according to Hindu mantra teaching facilitates the opening of the heart.[23] Combined with the articulation of four consonants this gives the mind enough 'activity' to hold attention and stop mental scattering. Main understood the mantra very practically as 'simply a means of turning our attention beyond ourselves – a way of unhooking us from our own thoughts and concerns'.[24] However it also provides 'the integrating power' that restores the unity of mind and heart acting 'like a harmonic that we sound in the depth of our spirit' (WS 14). The power and value of the mantra is related to the rhythm of its sound, its phonetic quality, as well as its root in tradition:

> The importance of 'Ma-ra-na-tha' is both that it is one of the most ancient prayer words there is and that it possesses the right sound to bring us to the silence and stillness necessary for meditation [...] As a prayer word its meaning is important, but during the time of meditation we do not think of its meaning but recite it as four equally stressed syllables. (MC 5)

Swami Satyananda also taught how a 'saying' of the mantra deepens into a 'sounding' of it that in turn deepens, as the mantra takes root, into a 'listening'. At this level repetition moves from an act of the will, or *intention*, into an act of *attention*: 'Meditation,' Main says, 'is in essence the art of concentration precisely because the higher we toil up the mountainside the fainter becomes the mantra sounding in the valley below us' (WS 53). This was the teaching of Swami Satyananda:

> My teacher used to say to me: 'When you get to this listening stage it is as though you are toiling up a mountainside and the mantra is sounding in the valley down below you. The higher you mount, the fainter becomes the sound of the mantra. And then there comes the day when the mantra is out of earshot all together. (GT 42)

The final stage witnessed to in this inner journey is silence: 'An absolute silence,' John Main says, 'where we enter the 'cloud of unknowing' and no longer hear the mantra' (WS 53). This shows John Main's own experience, the witness of the Christian mystical tradition and the teaching of Swami Satyananda coming together and pointing to the 'beyond' where 'the mantra ceases to sound and we are lost in the eternal silence of God' (MC xi). Swami Satyananda believed that 'mental worship and repetition of the Holy Name' is succeeded by 'silent contemplation' and finally by 'becoming one with the Supreme Spirit.'[25] In the scholar Adalbert de Vogüé's opinion, John Main's perfect and seamless assimilation of Hindu mantra meditation through his discovery of John Cassian shows 'a convergence of independent monastic experiences rich in inter-religious significance.'[26]

What John Main and the monastic tradition generally reminds us of is the practical steps that can be taken to dispose ourselves for prayer: a good posture, awareness of the breath, use of a prayer phrase, handing over the active role to the Holy Spirit. There is a danger that mysticism can get over-focused on 'experiences' instead of entering into the experience of transcendence itself. John Main reminds us that mysticism is an unselfconscious experience, it involves taking attention off ourselves and reconnecting with a stream of prayer, a living tradition that has its root in the prayer of Jesus to the Father. In prayer, Main says, 'it is not we ourselves that are taking the initiative. We are not talking to God. We are listening to God's word within us. We are not looking for God, it is God who has found us.' (WS 48)

Mindfulness, in John Main's teaching, is our way of preparing, recollecting ourselves, so we can focus: 'The first step and in a sense the only step,' he says, 'is mindfulness, attention.'[27]

> We must collect ourselves together. We must become mindful, remember who we are and where we are and why we are. We need to find a peace within ourselves and a peace in our lives. This peace is mindfulness.[28]

For Main the place of mindfulness is the present, 'mindfulness not of what has been or what might be but what is' (DS 82). 'In stillness,' Main says, 'we are simply ourselves, neither remembering our past selves nor straining to become any other self' (31). Simple but not easy, as he wrote in his penultimate Spiritual Letter to the community that formed around Christian Meditation:

> Every moment is a dying to the past and a rising to a new present in which the past is not rejected but enfolded. We are who we have become through the experiences of a lifetime in which memory is allowed to crumble back into the dust. We have to forget, to un-know everything we have been if we are to come to completeness. The pain of overcoming the limitations of memory is that we have to let go of not just part of ourselves but of all self-consciousness.

We are only fully present to the now of the divine moment when we leave the past behind totally.[29]

Drawing from early monastic sources John Main taught a practice of stillness of body and use of a mantra:

> Meditation is a discipline of presence. By stillness of body and spirit we learn to be wholly present to ourselves, to our situation, to our place. It is not running away. By staying rooted in our own being we become present to its source. We become rooted in being it-self. Through all the changing circumstances of life, nothing can shake us. The process is gradual. It requires patience. And faithfulness. And discipline. And humility. The humility of meditation is to put aside all self-important questioning. To put aside self-importance means to experience ourselves poor, divested of ego, as we learn how to be: to be present to the presence. We learn, not out of our own cleverness, but from the source of wisdom itself, the Spirit of God. (DS 83)

At times he recommends saying the mantra in conjunction with our breathing:

> You can breathe it in one breath, and breathe out silently. Then in saying the mantra, it is as if you are accepting God's spirit, which is our life. We breathe it in. And breathing out in silence is like returning our life to God, ready to receive it again as gift [...] Our breath shows how meditation is firmly anchored in finding our being, letting go and receiving again, that is the Paschal mystery [...] It is nothing less than essential to meditate every day. Meditation is to the spirit what food and air are to the body.[30]

If recollection or mindfulness is the first step, and in a sense the only step *we* make, Main points out there is a further step into God that is a gift of grace.

> The second step is the second degree of the first step, but it is more like a leap or a plunge into the very basis of all that is. The second step is the realisation that God is. That God is present. That God is now and, perhaps most wonderful of all, that God is mindful of all. (DS 82)

Here the work of stillness bears fruit both in our bodies and in our mind. 'Gradually the whole of your sensory perception is deepened and refined,' he writes, 'You see things, you will hear things and touch things and smell things as you have never done before.'[31] This is not an experience *in* meditation but a new quality found in our everyday life. The attention practised during the time of meditation can be applied to all the other things we do and the people we meet during our day. Attention is love. We love someone when we give them our attention. Mindfulness is the living out of this in time; prayer is the practice of this with God. As Main says,

> Love teaches us about the relationship between time and eternity. The experience of prayer is an entry into the eternity of God – in the now. In meditation we become alive *now* with the life of Christ. We are enlivened with the life of Christ. We learnt that what is eternal is not out of time but is fully present. Past, present and future are drawn together in the centrality of the present moment of the now. It is important to be clear in our perception of time and eternity. Meditation leads into the experience of being so deeply rooted in the present moment that we pierce the veil of time. By being wholly at one with Christ in the present moment in prayer we transcend the limitations of our own separateness. (DS 50)

'The Mantra,' Main says, 'is our sacrament of the present moment' in both time and eternity. (DS 87)

Conclusion:

Making Depth Accessible

What we can learn from the Christian mystics is that there is not just one type of mindfulness. The real mindfulness need not stand up for there are many ways of understanding and practising such a universal human capacity. There is a deepening of attentiveness, however. In Christian spirituality this is often described as the journey from recollection to contemplation to union. In modern parlance: the three M's of mindfulness, meditation and mysticism. The Christian mystics give place for all, but favour a trajectory of progressive de-centring from the ego and re-centring on God. The way this happens in each person's life though is somewhat unique. 'Union differentiates.'[1] We become more ourselves as we hand over 'our way' to God. Where grace is active, 'Christ plays in ten thousand places.'[2] The ways and methods serve only to take us to the point where God takes over. However, as the handing over is ever-necessary time-tested practices of mindfulness, meditation and letting go never become obsolete. In fact, these practices, as good habits, make depth accessible. They make depth accessible not in that they 'make something happen' but they dispose us to receive grace as a gift. Disciplines for daily living become, therefore, ways in which we keep our body, heart, mind and soul open and fully alive.

From our study of the Christian mystics we can see that these are the four main mediums of mindfulness – the body; the heart;

the mind; and the soul (transcendence). There are clear parallels in this to the four foundations of mindfulness taught by the Buddha in the *Satipatthana Sutta:*

> [The Meditator] having overcome covetousness and repugnance towards the world of the body lives observing the activities of the body; having overcome covetousness or repugnance toward the world of feeling he lives observing feelings; having overcome covetousness or repugnance toward the world of the mind he lives observing the activities of the mind; having overcome covetousness or repugnance toward the world of mental objects he lives observing mental objects.[3]

The last stage is that of transcendence. Christians would call this 'seeing things from God's point of view'. In this transcendence we become children of our Father in heaven; like the sun he causes our consciousness to rise with equanimity on what we experience as good and evil in our lives.

These 'ways' are not distinct in Christian mysticism – let alone different – but are interrelated (as they are in Buddhism). Most of the practices reviewed in this book cover the body, heart and mind of the human person, Christian mysticism, however, does point beyond to the realm of the soul or human spirit, where the body, heart and mind are given over to entirely 'resting in the presence of God'. For Christians 'resting in the spirit' is the end point of all mindfulness and meditation practice. This is not to diminish the importance of guidance in mindfulness through the vehicles of the body, heart or mind. Indeed, the mystics we have looked at were grounded in their practice of self-awareness. Any sense of ourselves as a whole person, as a holy person, must come from a clear honest exposure of the body, heart and mind to their condition. Mindfulness is the tuning our physical, emotional and mental awareness so as to be open to the spirit within us. It involves dealing with the distractions and desires of the mind, body and heart as pre-requisite for transcendence.

The Christian mystics show us that the essence of mysticism is a combination of interiority and other-centeredness. The rediscovery of this tradition as a practical path that is neither narcissistic or unconcerned with the world but open to all people in their needs is evidenced in the Christian contemplative communities that have formed around the practice of silent prayer. The World Community for Christian Meditation following the teaching of John Main, the Bede Griffiths Sangha, Julian Groups following the inspiration of Julian of Norwich, Contemplative Outreach based on the practice of Centring Prayer, all show that contemplation is no longer a prerogative of the monasteries. They also show there is no one practice for everyone but varying ways to enter a common tradition rooted in the prayer of Christ. Pluralism, however, is tempered by each person's commitment to a particular path and the companions they find on that journey. A new emphasis on practice and regularity has helped free mysticism from a solipsistic concern with 'experiences'. A new emphasis on attention and mindfulness has freed it from a sometimes over-florid emotionalism. All these show that Christian contemplation can learn from the contemplative practice and wisdom traditions of Eastern Christianity and of other religions.

There is no one narrative but there is the recovery of a tradition. And there is an opening to new ways of interpreting and living it. This book offers a rapprochement between the Christian tradition of meditation and the Mindfulness practice that has become popular today. Both can share in what Thomas Aquinas called 'the simple enjoyment of the truth.'[4] As mind, heart and body work together, truth is never separated from compassionate action and concern for others. Contemporary interest in mindfulness can help mysticism to find its place again at the heart of Christian faith. Mindfulness can remind Christians that prayer is not something we do but something that is happening in us all the time, if we could but be aware of the Spirit. But mindfulness can also remind

Christians that it is necessary to take the practical steps to uncover the gift of transcendence from the physical, emotional and mental blocks that keep us locked in the ego or limited sense of self. As John Main says,

> There is no part-time or partial prayer, as if the Spirit were not always alive in our heart. But there are times, our twice-daily meditation, when we make a complete turn of consciousness towards this ever-present reality. There comes a level of awakening when our awareness of this reality is constant, throughout our most diverse activities and concerns. (WS 37)

That is Christian Mindfulness.

Mindfulness in its therapeutic form has come as a response to levels of stress in the modern world. To let go of anxious thoughts has always been a refrain of the Gospel. 'Do not let your hearts be troubled, neither let them be afraid,' Jesus said to his disciples (Jn 14:27). But in the face of the real worries of life how does one do this? Mindfulness teaches us to let go of our anxieties by coming back to a felt-sense of self, learning to enjoy being alive in the present moment. Belief in God can be an extra resource for calming a troubled mind. Calling to the Lord in our distress is a refrain of the Psalms. 'Cast all your anxiety upon God,' St Peter writes, 'because he cares for you' (1Pet 5:7). The sense of God's concern for us is at the root of petitionary and intercessory prayer. Both are a way of opening difficult life situations up to a source of goodness that is greater than our control or achievement. They help us hand over our worries in a state of trust. Contemplative prayer or meditation goes deeper though enabling us to open our whole being to God's love. This is the way of the mystics. Many of the mystics we have looked at were monks and nuns but not all. Jesus himself came from no 'professional' religious environment, he was known as the carpenter from Nazareth. Today meditation as the key to mystical Christianity is being made accessible to people in all walks of life.

One of the reasons why meditation was not well known among the laity in the past was that it was essentially an oral tradition handed down within the monastic context. It was rarely taught outside the religious orders. It was not that this practice was forgotten in Christian history but it was hidden. It was considered the preserve of specialists in prayer. As a practice within the monastic order, because of the personal quality of the practice, it was mostly passed down in an oral teaching from teacher to disciples. The 'how to do it' aspect of Christian teaching on prayer was often transmitted as a lived experience. Part of the contemporary rediscovery of this teaching, especially in the teaching of John Main and The World Community for Christian Meditation is a new openness to its practice in all walks of life. The revival of this way of prayer today among Christians has notably been among the laity. Contemplative practice in Christianity is no longer the preserve of monks and nuns but all who seek God, or who seek life, truth and a way. The simplicity of meditation means that no theological sophistication is necessary. In fact children often take very easily to it. Communities of men, women and children, like the World Community for Christian Meditation, who practise mindful living and awareness of other's needs are natural vehicles for the passing on of this way of contemplative prayer which may be the greatest need of the world today.

Notes

Introduction: Minding the Gaps

1. Shaun Lambert, *A Book of Sparks: A Study of Christian Mind*Full*ness* (Watford: Instand Apostle, 2012), p. 5.
2. Thich Nhat Hanh, *Living Buddha, Living Christ* (New York: Riverhead, 1997), p. 9.

Chapter 1: Jesus, Teacher of Mindfulness

1. Simone Weil, *Waiting on God* (London: Routledge and Kegan Paul, 1951), p. 45.
2. Jean Vanier, *Signs of the Times: Seven Paths of Hope for a Troubled World* (London: DLT, 2013), p. 62.
3. The Gospel of Truth in *The Nag Hammadi Library in English*, trans. James Robinson (2nd edn. Leiden: Brill, 1984), p. 40.
4. Kallistos Ware, *The Orthodox Way* (New York: Vladimir Press, 1979), pp. 113-114.
5. Mk 4:9,12,23 & 7:16, Mt 11:15; 13:9, Lk 8:8; 14:35. It occurs in the Book of Revelation ('the revelation of Jesus Christ') as a refrain for hearing what the spirit says to the Churches 2:7,17 & 3:6,13,22 & 13:9.
6. William Blake, 'The Marriage of Heaven and Hell', Plate 14, *The Complete Poems* (Harmondsworth: Penguin, 1987), p. 118.
7. Paul is quoting the Greek poet Epimenides.
8. Thich Nhat Hanh, *Living Buddha, Living Christ* (New York: Riverhead, 1997), p. 179.
9. Ware, *Orthodox Way,* p. 114.
10. Jn 2:21, 1Cor 6:19.
11. Blake, 'The Marriage of Heaven and Hell', 14, *Complete Poems*, p. 118.
12. Hanh, *Living Buddha,* pp. 74, 92.

13. Alan Wallace, *Mind in the Balance: Meditation in Science, Buddhism and Christianity* (New York: Columbia University Press, 2009), pp. 177–178.

14. *The Prayers of St. Catherine of Siena,* ed. Suzanne Noffke (New York: Paulist Press, 1983), p. 180.

15. Jon Kabat-Zinn, *Full Catastrophe Living: How to Cope with Stress, Pain and Illness Using Mindfulness Meditation* (London: Piaktus, 1996), p. 94.

16. Hanh, *Living Buddha,* p. 130.

17. *Nostra Aetate,* 28th October 1965, *Vatican Council II: Constitutions, Decrees, Declarations,* ed. A. Flannery (Dublin: Dominican Publications, 1996), p. 571.

18. Ibid.

19. Elizabeth West, *Happiness Here and Now: The Eightfold Path of Jesus Revisited with Buddhist Insights* (London: Continuum, 2000), pp. 135–139.

20. See *The Wiley-Blackwell Handbook of Transpersonal Psychology,* ed. Harris Friedman and Glen Hartelius (2013), Ch. 9.

21. Thomas Keating, *Open Mind, Open Heart: The Contemplative Dimension of the Gospel* (New York: Continuum, 2003), pp. 93–98.

22. The early Buddhist text the *Dhammapada* opens by saying, 'All that we are is the result of what we have thought: it is founded on our thoughts, it is made up of our thoughts.' ed. Anne Bancroft (Rockport, MA: Element, 1997), p. 12.

23. Jean-Pierre de Caussade, *Self-Abandonment to Divine Providence,* trans. Alger Thorold (Rockfort, Illinois: Tan Books, 1959), p. 69.

24. In translation both endings are valid. This relation of what is interior with what is interpersonal is paralleled in Buddhist reflection on the relation of emptiness and inter-dependence. See Wallace, *Mind in the Balance,* p.174.

25. Jon Kabat-Zinn, *Wherever You Go There You Are: Mindfulness Meditation (for Everyday Life)* (New York: Hyperion, 1994), pp. 12, 18, 20.

26. Ibid., p. 25.

27. See Christine Rosen, 'The Myth of Multitasking', *The New Atlantis: Journal of Technology and Society,* Spring 2008, 105-110.

28. 10:39 'at the Lord's feet' πρός τούς πόδας is nearly identical with Luke's reference to Paul 'at the feet of Gamaliel' παρά τούς πόδας in Acts 22:3.

29. There is a parallel to this story in John's account of Jesus washing his disciple's feet (13:1-17) where Peter, taking the traditional stance of Master–Disciple relations, has to be led into the meaning of Christ's servanthood.

30. *Dhammapada*, verse 277, p. 81.

31. *The Ancient Hebrew Lexicon of the Bible: Hebrew letters, words and roots defined within their ancient Cultural context*, Jeff Benner (Texas: Virtualbookworm, 2005), p. 37.

32. William Blake, *Gnomic Verses and Epigrams*, from 'The Rossetti Manuscript' (c. 1793–1810). *Blake: Selected Poems* (London: Penguin, 1996), p. 196.

33. John Main, *In the Beginning*, Audio Talks 3, Medio Media.

34. In 'Centring Prayer' the word expresses the intention of our heart for God.

35. Joel 2:32. 2Tim 2:22 (see also Rom 10:12-13). Calling on the Lord's name is witnessed to by Abraham (Gen 12:8), Isaac (Gen 26:25), Moses (Deut 4:7), Job (12:4), Jabez (1Chron 4:10), Samson (Judg 16:28), Samuel (1Sam 12:18), David (2Sam 22:4), Jonah (1:6) and Elijah (1Kings 18:24). Not only did the Old Testament saints call on the Lord, they prophesied that others would call on His name (Zeph 3:9; Zech 13:9).

36. Richard Rohr, *The Naked Now: Learning to See as the Mystics See* (New York: Crossroads, 2009), pp. 25–26.

37. Mk 14:36. The other Gospels translate it as 'Father': Mt 26:39 & 42, Lk 22:42, Jn 17. The centrality of Jesus' experience of God as *Abba* is argued by Edward Schillebeeckx, *Jesus an Experiment in Christology* (New York: Seabury, 1979), pp. 256-271.

38. See Exodus 39:30, Leviticus 16.

39. It is the equivalent of the Hebrew name *Immanuel*, meaning 'God is with us', a 'name' associated with the Messianic hope of the Jews. See Isaiah 7:14.

40. Meister Eckhart, *German Sermon 53*.

41. Simone Weil, 'Forms of Implicit Love of God', *Waiting on God*, pp. 82–115, 131–136.

42. Evagrius Ponticus, *Chapters on Prayer*, Saying 70.

43. *The Rule of Benedict*, 'Prologue'. Benedict rethinks positively the horrific closing verses of Psalm 136.

44. Keating, *Open Mind, Open Heart*, p. 93.

Chapter 2: What is Mindfulness?

1. Simone Weil, *The Notebooks of Simone Weil*, trans. A. Wills (New York: Routledge, 2004 – first published 1956), p. 378.

2. See Melanie McDonagh, 'The Cult of Mindfulness: Separating meditation from faith might not be as harmless as it seems', *The Spectator*, November 2014, p. 15.

3. http://www.austin-institute.org/2015/01/23/are-religious-people-happier/ and Shanida Nataraja, *The Blissful Brain: Neuroscience and proof of the power of meditation* (London: Gaia, 2008).

4. Luke Vandenberghe and Fabricia Costa Prado, 'Spirituality and Religion in Psychotherapy: Views of Brazilian Psychotherapists', *International Perspectives in Psychology: Research, Practice, Consultation*, Vol. 1, No. 2 (2012), 79–93.

5. Jn 4:28 and *The Divine Names* 1:4. Cited in Martin Laird, *Into the Silent Land: A Guide to the Practice of Christian Contemplation* (New York: Oxford University Press, 2006), p. 37.

6. Quoted in Olivier Clément, *The Roots of Christian Mysticism: Text and Commentary* (London: New City Press, 1993), p. 204.

7. Alan Wallace, *Mind in the Balance: Meditation in Science, Buddhism and Christianity* (New York: Columbia University Press, 2009), pp. 62-63.

8. Ibid., p. 2.

9. Bernard McGinn, *The Presence of God: A History of Western Christian Mysticism*, 'General Introduction', Vol. I *The Foundations of Mysticism: Origins to the Fifth Century* (London, SCM, 1991), xiv–xv.

10. Thomas Merton, *Raids on the Unspeakable* (NY: New Directions, 1966), p. 45–52.

11. Viktor Frankl, *Man's Search for Meaning,* written in 1946 (Boston: Beacon Press, 2006), pp. 109–111.

12. Ibid., 98, 120-121.

13. St John of the Cross, *Ascent of Mount Carmel,* Book 2, Chapter 22.

14. See Simone Weil, *Gravity and Grace* (London, New York: Routledge, 2002 – first published 1947), p. 30.

15. C. S. Lewis, *Mere Christianity* (London: MacMillan, 1960), pp. 40–41.

16. A refrain of Patristic writing first expressed by St Irenaeus of Lyons, *Adversus Haereses,* Book 4, Preface, paragraph 4, and, in the way quoted here, by St Athanasius of Alexandria, *De Incarnatione,* Chapter 54, paragraph 3.

17. Thomas Aquinas, *Summa Theologica* Book 1, Question 1, Article 8.

18. Anselm, *Monologion,* Chapter 78.

19. Anselm, *Proslogion,* 1, echoing Augustine's *Commentary on the Gospel of St John,* 29:6.

20. Augustine, *Sermon* 117:5, repeated in Anselm, *Monologion,* Chapter 1.

21. Rupert Gethin, 'On Some Definitions of Mindfulness', *Contemporary Buddhism,* Vol. 12, No. 1, May 2001, p. 263. Pali is the original language of Buddha though Mahayana Buddhism uses Sanskrit terms.

22. Wallace, *Mind in the Balance,* pp. 62–65.

23. Ellen Langer, 'The Prevention of Mindlessness', *Journal of Personality and Social Psychology,* Vol. 53 (1987), 280–287.

24. Ellen Langer, *The Power of Mindful Learning* (London: Addison Wesley, 1997), p. 4.

25. Ellen Langer, *Mindfulness* (Cambridge MA: Perseus Books, 1989), p. 12.

26. Ellen Langer, *Counterclockwise: Mindful Health and the Power of Possibility* (New York: Ballantine Books, 2009), p. 11.

27. Ellen Langer, 'The Construct of Mindfulness', *Journal of Social Issues,* Vol. 56 (2000), 1–9 (3).

28. Langer, *Mindfulness,* p. 13.

29. Shaun Lambert, quote taken from article accessed 13/12/14: http://www.mindandsoul.info/Articles/357258/Mind_and_Soul/

Resources/Topics/Mindfulness/Mindfulness_without_Meditation.
aspx

30. Thich Nhat Hanh, *The Miracle of Mindfulness* (Boston: Beacon Press, 1976).

31. Thich Nhat Hanh, *Living Buddha, Living Christ* (New York: Riverhead, 1997), p. 14.

32. Legend recounted by Nikos Kazantzakis, *Saint Francis* (London: Faber, 1975), p. 120.

33. Alan Wallace, *Minding Closely: The Four Applications of Mindfulness* (New York: Snow Lion, 2011), p. 22.

34. Jon Kabat-Zinn, *Full Catastrophe Living: How to Cope with Stress, Pain and Illness Using Mindfulness Meditation* (London: Piatkus, 1996), p. 343.

35. Alan Wallace, 'A Mindful Balance: What did the Buddha really mean by *mindfulness?*' *Tricycle* (Spring 2008), 60–63, 109–111.

36. Aquinas, 'Prologue', *Exposition of Boethius,* Leonine Vol. 50, pp. 267-268. Comparable statement found in *Contra Gentiles,* III, 2:9.

37. McGinn, *Foundations of Mysticism,* xvii–xix.

38. John Main, *The Present Christ,* in *The Inner Christ* (London: DLT, 1987), p. 313. This echoes St Anthony of the Desert's saying, 'The monk who does not know that he is praying, is truly praying.' Following quotes pp. 277 & 256.

39. John Henry Newman, *An Essay in Aid of a Grammar of Ascent,* Chapter 4, Part 2.

40. Evelyn Underhill, *Mysticism: A Study in the Nature and Development of Man's Spiritual Consciousness* (New York: Dover Publications, 2002 – first published in 1911), p. 57.

41. Ibid., xiv.

42. Karl Rahner, 'The Spirituality of the Church of the Future, *Theological Investigations,* Vol. 20 (London: DLT, 11981), pp. 149–50.

43. C. S. Lewis, *The Screwtape Letters* (London: HarperCollins, 2000), p.76.

44. Thomas of Celano in 'Second Life of St Francis', *Through the Year with Francis of Assisi,* ed. Murray Bodo (Cincinnati: Messenger Press, 1993), p. 166.

45. Simone Weil, *Gravity and Grace,* p. 99.

46. Thomas of Celano, 'First Life of St Francis', *Through the Year,* p. 117.

Chapter 3: Cognitive Therapy of the Desert

1. *The Sayings of the Desert Fathers*: 'Anonymous Collection', ed. F. Nau, *Review de l'Orient Chrétien*, 12 (1907), p. 52.
2. *The Sayings of the Desert Fathers: The Alphabetical Collection*, trans. Benedicta Ward (Kalamazoo: Cistercian Publications, 1975), Saying 12, p. 233. (Anthony, 30, p. 7, Agathon, 19, p. 23.)
3. Jon Kabat-Zinn, *Wherever You Go There You Are: Mindfulness Meditation (for Everyday Life)* (New York: Hyperion, 1994), p. 107.
4. Quoted in Olivier Clément, *The Roots of Christian Mysticism: Text and Commentary* (London: New City Press, 1993), p. 204.
5. Abba Poemen in *The Sayings of the Desert Fathers*, 8, p. 167.
6. *The Wisdom of the Desert Fathers: Systematic Sayings from the Anonymous Series of the 'Apophthegmata Patrum'*, trans. Benedicta Ward (Fairacres: SLG Press, 1975), Saying 141, p. 40.
7. *The Sayings of the Desert Fathers*, p. 65.
8. *Evagrius Pontus*, trans. John Eudes Bamberger, Cistercian studies 4 (Spencer, Mass.: Cistercian Publications, 1970), Saying 48, p. 29.
9. *John Cassian: Conferences,* trans. Colm Luibheid (New York: Paulist Press, 1985), 2:5, pp. 64–65.
10. *The Life of St Benedict by Gregory the Great*, III: 5, trans. T. Kardong (Collegeville, Minnesota: Liturgical Press, 2009), p. 22.
11. *The Sayings of the Desert Fathers*, 10, p. 197.
12. Basil of Caesarea, 'Short Rule' 21, *Ascetical Works,* trans. Monica Wagner, *Fathers of the Church* series (New York: The Catholic University of America Press, 1950).
13. Ward, *Wisdom of the Desert Fathers*, 133, p. 39.
14. Ibid., 135.
15. See T.S. Eliot, *Ash Wednesday* 1.
16. Basil of Caeserea, 'Long Rule' 5:2.
17. 'Homily on the Martyr Julitta', *Bibliothek der Kirchenväter*, 47, p. 214. My translation from the German.

18. *Auf den Höhen des Geistes. Gespräche eines russischen Moenches über das Jesus-Gebet* (Vienna: Herta Renner, 1976), pp 18–20. My translation.

19. 'Reflections on the Eight Thoughts', *Early Fathers from the Philokalia*, trans. E. Kadloubovsky and G. Palmer (London: Faber, 1954), p. 113.

20. Hesychius of Jerusalem in *The Art of Prayer: An Orthodox Anthology*, trans. Kadloubovsky and Palmer (London: Faber, 1966), p. 20.

21. *The Philokalia* IV, trans. G. Palmer, P. Gerard and K. Ware (London, New York: Faber, 1995), p. 337.

22. Pseudo-Macarius, *Fifty Spiritual Homilies and The Great Letter*, trans. G. A. Maloney, Classis of Western Spirituality (New York: Paulist Press, 1992), p. 194.

23. *The Ladder of Divine Ascent*, 'Step 28', trans. Colm Luibheid and Norman Russell (New York: Paulist Press, 1982), p. 276.

24. *The Little Flowers of St Francis*, trans. W. Heywood (Philadelphia: Dolphin Press, 1906), p. 3.

25. *The Anonymous Sayings of the Desert Fathers*, trans. Paul Evergetinos, ed. Victor Matthaiou (Athens: Monastery of the Transfiguration, 1964), p. 497.

26. See *The Sayings of the Desert Fathers*, 3, p. 57.

27. *The Way of a Pilgrim*, trans. Helen Bacovcin (London, New York: Doubleday, 2003), p. 5.

28. *The Sayings of the Desert Fathers*, 18, p. 23, 2, p. 102, 2, pp. 138–139, 3, p. 159.

29. Ibid., 3, pp. 202–203.

30. William Shakespeare, *Hamlet*, Act 1, Scene 5, lines 166–167.

31. See John Henry Newman, *An Essay on Development of Christian Doctrine* (1845), esp. Ch. 1.

32. Ward, *Wisdom of the Desert Fathers*, 145, p. 40.

33. Ibid., 86, p. 29.

34. Thomas Keating, *Open Mind, Open Heart: The Contemplative Dimension of the Gospel* (New York: Continuum, 2003), pp. 97–99.

35. Evagrius of Pontus, 'Miscellaneous Sayings', *Early Fathers from the Philokalia*, p. 109.

36. *The Sayings of the Desert Fathers,* 1, p. 82. Subsequent quotations taken from this book, respectively: 4, p. 83, 6, p. 84, 17, p. 234, 24, pp. 234–235, 18 & 19, p. 234, 6, p. 139.

37. *The Book of Mystical Chapters: Meditations on the Soul's Ascent from the Desert Fathers,* trans. J. A. McGuckin (Boston, Mass.: Shambhala, 2002), pp. 16–17.

38. These being gluttony, impurity, avarice, sadness, anger, acadia, vainglory, pride. Practikos 6–14, *Evagrius Pontus,* pp. 16–20. Henceforth in text Saying/Page.

39. *The Mind's Long Journey to the Holy Trinity: The 'Ad Monachos' of Evagrius Ponticus,* trans. with Intro. Jeremy Driscoll (Minnesota: Liturgical Press, 1993), 68, p. 51, translating *apatheia* as mindfulness. Subsequent quotations (except otherwise specified) from this book: 89/42, 70/35, 62/33, 79/36, 45/62.

40. 'Reflections on the Eight Thoughts', *Early Fathers of the Philokalia,* p. 113

41. Kabat-Zinn, *Wherever you Go,* p. 42.

42. Wallace, *Minding Closely,* p. 22.

43. *Evagrius Pontus: The Practikos and Chapters on Prayer,* trans. John Eudes Bamberger, Cistercian studies 4 (Spencer, Mass.: Cistercian Publications, 1970), Intro. lxxxii.

44. *Practikos* 2/15, 56/31. *Chapters on Prayer* 52/63.

45. 'Metaphysik und Mystik des Evagrius Ponticus', *Zeitschrift für Aszese und Mystik,* 14 (1939), p. 39.

46. There are two possible locations to the birthplace name given in *Lausiac History* 38:13.

47. His most speculative theology, the *Kephalaia Gnostica* was only recovered in 1952.

48. *Chapters on Prayer* 44(& 45)/62. Subsequent quotations 9&10/57, 69/66, 12/58.

49. Driscoll, Intro. *Ad Monachos,* p. 27.

50. *The Letter to Melania,* 5, trans. M. Parmentier, 'Evagrius of Pontus and the Letter to Melenia', Bijdragen, tijdschrift voor filosofie en theologie 46 (1985), 2-38 (12 lines 158-161).

51. Evagrius, 'Miscellaneous Sayings', *Early Fathers from the Philokalia,* p. 109.

Chapter 4: Making of Oneself a Stepping Stone

1. Augustine, *Revisions* 1:8 (3).
2. Bernard McGinn, *The Foundations of Mysticism: Origins to the Fifth Century* (London: SCM, 1991),, p. 231; Cuthbert Butler, *Western Mysticism: The Teaching of St Augustine, Gregory, and Bernard on Contemplation* (New York: Dutton, 1923), p. 24.
3. Mathew Fox, *Original Blessings* (New York: Bear & Co., 1983), pp. 21–24, 48–51, 267–269.
4. McGinn, *Foundations*, p. 230.
5. Augustine, *Sermon* 306:3. *Petrologic Latina*, 38, ed. Jacques Migne (1863).
6. Augustine, *The City of God*, trans. H. Bettenson (Middlesex: Penguin, 1972), 22:21.
7. Augustine, *City of God*, 21:14.
8. Margaret Miles, *Word Made Flesh: A History of Christian Thought* (Oxford: Blackwell, 2005), pp. 94–97.
9. Walter Hilton (1340–1396), an English Augustinian monk, said it would be no surprise if a man ran out of his house if when returning home he found only a smoking fire and a nagging wife! Gender roles may of course be reversed. *The Scale of Perfection,* Book 1, Ch. 53.
10. *Alcoholics Anonymous* (Aylesbury, Bucks: Hazell Books, 1976 – 3rd edition), p. 59.
11. Jon Kabat-Zinn, *Wherever You Go There You Are: Mindfulness Meditation (for Everyday Life)* (New York: Hyperion, 1994), p. 9.
12. *Dhammapada*, verses 276–277, p. 81. Emphasis mine.
13. Luke Vandenberghe and Fabricia Costa Prado, 'Law and Grace in St Augustine: A fresh perspective on mindfulness and spirituality in behavior therapy', *Mental Health, Religion and Culture*, 12:6 (2009), 587–600 (esp. 595–596).
14. Augustine, *The Trinity* (Book 14, 6:8), trans. Stephen McKenna (Washington D.C.: Catholic University of America Press, 1970), p. 420.
15. *Sermon* 117, iii, 5 (dated 418), *Petrologic Latina*, 38, p. 673. My translation.

16. Edward Howells calls this the 'mind's immediate self-presence – knowing oneself as interior to one's knowing.' 'Understanding Augustine's *On the Trinity* as a Mystical Work', Chapter 8 in *Christian Mysticism and Incarnational Theology,* ed. L. Nelstrop and S. Podmore (Farnham: Ashgate, 2013), p. 162.

17. *De Trinitate*, 4:18–24, 13:20–25.

18. Exposition on Psalm 130.12: Quoted in McGinn, *Foundations,* p. 242.

19. *Letter to Proba* (Letter 130, AD 412), Chapter 10.

20. Kabat-Zinn, *Wherever You Go,* p. 9.

21. *Letter to Proba,* 14.

22. In this, and following analysis I have been much helped by Margaret Lane, 'The role of *intentio* in Augustine's understanding of the soul's ascent to God: from *de animae quantitate* to *de trinitate*', unpublished PhD thesis, University of Durham, 2013, pp. 120–153.

23. Albert Einstein, *Relativity: The Special and General Theory* (1920).

24. Einstein, 'Letter to Michele Besso's Family' (1955).

25. Stephen Hawking, *A Brief History of Time: From the Big Bang to Black Holes* (London, New York: Bantam, 1988), pp. 144–153.

26. *Sermon 117,* iii, 5, *Patrologia Latina,* 38, p. 673.

27. *Sermon on Psalm* 41:7-8.

28. *Letter to Proba,* 10.

29. *On the Usefulness of Fasting,* 4. Quoted in Miles, *Word Made Flesh,* p. 97.

30. *Augustine on the Body,* AAR Dissertation Series 31 (Missoula, Montana: Scholars Press, 1979), pp. 12–15, 46, 70. Emphasis Miles's (p. 12).

31. The anthropological model here is tripartite; the higher reason (*mens*), lower reason (*spiritus*) and the bodily senses. In this and on-going analysis I am helped by Miles, *Augustine on the Body,* pp. 18–28, 55, 69, 109, 129–131.

32. *Ascesis* meaning 'training' can be applied outside of religious context.

33. *Sermons,* III/8, Sermon 277, ed. John Rotelle, tr. Edmund Hill (New York: New City Press, 1994), p. 37.

34. Ramana Maharshi, *The Teachings of Ramana Maharshi in His Own Words,* ed. A. Osborne (Tiruvanamalai: V.S. Ramanan, 2005), p. 4.

35. Ibid., p. 10.

36. *Sermons on the New Testament* 54, http://www.newadvent.org/fathers/160354.htm. Accessed 21/4/15.

37. *Teachings of Ramana*, pp. 28–29.

Chapter 5: Letting Go, Letting God

1. *Meister Eckhart: Sermons and Treatises*, Vols. I, II & III, trans. Maurice O'C. Walshe (I & II, London: Watkins, 1979; III, Shaftsbury: Element Books, 1979). *Talks of Instruction* - III, 6, p.18. Internal referencing gives Volume, Sermon or Treatise Section, page reference.

2. 'The language of philosophers,' Heidegger said.

3. In the Holy Roman Empire nobility was broader and more localised than in medieval nation states including landowners (gentry) who had no courtly function.

4. Saxony as an ecclesiastical province stretched from the Netherlands to Prague, containing forty-seven monasteries and nine large convents for women.

5. 'Fragments', *Meister Eckhart: A Modern Translation*, trans. Raymond Blakney (London: Harper & Row, 1941, reissued by Kessinger, 2003), p. 241.

6. Eckhart 'On Detachment' in *Meister Eckhart from Whom God Hid Nothing: Sermons, Writings, and Sayings,* ed. David O'Neal (Boston and London: Shambhala, 1996), pp. 119–120.

7. 'Sermon 53', *Meister Eckhart: The Essential Sermons, Commentaries, Treatises, and Defense,* trans. Edmund Colledge and Bernard McGinn (New York: Paulist Press, 1981), p. 203.

8. Beware of yourself, then you have taken good care.

9. Jon Kabat-Zinn, *Wherever You Go There You Are: Mindfulness Meditation (for Everyday Life)* (New York: Hyperion, 1994), p. 95.

10. Brian J. Pierce, OP, *We Walk the Path Together: Learning from Thich Nhat Hanh and Meister Eckhart* (New York: Orbis, 2005), pp. 74–75, 119.

11. Quoted by Oliver Davies, *God Within: The Mystical Tradition of Northern Europe* (London: DLT, 1988), p. 62. The Biblical template is poverty of spirit (Mt 5:3).

12. *Meister Eckhart from Whom God Hid Nothing,* pp. 5–6.
13. 'Talks of Instruction', Davies, *God Within,* p. 63.
14. Latin Sermon 6:1 in *Meister Eckhart: Teacher and Preacher,* ed. B. McGinn (New York: Paulist Press, 1986), p. 212.
15. German Sermon 12, Ibid., p. 269.
16. 'Talks of Instruction', Davies, *God Within,* pp. 63–64.
17. Kabat-Zinn, *Wherever You Go,* p. 58.
18. Quoted by Cyprian Smith, *The Way of Paradox: Spiritual Life as Taught by Meister Eckhart* (London: DLT, 1987), p. 95 (in 2004 edition)
19. Colledge and McGinn, *Meister Eckhart: The Essential Sermons,* p. 241.
20. Ibid., p. 203
21. The translation is of Dionysius the Aeropagite's *Mystical Theology* (original 5th Century Greek, though the author translates from a Latin version).
22. Internal referencing takes page and line from the critical edition of the Middle English text, *The Cloud of Unknowing and Related Treatises,* ed. Phyllis Hodgson (Exeter: Catholic Records Press, 1982). Translation into modern English mine.
23. For the former see Hodgson, 'Introduction', *Cloud,* xi-xii. For the latter theory see Julia Bolton Holloway, *Anchoress and Cardinal: Julian of Norwich and Adam Easton O.S.B, Analecta Cartusiana,* Vol. 20 (Salzburg, 2008), pp. 97-100.
24. 'Introduction', *The Cloud of Unknowing* (Rockport MA: Element Books, 1997), pp. 12-13.
25. John Main, *The Way of Unknowing* (Norwich: Canterbury Press, 2011), p. 60.
26. *The Epistle of Privy Counselling,* ed. Hodgson, in *Cloud,* 83:31–35.
27. See, for example, Eckhart Tolle, *The Power of Now* (London: Hodder & Stoughton, 2001), pp. 78, 95, 102. Tolle's teaching is nuanced though as we will see.
28. Ibid., p. 92.
29. This distinction has been explored in phenomenological studies of the body. See Hans Jonas *The Phenomenon of Life* (Chicago: University of Chicago Press, 1966), pp. 145–9; Maurice Merleau-Ponty, *Phenomenology of Perception,* tr. Colin Smith (London: Routledge and Kegan Paul, 1962), pp. 346–365 and *The Visible and*

the Invisible, tr. Alphonso Lingis (Evanston, Illinois: Northwestern University Press, 1968), pp. 130–155.

30. *Power of Now*, pp. 96–97. Emphasis his.

31. Ibid., pp. 101, 109. Emphasis his.

32. 97:6–13(9), Middle English: 'blithely bowing & so plesauntly pliing."

Chapter 6: Yoga and Loving-Kindness Meditation

1. Teresa of Avila (1515–1582), *The Interior Castle*, Mansion 1, Chapter 2, para 8.

2. Exceptions like Iyengar and Sivananda Yoga retain the idea of physical work as preparation for meditation and even retain aspects of Hindu devotion.

3. *Yoga Sutras*, Book 3, Verses 37 & 44.

4. *The Nine Ways of Prayer of Saint Dominic*, trans. Simon Tugwell (Dublin: Dominican Publications, 1978).

5. Louis Hughes, *Body, Mind and Spirit: to Harmony through Meditation* (Dublin: 23rd Publications, 1991).

6. Nancy Roth, *A New Christian Yoga* (Cambridge MA: Cowley Publications, 1991), illustrated p. 104.

7. *Incendium Amoris*, ed. Margaret Deanesly (London, New York: Manchester University Press, 1915), Ch. 11, p. 176. My translations from Latin.

8. *Incendium*, 37, p. 257.

9. *Melos Amoris*, ed. E. J. F. Arnould (Oxford: Blackwell, 1957), p. 12, lines 15–16.

10. *Incendium*, 14, p. 185.

11. *Richard Rolle: Prose and Verse*, Early English Text Society, ed. S. J. Ogilvie-Thompson (Oxford: OUP, 1988), pp. 23–24, lines 826, 829-833. My translation.

12. Kallistos Ware, *The Power of the Name: The Jesus Prayer in Orthodox Spirituality* (Oxford: SLG Press, 1986), p. 21.

13. In *The Philokalia*, trans. G. Palmer, P. Sherrard and K. Ware (London: Faber, 1995), IV, p. 337.

14. Gregory Palamas, *The Triads*, Book 2, Chapter 2, Paragraph 12, trans. N. Gendle (New York: Paulist Press, 1983), pp. 51–52.

15. Laurence Freeman, *Aspects of Love,* Meditatio Talks Series 2014A, p. 12.

16. It is now generally accepted she was not an anchoress at the time of her revelations. Veronica Mary Rolf in *Julian's Gospel* (New York: Orbis, 2013) proposes Julian was a widow at the time of her revelations and only entered anchoritic life in the 1400s. For an overview of what without imaginative embellishments we can say about Julian's life see Nicholas Watson, 'The Composition of Julian of Norwich's Revelations', *Speculum,* 68 (1993), 637–83.

17. For proto-typical 'fire and brimstone' preaching at the time of the plague see R. Horrox, *The Black Death* (Manchester: Manchester University Press, 1994), pp. 116, 118, 130–131,144–148.

18. Internal referencing takes page and line from the critical edition of the Middle English text, *The Writings of Julian of Norwich: A Vision Showed to a Devout Woman and a Revelation of Love,* ed. Nicholas Watson and Jacqueline Jenkins (Pennsylvania: Pennsylvania State University, 2006), using the Paris manuscript (c. 1580), the earliest extant version of Julian's 'Long Text' (c. 1390–1410). Modern English translation mine.

19. These twin pillars of Buddhist practice have parallels in the two commandments of Christ: 'Love the Lord your God with all your heart and with all your soul and with all your mind and with all your strength' and 'love your neighbour as yourself.' By transferring our desire and attachment from 'things' to the 'no-thing-ness' of God we pass from a self-centred to a God centred perspective on life, where all people are as real, valuable and worthy of care as we are.

20. Thich Nhat Hanh, *Living Buddha, Living Christ* (New York: Riverhead, 1997), p. 117.

21. Jon Kabat-Zinn, *Wherever You Go There You Are: Mindfulness Meditation (for Everyday Life)* (New York: Hyperion, 1994), p. 68.

22. This and following quotations (unless stated otherwise) from Kabat-Zinn, *Wherever You Go*, pp. 67–68.

23. *The Book of Margery Kempe,* translated into modern English by B. A. Windeatt (London: Penguin, 1985), p. 187.

24. Kabat-Zinn, *Wherever You Go*, p. 14.
25. There are will bequests to Julian as an anchoress in 1416. If Julian, as she says, was thirty in 1373 this means she lived to at least the age of 73 and maybe many years longer.
26. Authored by Reinhold Niebuhr (1892–1971)
27. See Raphael Langham, *The Jews in Britain: A Chronology* (New York: Palgrave Macmillan, 2005) pp. 24–33.

Chapter 7: God among the Pots and Pans

1. Thich Nhat Hanh, *The Miracle of Mindfulness* (Boston: Beacon Press, 1976), p. 24.
2. Teresa of Avila, *The Book of Foundations*, Chapter 5, para 8. Quotations are taken from *The Collected Works of St Teresa of Avila*, trans. K. Kavanaugh and O. Rodriguez, 3 vols (Washington DC: Institute of Carmelite Studies, 1980–1987). In text references with Book, chapter and paragraph.
3. For more on the apparently apocryphal nature of this story see Tomas Alvarez, *St Teresa of Avila: 100 Themes on Her Life and Work*, trans. K. Kavanaugh (Washington DC: Institute of Carmelite Studies, 2011), Ch. 59 'The Teresian Legend'.
4. *The Way of Perfection* (WP), 19:2 & 28:4.
5. *The Life of St Teresa* (L), 4:7; WP 28:4.
6. See Peter Tyler, *Teresa of Avila: Doctor of the Soul* (London: Continuum, 2013), p. 193.
7. *Letter to Don Lorenzo de Cepeda* (2nd January 1577). Quoted in Tyler, *Teresa*, p. 192.
8. John of the Cross, *The Ascent of Mount Carmel*, Book 2, Chapter 13, para 4. Quotations taken from *The Collected Works of John of the Cross*, trans. K. Kavanaugh and R. Rodriguez (Washington DC: Institute of Carmelite Studies, 1979).
9. Jon Kabat-Zinn, *Full Catastrophe Living: How to Cope with Stress, Pain and Illness Using Mindfulness Meditation* (London: Piaktus, 1996), p. 35.
10. St John of the Cross, *The Living Flame of Love*, Chapter 3, para 33.

11. St John of the Cross, *The Spiritual Canticle*, Red A., str. 38.

12. *The Spiritual Exercises of St Ignatius,* trans. A. Mottola (New York, London: Image/Doubleday, 1989), p. 108.

13. Ibid., p. 104. See 'Introduction' by Robert Gleason, p.15.

14. *Letters of St Ignatius of Loyola* (Chicago: Loyola Press, 1959), p. 240.

15. Quoted by Evelyn Underhill, *The Mystics of the Church* (Cambridge: James Clarke, 1925), p. 200.

16. St Francis de Sales, *Introduction to the Devout Life,* trans. J. Ryan (New York: Doubleday, Image, 1972), p. 95.

17. Ibid., pp. 213 and 214.

18. Joseph de Beaufort, 'The Character of Brother Lawrence', *The Practice of the Presence of God,* trans. Harold Chadwick (Gainsville, FL: Bridge-Logos, 2001), p. 12. In-text page references.

19. See Simon Tugwell, *Ways of Imperfection: Exploration of Christian Spirituality* (Springfield, IL: Templegate, 1985), Chapter 17.

20. 'Letter 9', in *Self-Abandonment to Divine Providence and Letters of Father De Caussade on the Practice of Self-Abandonment,* trans. Algar Thorold (Rockford, Illinois: Tan Books, 1959), p. 122. In-text references give letter and page number.

21. *Self-Abandonment,* Chapter 1, Section 2, p. 5. In text references give chapter/section and page.

22. Canon 6 'On the Sacraments in General' (Trent, March 3rd 1547).

23. From his treatise *On the Prayer of the Heart,* quoted by Tugwell, *Ways of Imperfection,* p. 211.

24. 2/11:37–38. The reference from not squeezing into corners comes directly from St Teresa *Interior Castle* 1.2.8. Teresa was an authority for the Visitation Order through their foundress St Jeanne-Françoise de Chantal who had been a Carmelite.

25. *Letters,* Book VIII, 1/433.

26. Ida Görres, *Das Verborgene Antlitz* (1944), published in English as *The Hidden Face* (San Francisco: Ignatius Press, 1959).

27. Monica Furlong, *Thérèse of Lisieux* (New York: Pantheon, 1987), p. 96.

28. Quoted by John Donohue, 'Thérèse of Lisieux, Doctor of the Church', *America,* 177 (December 13, 1997), 16.

29. Letter of 25th April 1993 & 6th July 1893, *Collected Letters of Saint Thérèse of Lisieux,* trans. F. Sheed (London: Sheed & Ward, 1949), p. 163 and 167–168.

30. Hans Urs von Balthasar, *Two Sisters in the Spirit: Thérèse of Lisieux and Elizabeth of the Trinity,* trans. D. Nichols and A. Englund (San Francisco: Ignatius Press, 1970), pp. 66–67.

31. *The Little Way of St Thérèse of Lisieux: From the Saint's Own Writings,* CTS pamphlet (London: Ludo Press, 1995), Preface.

32. *Story of a Soul: The Autobiography of St. Thérèse of Lisieux,* trans. John Clarke (Washington DC: ICS, 1996), Chapter 10, pp. 207-208. In text references give chapter and page.

33. *The Little Way of St Thérèse of Lisieux,* CTS Pamphlet, p. 12.

34. Ibid., p. 13.

35. Saying from 26th August 1896 quoted in *The Spirit of Saint Thérèse: Writings and the Testimony of Eyewitnesses* (London: Burns Oates, 1925), p. 184. (Henceforth *Sayings*)

36. *Sayings,* June 4th 1896

37. Quoted by Francois Jamart, *Complete Spiritual Doctrine of St Therese of Lisieux* (New York: Alba, 1961), p. 259.

38. Ibid., p. 31.

39. *The Little Way of St Thérèse of Lisieux,* CTS Pamphlet, p. 20.

40. *Sayings,* 23rd July 1897, full quotation in Jamart, *Complete Spiritual Doctrine,* p. 131.

41. 26th April 1888, *Collected Letters,* p. 88.

42. *Poems,* trans. A. Bancroft (London: HarperCollins, 1996), p. 17.

43. *St Therese of Lisieux: Her Last Conversations,* trans. John Clarke (Washington DC: ICS, 1977), p. 193.

44. Letter to Céline 26th April 1888, *Collected Letters,* p. 88.

45. *Sayings,* 27th July 1889, p. 160.

46. *Sayings,* 15th July 1897, pp. 163-164.

47. *Sayings,* 5th August 1897, p. 163.

48. *Sayings,* 8th August 1897, pp. 197-198.

49. *Sayings,* 19th August 1896, p. 191

50. This, and following, taken from *Last Conversations,* pp. 191, 196, 224 and 228.

Chapter 8: The Way of Attention

1. John Main, *Word into Silence* (1980) (Norwich, Canterbury Press, 2006), p. 67. In text WS.
2. Nov 24th 1854, *The Journals of Søren Kierkegaard*, trans. A. Dru (Oxford: OUP, 1938), pp. 542-543.
3. 'Upbuilding Discourses in Various Spirits', 1847, *Spiritual Writings*, trans. George Pattison (New York, London: HarperCollins, 2010), p. 112. In text page references.
4. See Daphne Hampson, *Kierkegaard: Exposition & Critique* (Oxford: OUP, 2013), p. 169.
5. Quoted in Hampson, *Exposition & Critique*, p. 195.
6. July 11th 1840, *Journals*, p. 82.
7. cf. Chapter 2.
8. T. S. Eliot, *Four Quartets*, 1:1.
9. Kierkegaard, 'Christian Discourses', 1848, *Spiritual Writings*, p. 151.
10. Ibid., pp. 155–156.
11. Simone Weil, 'Spiritual Autobiography', *Waiting on God*, p. 17. In text WG.
12. Simone Weil, *Gravity and Grace*, p. 179. In text GG.
13. 'The love of those things which are outside visible Christianity keeps me outside the Church.' 'Letter 6', WG, p. 42.
14. Simone Weil, *On Science, Necessity and the Love of God* (Oxford: OUP, 1968), p. 158.
15. Ellen Langer, *Counterclockwise: Mindful Health and the Power of Possibility* (New York: Ballantine Books, 2009), p. 13.
16. Thich Nhat Hanh, 'The Four Immeasurable Minds', *The Mindfulness Bell* no. 18 (Jan-April 1997), 5.
17. Langer, *Counterclockwise*, pp.14, 16.
18. Weil, 'Right Use of School Studies', WG, p. 58, also p. 59: 'To love our neighbour in all its fullness simply means being able to say to him: what are you going through?"
19. Eliot, *Four Quartets*, 1:2,4.
20. Neil McKenty, *In the Stillness Dancing: The Life of Father John Main* (London: DLT, 1986), p. 49.

21. John Main, *Christian Meditation: The Gethsemani Talks* (Tucson AZ: Medio Media, 1999), p. 10. In text GT.

22. See Bede Griffiths, *New Creation in Christ* (Springfield IL: Templegate, 1992), pp. 52–53.

23. See Pandit Rajmani Tigunait, *The Power of Mantra Meditation* (Himalayan Institute, 1996), pp. 110–112.

24. John Main, 'Foreword' to *Moment of Christ* (1984) (Norwich: Canterbury Press, 2010), xi. In text MC.

25. See *The Pure Life Society Silver Jubilee Magazine* (Kuala Lumpur, 1975).

26. Adalbert de Vogüé, 'From John Cassian to John Main', *Monastic Studies* XV (1984) (Benedictine Priory of Montreal), 69.

27. John Main, 'Being Present Now', *Door to Silence* (Norwich: Canterbury Press, 2006), p. 82. In text DS.

28. John Main, *The Heart of Creation* (London: DLT, 1988), p. 83.

29. John Main, 'Beyond Memory', Letter 23, *Monastery Without Walls: the Spiritual Letters of John Main*, ed. Laurence Freeman (Norwich: Canterbury Press, 2006), p. 216.

30. John Main, 'Making Nothing Happen', *Word Made Flesh* (London: DLT, 1993), p. 21.

31. Main, *Heart of Creation*, p. 89.

Conclusion: Making Depth Accessible

1. Teilhard de Chardin, *The Human Phenomenon*, trans. Sarah Appleton-Weber (Brighton/Portland: Sussex Academic Press, 2003), p. 186.

2. Gerard Manley Hopkins, 'As Kingfishers Catch Fire, Dragonflies Draw Flame'.

3. Walpola Rahula, *What the Buddha Taught* (Bedford: Gordon Frazer, 1985), p. 110.

4. Aquinas, *Summa Theologica*, Book 2, *Quaestio* 2 (Allen, Texas: Christian Classics, 1948), p. 180.

Suggested Reading

Chapter 1: Jesus, Teacher of Mindfulness

For the Gospel of John: Raymond Brown: *The Community of the Beloved Disciple* (New York: Paulist Press, 1979).

For the Gospel of Thomas: Elaine Pagels, *Beyond Belief: The Secret Gospel of Thomas* (New York: Macmillan, 2003), pp. 114–142.

For Karl Rahner's notion of Anonymous Christianity and its reception: John Pasquini, *Atheism and Salvation: Atheism from the Perspective of Anonymous Christianity* (Oxford: University Press of America, 2000), esp. pp. 54–55.

For Jesus' presence in the wisdom of other religions: Raimundo Panikkar, *The Unknown Christ of Hinduism: Towards an Ecumenical Christophany* (London: DLT, 1981).

Chapter 2: What is Mindfulness?

For the possibility of secular ethics: The Dalai Lama, *Beyond Religion: Ethics for a Whole World* (London: Rider, 2012).

Hans Kung, *A Global Ethic for Global Politics and Economics* (Oxford: OUP, 1998).

For Buddhism and Christianity: *The Good Heart: His Holiness the Dalai Lama explores the Heart of Christianity* (London: Rider, 2002), pp. 23–25.

On the schools and traditions within Christian mysticism: Kim Natarajah (ed.) *Journey to the Heart: Christian Contemplation through the Centuries* (Norwich: Canterbury Press, 2011).

On the distinction between faith and belief: Laurence Freeman, *First Sight: The Experience of Faith* (London: Continuum, 2011), p. 6.

For the use of spirituality within therapy: Luke Vandenberghe and Fabricia Costa Prado, 'Spirituality and Religion in Psychotherapy: Views of Brazilian Psychotherapists', *International Perspectives in Psychology: Research, Practice, Consultation*, Vol. 1, No. 2 (2012), 79–93.

For the use of *Communicatio Idiomatum* **among the Church Fathers**: Henry Chadwick, *Heresy and Orthodoxy in the Early Church* (Aldershot, Hampshire: Variorum, 1991), Chapter 18 'The Calcedonian Definition'.
J. A. McGuckin, *The Christology of Cyril of Alexandria* (London: St Vladimir's Seminary Press, 1994), pp. 154–155, 190–193, 212.
R. A. Norris, *Manhood and Christ* (Oxford: Clarendon Press, 1963), pp. 190–200.
A. Grillmeier, *Christ in the Christian Tradition,* Volume 1 (London: Mowbray & Co., 2nd edition 1975), pp. 105, 452–453.
For Mindfulness-based Cognitive Behaviour Therapy: S. Hayes, K. Strosahl and K. Wilson, *Acceptance and Commitment Therapy: An Experiential Approach to Behavior Change* (New York: Guilford, 1999).
L. Fletcher and S. Hayes, 'A Functional Analytic Definition of Mindfulness', *Journal of Rational-Emotive and Cognitive Behavior Therapy,* 23 (2005), 315–336.
For Mindfulness based Stress Relief: Jon Kabat-Zinn, *Full Catastrophe Living: How to Cope with Stress, Pain and Illness Using Mindfulness Meditation* (London: Piatkus, 1996).
Modern presentations of key Buddhist texts on Mindfulness: Thich Nhat Hanh, *Transformation and Healing: The Sutra on the Four Establishments of Mindfulness* (Berkeley, CA: Parallax Press, 1990), *Breathe! You are Alive: Sutra on the Full Awareness of Breathing* (London, Rider, 1992), *Our Appointment with Life: The Buddha's Teaching on Living in the Present Moment* (Berkeley, CA: Parallax Press, 1990).

Chapter 3: Cognitive Therapy of the Desert

On the Desert Mysticism: Thomas Merton, *The Wisdom of the Desert* (New York: New Directions 1960).
Simon Tugwell, *Ways of Imperfection* (Springfield, IL: Templegate, 1985), pp. 13–27.
Andrew Louth, *The Origins of the Christian Mystical Tradition* (Oxford: OUP, 1981), pp. 95–127.

On Benedictine 'mindfulness': Pia Luislampe, 'Living in the Presence of God: Comments on a Discipline of Benedictine Life', *The American Benedictine Review*, 40:4 (Dec 1989), 416–442.

Chapter 4: Making of Oneself a Stepping Stone

Augustine as Mystic: Bernard McGinn, *Early Christian Mystics* (New York: Crossroad, 2003), pp. 153–161, *Foundations of Mysticism: Origins to the Fifth Century* (New York: Crossroads, 2002), pp. 228–263.
Cuthbert Butler, *Western Mysticism: The Teaching of St Augustine, Gregory, and Bernard on Contemplation* (New York: Dutton, 1923).
Andrew Louth, *The Origins of the Christian Mystical Tradition* (Oxford: OUP, 1981), pp. 128–153.

Chapter 5: Letting Go, Letting God

Introduction to Eckhart: Cyprian Smith, *The Way of Paradox: Spiritual Life as Taught by Meister Eckhart* (London: DLT, 1987).
Meister Eckhart and Buddhism: Brian Pierce, *We Walk the Path Together: Learning from Thich Nhat Hanh and Meister Eckhart* (New York: Orbis, 2005).
Introduction to *The Cloud of Unknowing*: Graeme Watson, *Strike the Cloud: Understanding and practising the teaching of The Cloud of Unknowing* (London: SPCK, 2011).

Chapter 6: Yoga and Loving-Kindness Meditation

Breathing and yoga exercises in Christian prayer: Jean-Marie Dechanet, *Christian Yoga* (London and New York: Continuum, 1965).
Anthony de Mello, *Sadhana: A Way to God – Christian Exercises in Eastern Form* (New York: Doubleday, 1978). Bede Griffiths, *Return to the Centre* (Norwich: Canterbury Press, 1982).
Swami Amaldas, *Christian Yogic Meditation* (Collegeville, MN: Michael Glazier, 1984).

On Julian: Grace Jantzen, *Julian of Norwich: Mystic and Theologian* (New York: Paulist Press, 2000).

Denise Baker, *Julian of Norwich's Showings: From Vision to Book* (Princeton NJ: Princeton University Press, 1994).

Julian's Experience of the Eternal Now: Brant Pelphrey, 'Leaving the Womb of Christ: Love, Doomsday and Space/Time in Julian of Norwich and Eastern Orthodox Mysticism', *Julian of Norwich: A Book of Essays*, ed. Sandra McEntire (New York and London: Routledge, 1998), pp. 291–320.

Chapter 7: God among the Pots and Pans

Mindfulness for Teresa of Avila: Peter Tyler, *Teresa of Avila: Doctor of the Soul* (London: Continuum, 2013), pp. 184–203.

Early modern French mysticism: Evelyn Underhill, *The Mystics of the Church* (Cambridge: James Clarke, 1925), pp. 187–211.

Ursula King, *Christian Mystics: Their Lives and Legacies Through the Ages* (New Jersey: HiddenSpring, 2001), pp. 157–175.

Thérèse of Lisieux: Ida Görres, *The Hidden Face* (San Francisco: Ignatius Press, 1959). Monica Furlong, *Thérèse of Lisieux* (New York: Pantheon, 1987).

Chapter 8: The Way of Attention

Sören Kierkegaard, *Provocations: Spiritual Writings of Kierkegaard* (New York: Plough Publishing House, 2002).

Christopher Barnett, *From Despair to Faith: The Spirituality of Sören Kierkegaard* (Minneapolis, MN: Augsburg Fortress Publishers, 2014).

Mysticism in the Protestant tradition: Evelyn Underhill, *Mystics of the Church*, pp. 212–237.

Simone Weil: Mario von der Ruhr, *Simone Weil: An Apprenticeship in Attention* (London: Continuum, 2006).

John Main: Laurence Freeman, 'Introduction', *John Main: Essential Writings* (New York: Orbis, 2002), pp. 11–51.

Suggested Reading

John Main by those who knew him, ed. Paul Harris (Singapore: Medio Media, 2007).

Bibliography of Main Texts

Aquinas, Thomas
Summa Theologica (Allen, Texas: Christian Classics, 1948)

Augustine of Hippo
The City of God, trans. H. Bettenson (Middlesex: Penguin, 1972)
The Trinity, trans. Stephen McKenna (Washington D.C.: Catholic University of America Press, 1970)
Sermons (ed. John Rotelle, tr. Edmund Hill (New York: New City Press, 1994)

Basil of Caesarea
Ascetical Works, trans. Monica Wagner, *Fathers of the Church* series (New York: Fathers of the Church, 1950)

Blake, William
The Complete Poems (Harmondsworth: Penguin, 1987)

Butler, Cuthbert
Western Mysticism: The Teaching of St Augustine, Gregory, and Bernard on Contemplation (New York: Dutton, 1923)

Cassian, John
Conferences, trans. Colm Luibheid (New York: Paulist Press, 1985)

Catherine of Siena
The Prayers of St. Catherine of Siena, ed. Suzanne Noffke (New York: Paulist Press, 1983)

Caussade, Jean Pierre De
Self-Abandonment to Divine Providence, trans. Alger Thorold (Rockfort, Illinois: Tan Books, 1959)

Clément, Olivier
The Roots of Christian Mysticism: Text and Commentary (London: New City Press, 1993)

Climacus, John
The Ladder of Divine Ascent, trans. Colm Luibheid and Norman Russell (New York: Paulist Press, 1982)

***Cloud*-author**
The Cloud of Unknowing and Related Treatises, ed. Phyllis Hodgson (Exeter: Catholic Records Press, 1982)

Davies, Oliver
God Within: The Mystical Tradition of Northern Europe (London: DLT, 1988)

Desert Fathers and Mothers
The Sayings of the Desert Fathers: The Alphabetical Collection, trans. Benedicta Ward (Kalamazoo: Cistercian Publications, 1975)
The Wisdom of the Desert Fathers: Systematic Sayings from the Anonymous Series of the 'Apophthegmata Patrum', trans. Benedicta Ward (Fairacres: SLG Press, 1975)
The Book of Mystical Chapters: Meditations on the Soul's Ascent from the Desert Fathers, trans. J. A. McGuckin (Boston, Mass.: Shambhala, 2002)

Dominic, St
The Nine Ways of Prayer of Saint Dominic, trans. Simon Tugwell (Dublin: Dominican Publications, 1978)

Eckhart, Meister
Sermons & Treatises, Vols. I, II & III, trans. Maurice O'C. Walshe (I & II, London: Watkins, 1979; III, Shaftsbury: Element Books, 1979)
Meister Eckhart: The Essential Sermons, Commentaries, Treatises, and Defense, trans. Edmund Colledge and Bernard McGinn (New York: Paulist Press, 1981)

Meister Eckhart: Teacher and Preacher, ed. B. McGinn (New York: Paulist Press, 1986)

Evagrius
Evagrius Pontus, trans. John Eudes Bamberger, Cistercian studies 4 (Spencer, Mass.: Cistercian Publications, 1970)
The Mind's Long Journey to the Holy Trinity: The 'Ad Monachos' of Evagrius Ponticus, trans. with Intro. Jeremy Driscoll (Minnesota: Liturgical Press, 1993)
The Letter to Melania, 5, trans. M. Parmentier, 'Evagrius of Pontus and the Letter to Melenia', Bijdragen, tijdschrift voor filosofie en theologie 46 (1985), 2–38

Francis of Assisi
Through the Year with Francis of Assisi, ed. Murray Bodo (Cincinnati: Messenger Press, 1993)

Frankl, Viktor
Man's Search for Meaning, written in 1946 (Boston: Beacon Press, 2006)

Gregory the Great
The Life of St Benedict, III: 5, trans. T. Kardong (Collegeville, MN: Liturgical Press, 2009)

Griffiths, Bede
New Creation in Christ (Springfield IL, Templegate, 1992)

Hanh, Thich Nhat
Living Buddha, Living Christ (New York: Riverhead, 1997)

Hampson, Daphne
Kierkegaard: Exposition & Critique (Oxford: OUP, 2013)

Howells, Edward
'Understanding Augustine's *On the Trinity* as a Mystical Work', Chapter 8 in *Christian Mysticism and Incarnational Theology,* ed. L. Nelstrop and S. Podmore (Farnham: Ashgate, 2013)

Hughes, Louis
Body, Mind and Spirit: to Harmony through Meditation (Dublin: 23rd Publications, 1991)

Ignatius of Loyola
The Spiritual Exercises of St Ignatius, trans. A. Mottola (New York, London: Image/Doubleday, 1989)
Letters of St Ignatius of Loyola (Chicago: Loyola Press, 1959)

Jamart, Francois
Complete Spiritual Doctrine of St Therese of Lisieux (New York: Alba, 1961)

John of the Cross
The Collected Works of John of the Cross, trans. K. Kavanaugh and R. Rodriguez (Washington DC: Institute of Carmelite Studies, 1979)

Julian of Norwich
The Writings of Julian of Norwich: A Vision Showed to a Devout Woman and a Revelation of Love, ed. Nicholas Watson and Jacqueline Jenkins (Pennsylvania: Pennsylvania State University, 2006)

Kabat-Zinn, Jon
Wherever You Go There You Are: Mindfulness Meditation (for Everyday Life) (New York: Hyperion, 1994)

Keating, Thomas
Open Mind, Open Heart: The Contemplative Dimension of the Gospel (New York: Continuum, 2003)

Kierkegaard, Søren
The Journals of Søren Kierkegaard, trans. A. Dru (Oxford: OUP, 1938)
Spiritual Writings, trans. George Pattison (New York, London: HarperCollins, 2010)

Laird, Martin
Into the Silent Land: A Guide to the Practice of Christian Contemplation (London, DLT, 2006)

Lambert, Shaun
*A Book of Sparks: A Study of Christian Mind*Full*ness* (Watford: Instand Apostle, 2012)

Langer, Ellen
'The Prevention of Mindlessness', *Journal of Personality and Social Psychology*, Vol. 53 (1987), 280–287.
The Power of Mindful Learning (London: Addison Wesley, 1997)
Mindfulness (Cambridge MA: Perseus Books, 1989)
Counterclockwise: Mindful Health and the Power of Possibility (New York: Ballantine Books, 2009)
'The Construct of Mindfulness', *Journal of Social Issues*, Vol. 56 (2000), 1–9

Lawrence, Brother
The Practice of the Presence of God, trans. Harold Chadwick (Gainsville, FL: Bridge-Logos, 2001)

Macarius
Fifty Spiritual Homilies and The Great Letter, trans. G. A. Maloney, Classics of Western Spirituality (New York: Paulist Press, 1992)

Main, John
The Inner Christ (London: DLT, 1987)
Word into Silence (first published 1980) (Norwich: Canterbury Press, 2006)
Christian Meditation: The Gethsemani Talks (Tucson, AZ: Medio Media, 1999)
Moment of Christ (first published 1984) (Norwich: Canterbury Press, 2010)
Door to Silence (Norwich: Canterbury Press, 2006)
Monastery Without Walls (Norwich: Canterbury Press, 2006)
Word Made Flesh (London: DLT, 1993)
Heart of Creation (London: DLT, 1988)

Bibliography of Main Texts

McGinn, Bernard
The Presence of God: A History of Western Christian Mysticism, Vol. I *The Foundations of Mysticism: Origins to the Fifth Century* (London, SCM, 1991)

Merton, Thomas
Raids on the Unspeakable (New York: New Directions, 1966)

Miles, Margaret
Word Made Flesh: A History of Christian Thought (Oxford: Blackwell, 2005)
Augustine on the Body, AAR Dissertation Series 31 (Missoula, Montana: Scholars Press, 1979)

Rahula, Walpola
What the Buddha Taught (Bedford: Gordon Frazer, 1985)

Ramana, Maharshi
The Teachings of Ramana Maharshi in His Own Words, ed. A. Osborne (Tiruvanamalai: V.S. Ramanan, 2005)

Rohr, Richard
The Naked Now: Learning to See as the Mystics See (New York: Crossroads, 2009)

Rolle, Richard
Incendium Amoris, ed. Margaret Deanesly (Manchester: Manchester University Press, 1915)
Prose and Verse, Early English Text Society, ed. S. J. Ogilvie-Thompson (Oxford: OUP, 1988)
Melos Amoris, ed. E. J. F. Arnould (Oxford: Blackwell, 1957)

Rosen, Christine
'The Myth of Multitasking', *The New Atlantis: Journal of Technology and Society,* Spring 2008, 105–110

Roth, Nancy
A New Christian Yoga (Cambridge MA: Cowley Publications, 1991)

Sales, Francis De
Introduction to the Devout Life, trans. J. Ryan (New York: Doubleday, Image, 1972)

Teresa of Avila
The Collected Works of St Teresa of Avila, trans. K. Kavanaugh and O. Rodriguez, 3 vols (Washington DC: Institute of Carmelite Studies, 1980–1987)

Thérèse of Lisieux
Collected Letters of Saint Thérèse of Lisieux, trans. F. Sheed (London: Sheed & Ward, 1949)
Story of a Soul: The Autobiography of St. Thérèse of Lisieux, trans. John Clarke (Washington DC: ICS, 1996)
The Spirit of Saint Thérèse: Writings and the Testimony of Eyewitnesses (London: Burns Oates, 1925)
St Thérèse of Lisieux: Her Last Conversations, trans. John Clarke (Washington DC: ICS, 1977)
Poems, trans. A. Bancroft (London: HarperCollins, 1996)

Tolle, Eckhart
The Power of Now (London: Hodder & Stoughton, 2001)

Underhill, Evelyn
Mysticism: A Study in the Nature and Development of Man's Spiritual Consciousness (first published 1911) (New York: Dover Publications, 2002)
The Mystics of the Church (Cambridge: James Clarke, 1925)

Vandenberghe, Luke and Prado, Fabricia Costa
'Law and Grace in St Augustine: A fresh perspective on mindfulness and spirituality in behavior therapy', *Mental Health, Religion and Culture*, 12:6 (2009), 587–600

Vanier, Jean
Signs of the Times: Seven Paths of Hope for a Troubled World (London: DLT, 2013)

Vogüé, Adalbert De
'From John Main to John Cassian', *Monastic Studies* V (Benedictine Priory of Montreal)

Wallace, Alan
Mind in the Balance: Meditation in Science, Buddhism and Christianity (New York: Columbia University Press, 2009)
Minding Closely: The Four Applications of Mindfulness (New York: Snow Lion, 2011),
'A Mindful Balance: What did the Buddha really mean by *mindfulness*?' *Tricycle* (Spring 2008), 60-63, 109–111

Ware, Kallistos
The Orthodox Way (New York: Vladimir Press, 1979)
The Power of the Name: The Jesus Prayer in Orthodox Spirituality (Oxford: SLG Press, 1986)

Weil, Simone
Waiting on God (London: Routledge and Kegan Paul, 1951)
The Notebooks of Simone Weil, trans. A. Wills (New York: Routledge, 2004 – first published 1956)
Gravity and Grace (London, New York: Routledge, 2002 – first published 1947)
On Science, Necessity and the Love of God (Oxford: OUP, 1968)

West, Elizabeth
Happiness Here and Now: The Eightfold Path of Jesus Revisited with Buddhist Insights (London: Continuum, 2000)